'*Requiem for a Species* is a remarkable publication which brings together the scientific imperatives of taking action in the field of climate change. Hamilton highlights the political inertia which is currently acting as a roadblock. In the wake of the weak outcome of Copenhagen, this book assumes added significance in breaking the resistance to the truth about climate change.'
R K Pachauri, Chair, Intergovernmental Panel on Climate Change (IPCC), and Director-General, TERI

'Clive Hamilton, as usual, has courageously challenged the current nature of our society in this inspirational new book.'
Graeme Pearman, former head of the CSIRO Division of Atmospheric Research

'*Requiem* offers an insightful and informative look at why the human species can't come to terms with a changing climate. And Hamilton's conclusion – to despair, accept, then act – is an important call for us to respond to climate change immediately and decisively or spend the rest of our lives reacting to a warming world and an unravelling civilization.'
Erik Assadourian, Project Director, *State of the World 2010* and Senior Researcher, Worldwatch Institute

'Listen to this *Requiem* and weep, if it helps. False hope is as dangerous as despair. But don't get mired in helplessness. Above all, *Requiem* is a call to arms; to the urgent task of overhauling democracy in pursuit of survival. At stake, the biggest prize of all: our own humanity.'
Tim Jackson, author of *Prosperity Without Growth*

'I am afraid Clive Hamilton has it right about climate change – deeply afraid. *Requiem* is a brave and searingly honest book by a brilliant scholar. Ignoring it will only make a bad situation worse, so, please, read this book now.'
James Gustave Speth, author of *The Bridge at the Edge of the World: Capitalism, the Environment and Crossing from Crisis to Sustainability* and Dean Emeritus, Yale School of Forestry and Environmental Studies

‘Clive Hamilton investigates – in real time – our society’s choice not to act to protect ourselves from devastating climate change. We know the science, but “scientific facts are fighting against more powerful forces” – power, money, bureaucratic inertia and our innate desire to ignore what we don’t want to believe. “It’s too late,” he says. “Humanity failed.” That past tense is devastating.’
Fred Pearce, writer and author of *The Last Generation: How Nature Will Take Her Revenge for Climate Change*

‘Hamilton’s book presents a powerful statement of the problems confronting us – not just the problem of climate change itself, but the tendency to wish the problem away by denial (which in less extreme circumstances can arguably be an adaptive response to difficult situations). And all compounded by the fact that neither our institutions nor we ourselves have experience in acting on behalf of a seemingly distant future. Read this book.’
Robert M May OM AC FRS

‘When future generations look out on a planet ravaged by climate change, they will ask of our generation “When you knew what was happening – surely the greatest debacle since we came out of our caves – why didn’t you stop it?” Clive Hamilton proposes the problem lies with “the perversity of our institutions, our psychological dispositions, our strange obsessions, our penchant for avoiding facts, and, especially, our hubris.” It all makes for a riveting read because (alas) it is all too true – just like Greek tragedy.’
Norman Myers, 21st Century School, University of Oxford

‘*Requiem for a Species* magnificently captures the idea that, by and large, none of us want to believe that climate change is real. It explains our inability to seriously weigh the evidence of climate change, and to take appropriate action to ensure our own survival.’
Tim Costello, CEO, World Vision Australia

Clive Hamilton is professor of public ethics at the Centre for Applied Philosophy and Public Ethics based at the Australian National University. For 14 years until early 2008 he was the executive director of Australia's foremost progressive think tank. He has held visiting academic positions at the University of Cambridge and Yale University, and is author of the bestselling *Affluenza* and *Growth Fetish, Scorcher* and most recently *The Freedom Paradox.*

REQUIEM FOR A SPECIES

WHY WE RESIST THE TRUTH ABOUT CLIMATE CHANGE

CLIVE HAMILTON

publishing for a sustainable future

London • Washington, DC

First published in 2010 by Earthscan

Earthscan Ltd, Dunstan House, 14a St Cross Street, London EC1N 8XA, UK
Earthscan LLC, 1616 P Street, NW, Washington, DC 20036, USA
Earthscan publishes in association with the International Institute for Environment and Development

For more information on Earthscan publications, see www.earthscan.co.uk or write to earthinfo@earthscan.co.uk

ISBN: 978-1-84971-081-7

Typeset by Midland Typesetters, Australia
Cover design by Susanne Harris

A catalogue record for this book is available from the British Library

Library of Congress Cataloging-in-Publication Data

Hamilton, Clive.
Requiem for a species / Clive Hamilton.
p. cm.
Includes bibliographical references and index.
ISBN 978-1-84971-081-7 (hbk.)
1. Climatic changes—Social aspects. 2. Global warming—Social aspects.
3. Twenty-first century—Forecasts. I. Title.
QC903.H2185 2010
363.738'74—dc22

2010000214

At Earthscan we strive to minimize our environmental impacts and carbon footprint through reducing waste, recycling and offsetting our CO_2 emissions, including those created through publication of this book. For more details of our environmental policy, see www.earthscan.co.uk.

FSC
Mixed Sources
Product group from well-managed forests and other controlled sources
Cert no. SGS-COC-2482
www.fsc.org
© 1996 Forest Stewardship Council

Printed and bound in the UK by TJ International, an ISO 14001 accredited company. The paper used is FSC certified and the inks are vegetable based.

CONTENTS

Acknowledgments

In preparing this book I have been more than usually reliant on the expertise of others. Drafts of the first chapter have been read by a number of experts in climate science—Alice Bows, Graeme Pearman and Mike Raupach. David Spratt also provided very helpful insights. As the argument of the book depends on the science reported in Chapter 1, I am greatly indebted to them.

Chapter 4, on forms of denial, has benefited greatly from comments provided by Tim Kasser, Robert Manne, Tony Leiserowitz and Scott Cowdell.

Chapter 5, on our disconnection from Nature, has been thoroughly enriched by comments from my colleagues Wayne Hudson, James Haire and Scott Cowdell, as well as from participants in seminars at the Centre for Applied Philosophy and Public Ethics at the Australian National University and the School of Forestry and Environmental Studies at Yale University. I also benefited from discussions with Mary Evelyn Tucker and John Grimm.

Chapter 7, a report on a conference at the University of Oxford, has been improved after comments on a draft from Peter Christoff, David Karoly and Mark Stafford Smith.

Chapter 8, the most difficult to write, has benefited from comments provided by Scott Cowdell and David McKnight.

I would like to extend special thanks to Andrew Glikson, who provided helpful advice throughout, particularly on the science, and Cordelia Fine, who generously devoted time to reading most of the manuscript and providing feedback.

I'm grateful to Gus Speth for facilitating a visit to Yale University where a large portion of the book was written. Charles Sturt University has shown an admirable commitment to promoting public debate by providing me with the freedom to research and write this book unencumbered by other obligations.

As always, Elizabeth Weiss at Allen & Unwin has been a fount of support and good advice. The teams at Allen & Unwin and Earthscan have been a pleasure to work with.

Preface

Sometimes facing up to the truth is just too hard. When the facts are distressing it is easier to reframe or ignore them. Around the world only a few have truly faced up to the facts about global warming. Apart from the climate 'sceptics', most people do not disbelieve what the climate scientists have been saying about the calamities expected to befall us. But accepting intellectually is not the same as accepting emotionally the possibility that the world as we know it is heading for a horrible end. It's the same with our own deaths; we all 'accept' that we will die, but it is only when death is imminent that we confront the true meaning of our mortality.

Over the last five years, almost every advance in climate science has painted a more disturbing picture of the future. The reluctant conclusion of the most eminent climate scientists is that the world is now on a path to a very unpleasant future and it is too late to stop it. Behind the facade of scientific detachment, the climate scientists themselves now evince a mood of barely suppressed panic. No one is willing to say publicly what the climate science is telling us: that we can no longer prevent global warming that will this century bring about a radically transformed world that is much more hostile to the survival and flourishing of life. As I will show, this is no longer an expectation of what might happen if we do not act soon; this will happen, even if the most optimistic assessment of how the world might respond to the climate disruption is validated.

The Copenhagen Conference in December 2009 was the last hope for humanity to pull back from the abyss. But a binding commitment from the major polluting nations to shift their economies immediately onto a path of rapid emission cuts proved too hard. In light of the fierce urgency to act, there was a sense at the Copenhagen conference that we were witnessing not so much the making of history, but the ending of it.

Some climate scientists feel guilty that they did not ring the alarm bells earlier, so that we could have acted in time. But it's not their fault. As I will argue, despite our pretensions to rationality, scientific facts are fighting against more powerful forces. Apart from institutional factors that have prevented early action—the power of industry, the rise of money politics and bureaucratic inertia—we have never really believed the dire warnings of the scientists. Unreasoning optimism is one of humankind's greatest virtues and most dangerous foibles. Primo Levi quotes an old German adage that encapsulates our psychological resistance to the scientific warnings: 'Things whose existence is not morally possible cannot exist.'[1]

In the past, environmental warnings have often taken on an apocalyptic tone, and it is to be expected that the public greets them with a certain weariness. Yet climate change is unique among environmental threats because its risks have been systematically understated by both campaigners and, until very recently, most scientists. Environmental campaigners, naturally optimistic people, have been slow to accept the full implications of the science and worry about immobilising the public with too much fear. With the growth of global greenhouse gas emissions now exceeding the worst-case scenarios of a few years ago, and the expectation that we will soon pass tipping points that will trigger irreversible changes to the climate, it is now apparent that the Cassandras—the global warming pessimists—are proving to be right and the Pollyannas—the optimists—wrong. In the Greek myth Cassandra was given the gift of prophecy by Apollo, but when she failed to return his love Apollo issued a curse so that her prophecies would not be believed. I think the climate scientists, who for two decades have been sending warnings about global warming and its impacts, must sometimes feel like Cassandras cursed by Apollo, and never more so than now.

There have been any number of books and reports over the years explaining just how ominous the future looks and how little time we have left to act. This book is about why we have ignored those warnings. It is a book about the frailties of the human species, the perversity of our institutions and the psychological dispositions that have set us on a self-destructive path. It is about our strange obsessions, our penchant for avoiding the facts, and, especially, our hubris. It is the story of a battle within us between the forces that should have caused us to protect the Earth—our capacity to reason and our connection to Nature—and those that in the end have won out—our greed, materialism and alienation from Nature. And it is about the twenty-first century consequences of these failures.

For some years I could see intellectually that the gap between the actions demanded by the science and what our political institutions could deliver was large and probably unbridgeable, yet emotionally I could not accept what this really meant for the future of the world. It was only in September 2008, after reading a number of new books, reports and scientific papers, that I finally allowed myself to make the shift and to admit that we simply are not going to act with anything like the urgency required. Humanity's determination to transform the planet for its own material benefit is now backfiring on us in the most spectacular way, so that the climate crisis is for the human species now an existential one. On one level, I felt relief: relief at finally admitting what my rational brain had been telling me; relief at no longer having to spend energy on false hopes; and relief at being able to let go of some anger at the politicians, business executives and climate sceptics who are largely responsible for delaying action against global warming until it became too late. Yet capitulating to the truth initiated a period of turmoil that lasted at least as long as it took to write this book. So why write it? I hope the reasons will become apparent.

Accepting the reality of climate change does not mean we should do nothing. Cutting global emissions quickly and deeply can at least delay some of the worst effects of warming. But sooner or later we must face up to the truth and try to understand why we have allowed the situation that now confronts us. Apart from the need to understand how we arrived at this point, the main justification for the book is that by setting out what we face we can better prepare ourselves for it.

Undoubtedly I will be accused of doom-mongering. Prophecies of doom have always been of two types. Some, like those of doomsday cults, have been built on a belief in a 'truth' revealed by a supernatural force or the delusions of a charismatic leader.

Sooner or later the facts assert themselves and the prophecy is proven wrong. The second type is based on the possibility of a real disaster but one whose probability is exaggerated. Survivalist communities sprang up during the Cold War because those who joined were convinced that nuclear war would break out, leading to the end of civilisation. There was indeed a chance of that happening, but most people believed it was lower than expected by survivalists and the latter were legitimately accused of doom-mongering. The same may be said for a number of real but small risks that have led some to forecast the end of the world—the Y2K bug and a collision with an asteroid come to mind.

Until recently, catastrophic global warming fell into the latter category, and anyone predicting the end of modern civilisation was arguably guilty of exaggerating the known risks because the prevailing warming projections indicated there was a good chance that early action could prevent dangerous climate change. But in the last few years scientists' predictions about climate change have become much more certain and much more alarming, with bigger and irreversible changes now expected sooner. After a decade of little real action, even with a very optimistic assessment of the likelihood of the world taking the necessary action and in the absence of so-called unknown unknowns, catastrophic climate change is now virtually certain.

In these circumstances refusing to accept that we face a very unpleasant future becomes perverse. Denial requires a wilful misreading of the science, a romantic view of the ability of political institutions to respond, or faith in divine intervention. Climate Pollyannas adopt the same tactic as doom-mongers, but in reverse: instead of taking a very small risk of disaster and exaggerating it, they take a very high risk of disaster and minimise it.

Chapter 1

No escaping the science

Alarm bells

One of the most striking features of the global warming debate has been how, with each advance in climate science, the news keeps getting worse. Although temporarily slowed by the effects of the 2008 global financial crisis, the world's greenhouse gas emissions have been growing much faster than predicted in the 1990s. In addition, since 2005 a number of scientific papers have described the likelihood of the climate system passing significant 'tipping points' beyond which the warming process is reinforced by positive feedback mechanisms—small perturbations that cause large changes.[1] This new understanding has upset the comforting idea of a 'dose–response' relationship between the amount of greenhouse gases we put into the atmosphere and the amount of global warming that follows. That idea has allowed us to believe that, although we may be slow to respond, once we decide to act we will be able to rescue the situation. In truth, it is likely that in the next decade or so, beginning with the melting of the Arctic's summer sea-ice, the Earth's climate will shift onto a new trajectory driven by 'natural' processes that will take millenniums to work themselves out.

The paleoclimate record shows the Earth's climate often changing abruptly, flipping from one state to another, sometimes within a few years.[2] It now seems almost certain that, if it has not occurred already, within the next several years enough warming will be locked in to the system to set in train feedback processes that will overwhelm any attempts we make to cut back on our carbon emissions. We will be powerless to stop the jump to a new climate on Earth, one much less sympathetic to life. The kind of climate that has allowed civilisation to flourish will be gone and humans will enter a long struggle just to survive.

It is hard to accept that human beings could so change the composition of Earth's atmosphere that civilisation, and even the existence of the species, is jeopardised. Yet that is what some climate scientists now believe. Scientists are naturally reticent; except for a few mavericks, they stick to what they know with a high degree of certainty, which in most circumstances is appropriate. Yet after a massive research effort over the last 20 years scientists are beginning to express the fear that now haunts them—that the consequences of global warming are much worse than we thought and the world will almost certainly not act in time to stop it. These fears were cemented by the agreement reached at Copenhagen in December 2009 which locked the world into only modest abatement action for the foreseeable future.

In 2007 James Hansen, the head of NASA's Goddard Institute for Space Studies and one of the world's foremost climate experts, wrote of the traditional caution of scientists that has led them to understate the risks of a sea-level rise of several metres due to the possible collapse of the West Antarctic and Greenland icesheets.[3] He argued that scientists are more worried about being accused of 'crying wolf' than they are of being accused of 'fiddling while Rome burns'. There are, of course, institutional and cultural barriers that interfere with the process of communicating science to political decision-makers. Scientific journals are more likely to publish papers if they are cautious and filled with caveats. And, for all of its virtues, the consensus process of the Intergovernmental Panel on Climate Change (IPCC), the basis for the official response to global warming, naturally favours conservatism and understatement of the dangers. Hansen wrote: [4]

> There is enough information now, in my opinion, to make it a near certainty that business-as-usual climate forcing scenarios would lead to a disastrous multi-metre sea level rise on the century time scale.

The accelerating rate of melting of the Arctic sea-ice has shocked the scientists studying it, with many believing that summer ice will disappear entirely within the next decade or two.[5] Some expect it to be gone even sooner. Mark Serreze, director of the US National Snow and Ice Data Center, has declared that 'Arctic ice is in its death spiral'.[6] The dark water surface that will replace the reflective white one in summer will absorb more solar radiation, setting off a positive-feedback process of further warming. This is expected to initiate a cascade of effects as the patch of warmth over the Arctic spreads in all directions, warming the surrounding oceans, melting the Siberian permafrost and destabilising the Greenland icesheet. In December 2007, after a summer that saw a dramatic decline in Arctic sea-ice, NASA climate scientist Jay Zwally said: 'The Arctic is often cited as the canary in the coal mine for climate warming. Now, as a sign of climate warming, the canary has died. It is time to start getting out of the coal mines.'[7] Another resorted to a biblical metaphor: 'Climate scientists have begun to feel like a bunch of Noahs.'[8]

The world's top climate scientists are now ringing the alarm bell at a deafening volume because the time to act has virtually passed, yet it is as if the frequency of the chime is beyond the threshold of human hearing. While the scientists are becoming more desperate, the world's emissions of greenhouse gases have been going through the roof. In the 1970s and 1980s global emissions of carbon dioxide (CO_2) from burning fossil fuels increased at 2 per cent each year. In the 1990s they fell to 1 per cent. Since the year 2000, the growth rate of the world's CO_2 emissions has almost trebled to 3 per cent a year.[9] At that rate annual emissions will double every 25 years.

While rates of growth in rich countries have fallen below 1 per cent, they have expanded enormously in developing countries, led by China where fossil fuel emissions grew by 11–12 per cent annually in the first decade of this century.[10] By 2005 China accounted for 18 per cent of the world's greenhouse gas emissions; by 2030 it is expected to be responsible for 33 per cent.[11] The Chinese Government takes climate change seriously—much more so than the United States under the Bush Administration—and has implemented a number of policies designed to cut the emissions intensity of electricity and transport, but the sheer expansion of the economy is swamping all attempts at constraining the growth of carbon pollution.

The hope in the 1990s that greater energy efficiency and a gradual shift to low-carbon sources of energy in the West could head off global warming has been battered by the extraordinary growth of China's economy, compounded by that of India, Brazil and a couple of other large developing economies. The energy that powers this growth has come predominantly from burning coal. In the years after 2000, coal consumption by developing countries rose by 10 per cent annually.[12] Rather than decarbonising the world is carbonising at an unprecedented rate, and it is doing so at precisely the time we know we have to stop it.

The recession that arrived in late 2008 slowed, and in some countries reversed, growth in annual carbon emissions, but the volume of greenhouse gases in the atmosphere continued to rise,[13] just as reducing the flow rate of tap water does not stop the bath filling up. Even if annual emissions stopped dead, the fact that most of past carbon emissions remain in the atmosphere for a long time would mean that the elevated global temperature would persist for many centuries.[14] There is every reason to expect that, without policy intervention, emissions will revert to pre-recession rates for some decades. As the pace of China's economic expansion inevitably slows over the next two decades or so, growth in other large developing countries is likely to accelerate. Over the last two centuries some 75 per cent of increased greenhouse gas emissions have been put into the atmosphere by rich countries;[15] over the next century more than 90 per cent of the growth in global emissions is expected to occur in developing countries.[16] It is little wonder that, according to one newspaper survey, more than half of climate scientists now believe that cutting emissions will no longer be enough to avoid the worst and we will be forced to pursue the radical and dangerous route of engineering the global climate, a prospect considered in Chapter 6.[17]

Worse than the worst case

The headline of the IPCC's *Third Assessment Report* in 2001 was that average global surface temperatures are projected to increase by anywhere between 1.4 and 5.8°C above pre-industrial levels over the period 1990 to 2100. Climate 'sceptics' attacked those who emphasised the upper limit as alarmist and scoffed at the possibility of 6°C of warming, suggesting that the width of the range was a measure of the lack of confidence of the IPCC in the science. In truth, most of the variability in the range was due not to uncertainties about how much warming is associated with a given concentration of greenhouse gases in the atmosphere,[18] but to the difficulty of forecasting the future path of the world's greenhouse gas emissions. The models of the economists rather than those of the scientists were to blame.

In the 1990s the IPCC developed a number of scenarios to reflect future influences on emissions and associated warming. Of the half-dozen or so main IPCC scenarios, the 'worst-case scenario' is known as A1FI. This scenario, the one that has given the highest estimates of warming in the IPCC reports, assumed strong rates of global economic growth with continued high dependency on fossil fuel-based forms of energy production over the next decades.

It is worth noting here that climate deniers and conservatives have frequently accused the IPCC of exaggeration and ridiculed environmentalists for fear-mongering when they refer to the possibility of warming reaching the upper boundaries of the IPCC projections. Bjorn Lomborg, whose book *The Skeptical Environmentalist* made him the darling of right-wing think tanks and newspaper columnists, declared in 2001 that the A1FI scenario was 'patently implausible' and that carbon emissions are much more likely to follow the lowest paths suggested by the IPCC.[19] On this basis, he extended the argument of his book to conclude that: [20]

> global warming is not an ever-worsening problem. In fact, under any reasonable scenario of technological change and without policy intervention, carbon emissions will not reach the levels of A1FI and they will decline towards the end of this century ...

Lomborg made this confident declaration just at the time it was becoming apparent that growth in global emissions had risen so high that the world had shifted onto a path that is worse than the worst-case scenario imagined by the IPCC. In its worst case the IPCC anticipated growth in CO_2 emissions of 2.5 per cent per annum through to 2030, yet we have seen that from around 2000 global emissions began growing at 3 per cent a year.[21] This worse-than-the-worst-case scenario should now be regarded as the most likely one in the absence of determined intervention.[22] It is not often in the history of public debate that a commentator has been proven as emphatically wrong as Bjorn Lomborg has been.

What are we facing under such a scenario? The IPCC's *Fourth Assessment Report*, published in 2007, narrowed the likely range of warming to 2.4 to 4.6°C above pre-industrial levels by 2100 if we do nothing.[23] The upper limit of 4.6°C became the most likely outcome for the A1FI scenario.[24] Climate scientists believe that the temperature threshold that would bring about the melting of the Greenland icesheet is between 1°C and 3°C, in other words well below the 4.6°C warming level expected under A1FI. As

I will argue next, the numbers show that even with urgent and sustained global action it seems unlikely that we will be able to keep the Earth's temperature from rising by anything less than 3°C. Melting of the Greenland icesheet would eventually result in the world's oceans rising by around seven metres, dramatically redrawing the geography of the Earth.

The carbon cycle

To understand the significance of the latest climate science we need a rudimentary understanding of the carbon cycle. The natural carbon cycle forms the core of the Earth's living system. Carbon circulates through the biosphere via the growth and death of plants, animals and microbes. It is also buried in sediments as fossil carbon (coal, oil and natural gas) and is absorbed in the oceans in the form of dissolved CO_2. Some of the ocean's CO_2 is taken up by marine life and eventually buried in sediments on the ocean floor. Carbon also occurs in the atmosphere as the gases CO_2 and methane (CH_4). The terrestrial biosphere forms a thin carbon-rich layer on the Earth's surface through which this element is exchanged between sediments beneath and the atmosphere and ocean above.

For nearly three million years the natural carbon cycle has ensured the atmosphere has contained less than 300 parts per million (ppm) of CO_2, just the right amount to keep the planet at a temperature suited to the flourishing of a rich variety of life. But human industrial activity over the last two to three centuries has disturbed this balance. When we dig up and burn coal, over half of the CO_2 released is absorbed by land and ocean sinks. The rest stays in the atmosphere, some of it for a very long time. A quarter will still be affecting the climate after a thousand years and around 10 per cent after a hundred thousand years. As David Archer, professor of geophysical sciences at the University of Chicago, points out, the effects of carbon we emit now will last longer than that of nuclear waste created today.[25] Throughout its history Earth has passed through long warm greenhouse periods and shorter ice age periods in response to changes in the distribution of continents and oceans around the globe, the rise and erosion of mountain ranges, the long-term increase in the brightness of the sun, and cyclic variations in solar radiation associated with changes in the Earth's orbital position relative to the sun. If humans were to put all of the economically recoverable fossilised carbon back into the atmosphere over the next couple of centuries, then the eventual impact on the Earth's climate would exceed that of an orbital shift. So humans have become a 'natural' planetary force comparable to those that have driven the great glacial cycles that define geological time.[26]

Climate scientists now know that increases of atmospheric greenhouse gases raise the heat-trapping potential of the atmosphere, which in turn interferes with the natural carbon cycle in ways that tend to amplify the greenhouse effect. This is known as a positive-feedback effect. Through global warming, changes in atmospheric carbon alter the rate of absorption and release of carbon from natural sinks in the oceans and land. Climate–carbon cycle feedback mechanisms include the reduced ability of warmer ocean waters to remove CO_2 from the atmosphere, and the decline in deep-ocean mixing and thus the transport of carbon into the deep ocean from the carbon-rich surface layer. In addition, warming is expected to cause more deforestation through droughts, fires and high temperatures inhibiting plant growth. A recent study concluded that a 4°C rise in the Earth's average temperature would kill off 85 per cent of the Amazon rainforest, and that even a 2°C rise, now seen as unavoidable, will see 20–40 per cent of it die off.[27]

When ocean and land sinks take up less carbon, a greater proportion of the CO_2 put into the atmosphere by humans stays there, strengthening feedback effects and causing more warming. Perhaps most worrying, the threshold for release of methane and CO_2 from the vast permafrost of Siberia is approaching, driven by temperature rise in the Arctic, which at nearly 4°C is three to four times the global average.

In the terrestrial biosphere the feedback effect works as follows. An increasing concentration of CO_2 in the atmosphere stimulates the growth of plants which draw CO_2 out of the atmosphere in the process of photosynthesis. However, this so-called fertilisation effect—an offsetting or negative feedback—works only up to a point. Changes in rainfall patterns and higher temperatures associated with global warming will begin to work in the opposite direction, reducing the absorptive capacity of vegetation. So boreal (northern) forests will extend further north, while tropical rainforests burn. The processes are complex and not fully understood but the weight of evidence indicates that, taken overall, the detrimental effects of climate change on the absorption of CO_2 by the biosphere will outweigh the beneficial effects (including plant growth stimulated by higher rainfall in northern latitudes), and more so as temperatures rise. Overall, the effectiveness of natural sinks at removing carbon dioxide from the atmosphere has declined by 5 per cent over the last 50 years, and the decline will continue.[28] Unless offset by some other process, warming amplified by positive-feedback effects will, over centuries and perhaps much sooner, melt all of the ice on Earth, causing the seas to rise by some 70 metres.

So humans are increasing atmospheric CO_2 both directly by burning fossil fuels and clearing forests and indirectly by interfering with the natural carbon cycle. If we are to achieve the goal of all international efforts and stabilise greenhouse gas emissions in the atmosphere at a level considered 'safe', the presence of climate–carbon cycle feedbacks means we must reduce our direct emissions by more than we would need to if we had to contend only with direct effects. The IPCC estimates that, in order to stabilise greenhouse gas concentrations in the atmosphere at 450 parts per million (ppm), the presence of carbon cycle feedbacks means that we will have to reduce our total emissions over the twenty-first century by 27 per cent *more* than we would otherwise.[29]

Scientific urgency versus political sluggishness

I am trying to keep the use of numbers and abbreviations to a minimum, but to get a true sense of what we are up against a few more figures are needed. Note here too that carbon dioxide is only the most prominent greenhouse gas. In order to analyse the effects of all greenhouse gases, the others—methane, nitrous oxide and a number of 'trace gases'—are converted into their 'global warming potential' and measured in carbon dioxide equivalent (CO_2-e). When I refer to 'greenhouse gases' I mean all of them, not just carbon dioxide. This is explained in the appendix on page 227, where there is also a table showing the correspondences between CO_2 concentrations and CO_2-e concentrations.

It is widely accepted in international negotiations that if global average temperatures increase by 2°C above the pre-industrial average then we will pass into the danger zone.[30] Warming of 2°C is the most likely outcome if greenhouse gas emissions in the atmosphere are allowed to increase to 450 ppm, as long as we exclude the effects of positive feedbacks. Resolved to decide what is meant by 'dangerous' warming in the Framework Convention, the European Union adopted 2°C as the target level below which warming must be kept.

As I will argue, the chances of stopping warming at 2°C above pre-industrial levels are virtually zero because the chances of keeping concentrations below 450 ppm are virtually zero.[31] In fact, in 2007 the concentration of greenhouse gases reached 463 ppm, although when the warming effect is adjusted to account for the cooling effect of aerosols the figure falls to 396 ppm.[32] Only air pollution is protecting us. The Earth's temperature is already 0.8°C above its long-term average, and existing levels of greenhouse gases in the atmosphere mean that another 0.7°C of heating is in the pipeline and unavoidable, even if emissions fell to zero tomorrow.[33]

Most leading climate scientists now believe that 2°C of warming would pose a substantial risk both because of its direct impacts on climatically sensitive Earth systems and because of the potential to trigger irreversible changes in those systems. The latter include the disappearance of Arctic summer sea-ice and melting of much of the Greenland and West Antarctic icesheets.[34] James Hansen has declared the goal of keeping warming at 2°C 'a recipe for global disaster'.[35] He believes the safe level of CO_2

in the atmosphere is no more than 350 ppm. The current level of CO_2 is 385 ppm, rising at around 2 ppm each year, so that we have already overshot our target and must somehow draw down large volumes of CO_2 from the atmosphere.[36]

In the history of life on Earth there have been ice-free eras—a planet with no glaciers and no polar ice caps. In these times sea levels have been some 70 metres higher than they are today. Paleoclimate studies of sediments and ice core records indicate the Antarctic icesheet started to form once atmospheric CO_2 levels fell below about 500 ppm, and the Greenland and West Antarctic icesheets formed when levels fell below about 400 ppm.[37] Once melting commences there is little humans can do to arrest it, except perhaps by simulating volcanic eruptions (an approach considered in Chapter 6). It is on this basis that Hansen and his fellow researchers conclude that 'if humanity wishes to preserve a planet similar to that on which civilization developed ... CO_2 will need to be reduced from its current 385 ppm to at most 350 ppm'.[38] Who could have predicted that at the beginning of the twenty-first century humanity would have to ask itself whether it can preserve a planet fit for civilisation?

Despite these serious doubts about the semi-official target, is aiming to limit warming to even 2°C a feasible goal? What do we have to do to stop emissions pushing temperatures above this level? Just before the Bali Climate Change Conference at the end of 2008 climate scientists released a new assessment arguing that, in order to have a good chance of avoiding the 2°C threshold, rich countries must by 2020 reduce their greenhouse gas emissions by 25–40 per cent below 1990 levels.[39] The 25 per cent target quickly became entrenched internationally as the benchmark against which the commitment of rich countries is judged.

The fact that aiming for 25 per cent instead of 40 per cent means developing countries will have to do a lot more was conveniently passed over.

We have seen that, rather than declining or even growing more slowly, global emissions have in fact been accelerating over the last decade. To have any hope of avoiding catastrophes, emissions must peak within the next few years and certainly no later than 2020, then begin a rapid decline to the point where all energy generation and industrial processes are completely carbon free. James Hansen has put it bluntly:[40]

> Decision-makers do not appreciate the gravity of the situation ... Continued growth of greenhouse gas emissions, for just another decade, practically eliminates the possibility of near-term return of atmospheric composition beneath the tipping level for catastrophic effects.

Meeting in March 2009, the world's leading climate scientists reached a similar conclusion: 'immediate and dramatic emission reductions of all greenhouse gases are needed if the 2°C guardrail is to be respected.'[41]

The urgent question we must now ask ourselves is whether the global community is capable of cutting emissions at the speed required to avoid the Earth passing a point of no return beyond which the future will be out of our hands. It is this irreversibility that makes global warming not simply unique among environmental problems, but unique among all of the problems humanity has faced. Beyond a certain point it will not be possible to change our behaviour to control climate change no matter how resolved we are to do so.

There are in fact two types of threshold beyond which the inertia of the system takes over. The usual thresholds are scientific; once the melting of Greenland is well underway no reduction in anthropogenic emissions will be able to stop it. But political inertia is also a barrier. Except in times of war, political institutions take time to respond to changed circumstances even if the problem is serious and urgent. The main players first have to be persuaded there is a problem. Then meetings must be called, inquiries held, objections accommodated, opposition overcome and public support won. Legislation has to be drafted, debated, amended and enacted, at which point policies can be implemented, a process that can take years even without serious resistance.

If the scientists are right, global emissions must reach a peak within five to ten years then decline rapidly until the world's energy systems are all but decarbonised. Are the institutions of government in the major nations of the world capable of recognising and responding to the urgency of the problem in time? Are the international institutions that must agree on a global plan sufficiently responsive to agree to, implement and enforce the necessary measures? These are questions on which climate scientists have little useful to say; they are in the domain of political and behavioural scientists.

Carbon futures

One way to think about the task of protecting the climate is to work out how much additional carbon we can put into the atmosphere in order to keep the concentration of greenhouse gases below an agreed target such as 450 ppm. Kevin Anderson and Alice Bows from the United Kingdom's Tyndall Centre for Climate Change Research (one of the top such centres) have set out the task we face in the most striking way.[42] It is the most important and confronting paper on climate change I have read. The authors present a range of possible global emission reduction paths and work out their implications for greenhouse gas concentrations and associated warming.

There are two ways of thinking about the task. First, we can set a particular target, such as stabilisation at 450 ppm, and work out how soon global emissions must peak and how quickly they must fall thereafter to meet it. Then we must ask whether the path so defined is politically possible given the national and international institutions that must decide on and implement the plan. Alternatively, we can make the most hopeful judgment about the emissions reduction path the world is likely to follow then ask how much warming it will entail. Anderson and Bows analyse the task both ways, but here I will focus on the second approach. In other words, we will make some optimistic assumptions about how soon and how quickly emissions can be reduced over the century and see what sort of world we would be left with.[43]

There are three broad types of activity that determine the volume of greenhouse gases that go into the atmosphere: emissions of CO_2 from burning fossil fuels for energy and in industrial processes; CO_2 emissions from cutting and burning forested areas; and emissions of greenhouse gases other than CO_2. Anderson and Bows first make some simple but plausible estimates of what we can expect from the second and third of these. Having made these estimates we can then concentrate on the big one, CO_2 emissions from fossil fuels.

Deforestation currently accounts for 12–25 per cent of the world's annual anthropogenic or human-induced CO_2 emissions.[44] Reducing deforestation will need to be a major focus of efforts to minimise climate change. If the world's decision-makers adopt a resolute attitude to tackling climate change then an optimistic assessment would see deforestation rates peak in 2015 and fall rapidly thereafter, to around half their current levels by 2040 and close to zero by 2060. If this happens then the total stock of carbon dioxide locked up in the world's forests will fall from 1060 billion tonnes[45] in the year 2000 to around 847 billion tonnes in 2100, a decline of 20 per cent. Over this century, then, deforestation would add 'only' 213 billion tonnes of CO_2 to the atmosphere. (A less optimistic scenario would see deforestation add 319 billion tonnes of CO_2 to the atmosphere.)

What about non-CO_2 greenhouse gases? What can we expect from them? Methane and nitrous oxide are the two main non-CO_2 greenhouse gases. In 2000 they accounted for about 23 per cent of the global warming effect of all greenhouse gas emissions.[46] They are mostly emitted from agriculture—methane from livestock and rice cultivation and nitrous oxide from the use of fertilisers. Emissions from agriculture are growing rapidly as more land is turned over to crops and pasture and diets shift to more meat as people in countries like China become better off. Population growth will make the task of reducing non-CO_2 emissions much harder because food is the first item of consumption humans must have. Like emissions from deforestation, agricultural emissions must peak soon then decline. Unlike emissions from deforestation they cannot be reduced to zero because of the nature of food production.

If the world's leaders take resolute action an optimistic assumption would be that non-CO_2 emissions will continue to rise until 2020, up from 9.5 billion tonnes annually (measured in CO_2-e) in 2000 to 12.2 billion tonnes, then fall to 7.5 billion tonnes by 2050, the level at which it stabilises.[47] If, as expected, the world population increases to a little over nine billion by the middle of the century, these 7.5 billion tonnes of CO_2-e allocated to food production must be spread across an additional 2.6 billion people,[48] which means that the emissions intensity of food production must be approximately halved over the next four decades.

Putting together these optimistic scenarios for deforestation and non-CO_2 greenhouse gas emissions, Anderson and Bows calculate that the total cumulative emissions from these sectors over this century will amount to just under 1100 billion tonnes of CO_2-e that will be emitted into the atmosphere. This provides the floor on which can be constructed emission scenarios for energy and industrial CO_2 emissions, the main game in tackling climate change. Two critical parameters will determine our fate—the date at which global emissions reach their peak and the rate at which emissions fall thereafter. These will determine the total amount of greenhouse gases that go into the atmosphere over this century, the resulting increased concentration of greenhouse gases, and the global temperature rise that follows. The later the peak, the more quickly emissions must fall to keep within an emissions budget.

A very optimistic assumption is that global emissions will peak in 2020.[49] Stopping global emissions growth will require that, from that year onwards, any increase in emissions from developing countries must be more than offset by decreasing emissions from developed countries.

Nevertheless, if we assume that overall emissions growth can be halted in 2020, what rate of emissions reduction could we expect in each year thereafter? As we will see in the next chapter, growth in emissions is a product of three factors: the rate of growth of income or output per person, population growth, and the technology used to generate and use energy, including the rate at which technological change can reduce emissions per unit of output. Population growth will continue its relentless march at least until the middle of the century, when it is expected to slow and perhaps stabilise at a little over nine billion souls. Demographic change occurs slowly, so even with sustained attempts to moderate population growth it is unlikely it could be contained much under this number over the next four decades. (The UN's low estimate is 7.8 billion people by 2050.[50]) Recession inevitably slows the growth of emissions, and may even cause them to fall. Yet economic slumps soon pass and emissions growth resumes, now driven predominantly by the large developing countries. In the next chapter I will explain why our obsession with economic growth makes it politically untouchable in the foreseeable future.

If cutting population growth and economic growth are not feasible over the next three or four decades, a huge burden is placed on new and existing technologies to decarbonise the world economy. Instead of taking the usual path of assessing the possible contributions of various technologies and then adding them up—as in the 'wedges' approach made famous by two Princeton University professors[51]—historical precedents provide a better guide as to how rapidly greenhouse gas emissions could fall. The Stern report includes a short but vitally important section that provides some precedents.[52] Economic collapse in the Soviet Union after the fall of the Berlin Wall in 1989 led to a decline in its greenhouse gas emissions of 5.2 per cent each year for a decade. During this period economic activity more than halved[53] and widespread social misery ensued. When France embarked on an aggressive program of building nuclear capacity—a 40-fold increase in 25 years from the late 1970s—annual emissions from the electricity and heat sector fell by 6 per cent, but total fossil emissions declined by only 0.6 per cent annually. In the 1990s, the 'dash for gas' in Britain saw a large substitution of natural gas for coal in electricity generation. Total greenhouse gas emissions fell by 1 per cent each year in the decade. Depressingly, Stern concluded that reductions in emissions of more than 1 per cent over an extended period 'have historically been associated only with economic recession or upheaval'.[54]

Given that some world leaders recognise the severity of the threat posed by global warming and the need, unprecedented except in wartime, for a rapid structural change in their economies, it might be reasonable to expect that the world could agree to reduce emissions by 3 per cent per annum after the 2020 peak until they reach the floor of 7.5 billion tonnes of CO_2-e set by the need to feed the world. Anderson and Bows show that, because we have already made some assumptions about rates of decline of emissions from deforestation and food production, the 3 per cent rate of decline of emissions overall will require a 4 per cent rate of decline in CO_2 emissions from energy and industrial processes.[55] Given that emissions in developing countries would be expected to continue growing, although at a slower rate, for some time after 2020 before peaking and beginning to fall, this means that emission reductions in rich countries will need to be much higher than 4 per cent—perhaps 6–7 per cent, a level higher than that associated with Russia's economic collapse in the 1990s.

It is hard to imagine even the most concerned and active government—Sweden's perhaps—introducing policies that would bring about such a rapid industrial restructuring. Nevertheless, let us put ourselves in the most optimistic frame of mind we can. If global emissions do peak in 2020 then decline by 3 per cent each year, with energy emissions in rich countries falling by 6–7 per cent, could we head off the worst effects of climate change, or even keep it to 'safe' levels? The answer provided by Anderson and Bows, and backed by other analyses,[56] is a very grim one indeed. If that is the path taken by the world then over the century we will pump out an extra 3000 billion tonnes of greenhouse gases,[57] which would not see atmospheric concentrations of greenhouse gases stabilise at the 'safe' level of 450 ppm. Nor would they stabilise at the very dangerous level of 550 ppm. They would in fact rise to 650 ppm!

Can this be right?

The conclusion that, even if we act promptly and resolutely, the world is on a path to reach 650 ppm is almost too frightening to accept. That level of greenhouse gases in the atmosphere will be associated with warming of about 4°C by the end of the century, well above the temperature associated with tipping points that would trigger further warming.[58] So it seems that even with the most optimistic set of assumptions—the ending of deforestation, a halving of emissions associated with food production, global emissions peaking in 2020 and then falling by 3 per cent a year for a few decades—we have no chance of preventing emissions rising well above a number of critical tipping points that will spark uncontrollable climate change. The Earth's climate would enter a chaotic era lasting thousands of years before natural processes eventually establish some sort of equilibrium. Whether human beings would still be a force on the planet, or even survive, is a moot point. One thing seems certain: there will be far fewer of us.

These conclusions are alarming, to say the least, but they are not alarmist. Rather than choosing or interpreting numbers to make the situation appear worse than it could be, following Kevin Anderson and Alice Bows I have chosen numbers that err on the conservative side, which is to say numbers that reflect a more buoyant assessment of the possibilities. A more neutral assessment of how the global community is likely to respond would give an even bleaker assessment of our future. For example, the analysis excludes non-CO_2 emissions from aviation and shipping. Including them makes the task significantly harder, particularly as aviation emissions have been growing rapidly and are expected to continue to do so as there is no foreseeable alternative to severely restricting the number of flights.[59] And any realistic assessment of the prospects for international agreement would have global emissions peaking closer to 2030 rather than 2020. The last chance to reverse the trajectory of global emissions by 2020 was forfeited at the Copenhagen climate conference in December 2009. As a consequence, a global response proportionate to the problem was deferred for several years.

Nor does the analysis account for the effect of aerosols, the tiny particles that mask some of the warming otherwise built in to the system. The clean-up of urban air pollution in China and India, through laws requiring cars to have catalytic converters fitted and power plants to have scrubbers installed, would bring on the warming more quickly. The only good news is provided by the global recession, which may provide a couple of years of breathing space. If, due to resolute action, global emissions still peak in 2020 they will peak at a lower level, which would reduce the rate of emission reduction required. On the other hand there is a good chance the recession will erode political resolve, leading to a postponement of the peak year so that its benefits are foregone.

As if this were not stunning enough, while the analysis incorporates conventional carbon–climate feedback effects—the weakening capacity of land and ocean sinks to soak up carbon[60]—it does not account for the possibility of others such as the ice-albedo effects from Arctic warming that may hasten the approach of a 650 ppm world and take us well beyond it.

These facts must cause us to rethink entirely how the future will play out because the presence of feedback effects and tipping points call into question one of the most fundamental assumptions of all climate change negotiations—that we can aim to limit emissions so as to 'stabilise' climate change.

The stabilisation myth

The belief that we can stabilise the climate at a specified concentration of greenhouse gases in the atmosphere, with an associated increase in average global temperature, has underpinned all international negotiations over global warming. The idea that greenhouse gas emissions must be limited to prevent 'dangerous' warming is embodied in the 1992 Framework Convention on Climate Change. The official European and Group of Eight goal of aiming to keep warming below 2°C is based on this idea, as are greenhouse gas concentration targets such as 450 ppm or 550 ppm advocated in the Stern report and Australia's Garnaut report. But it ought to be clear by now that the belief that humans can adopt policies that stabilise the climate rests on assumptions that are not well founded in the science. Stabilisation requires that annual emissions be eventually reduced to 'the level that balances the Earth's natural capacity to remove greenhouse gases from the atmosphere'.[61] The problem is that global warming is likely to trigger its own 'natural' sources of new emissions and interfere with the Earth's capacity to remove carbon from the atmosphere.

The Earth's climate is not like a machine whose temperature can be regulated by turning some policy knobs; it is a highly complex system with its own regulatory mechanisms. Humans cannot regulate the climate; the climate regulates us. For several years climate scientists have understood that some of the relationships among variables are non-linear, so that a slight increase in warming can cause a large shift in other aspects of the climate. Paleoclimatologists have known this for a long time, but it is only in the last few years that the idea has been linked explicitly to today's global warming.[62] If we look at a chart showing the climate history of the Earth stretching back over many millenniums we do not see smooth transitions from ice ages to 'interglacial' or warm periods (such as the one we are now in). The transitions are sometimes dramatic, with sharp changes in the world's climate occurring over mere decades, probably due to amplifying feedback effects. So climate states can end abruptly once certain thresholds are crossed, setting off accelerated warming that is stopped only when a natural limit is reached, such as the disappearance of ice from the Earth.[63]

I have already mentioned some tipping points which could induce positive-feedback effects that amplify warming and its effects, including the disappearance of summer sea-ice in the Arctic, the melting of the Greenland icesheet, the melting of the West Antarctic icesheet, the release of carbon from melting permafrost, and large-scale die-back of the Amazon rainforest.[64] As they occur these changes will be effectively irreversible, at least for thousands of years. A recent paper has destroyed any idea we might have that we can take radical corrective action once things become intolerable.[65] It reaffirms that a large proportion of the CO_2 we are putting into the atmosphere will still be there in a thousand years, so the level at which emissions peak makes a huge difference. Both the warming and the sea-level rise associated with that peak will not decline, even if emissions fell to zero, but will stay virtually constant for more than a millennium. The authors conclude:[66]

> It is sometimes imagined that slow processes such as climate change pose small risks, on the basis of the assumption that a choice can always be made to quickly reduce emissions and thereby reverse any harm within a few years or decades. We have shown that this assumption is incorrect ...

The lag between emissions and their effects on climate and the irreversibility of those effects make global warming a uniquely dangerous and intractable problem for humanity. Among other things, as we will see in the next chapter, these features of climate change render standard economic analysis of the problem hopelessly inappropriate. Indeed, it is positively dangerous.

Recognition of the non-linear nature of climate change has radically transformed the climate science debate in the last few years, although the message is still to filter out of the scientific community and into policy deliberations. It is the reason many climate scientists are no longer merely worried but panicked, although the panic is sometimes suppressed by a practised detachment. As late as 2007 the IPCC was still writing as if stabilisation were feasible, although buried in its report was a muted but ominous warning: 'The risk of climate feedbacks is generally not included in the above analysis. Therefore, the emission reductions to meet a particular stabilization level reported in the mitigation studies assessed here might be underestimated.'[67]

After their 2008 review of the dangers of climate tipping points, a group of leading climate scientists wrote: 'Society may be lulled into a false sense of security by smooth projections of global change.'[68] This is typical of the cool understatement of so much climate science. The extent to which policy-makers and their advisers have been lulled into a false sense of security is apparent from the sudden emergence of 'overshooting' strategies, now adopted explicitly or implicitly by almost every government in the world. The rot set in around 2005 when key policy advisers seem to have decided that aiming to stabilise atmospheric concentrations of greenhouse gases at 450 ppm of CO_2-e, the level associated with 'dangerous' warming of 2°C, would be too difficult. The capitulation was announced by the United Kingdom's chief scientist David King, who declared that aiming for 450 ppm would be 'politically unrealistic'.[69] The same conclusion was drawn by Nicholas Stern, who wrote in his 2006 report that aiming for stabilisation at 450 ppm 'would require immediate, substantial and rapid cuts in emissions that are likely to be extremely costly'.[70] Instead, the world should aim to stabilise at a politically achievable 550 ppm, a target also taken up by

Ross Garnaut in his 2008 report for the Australian Government. After all, the reasoning goes, we are already at 430 ppm CO_2-e, and stopping at 450 would meet fierce opposition from industry and voters. So we must aim instead for a concentration of 550 ppm and then bring it back down to 450 ppm in the following decades.

This is the path adopted by the Obama Administration too. Rich country emission cuts of 25–40 per cent below 1990 levels by 2020, which are necessary if the world is to aim for a target of 450 ppm, were immediately declared politically impossible by new US Special Envoy for Climate Change, Todd Stern.[71] The 'most ambitious' proposal the United States could aim for would be to return emissions to 1990 levels by 2020—a 'zero per cent' reduction instead of 25–40 per cent—although the climate change legislation passed by the House of Representatives in 2009 subsequently set a nominal target of 4 per cent below 1990 levels. 'At the same time we are being guided by the science and doing the math', said Mr Stern, 'we cannot forget that we are engaged in a political process and that politics, in the classic formulation, is the art of the possible. Of course we cannot afford to be passive in our understanding of that principle—we need always to push the envelope of what is possible.' The British and American Sterns were at one.

Faith in our ability to overshoot then return to a safer climate simply fails to understand the science—whatever we do we will be stuck with the results for a very long time. If carbon dioxide concentrations reach 550 ppm, after which emissions fell to zero, the global temperature would continue to rise for at least another century.[72] Moreover, once we reach 550 ppm a number of tipping points will have been crossed and all the efforts humans then make to cut their greenhouse gas emissions may be overwhelmed by 'natural' sources of greenhouse gases. In that case, rather than *stabilising* at 550 ppm, 550 will be just another level we pass through one year on a trajectory to who knows where—1000 ppm perhaps.

In September 2008 two scientists from the Scripps Institution of Oceanography in the United States published an analysis arguing that the world is already committed to 2.4°C of warming above pre-industrial levels.[73] With that degree of warming the Earth would pass at least three climate tipping points—the disappearance of Arctic summer sea-ice, the melting of the Himalayan-Tibetan glaciers and the melting of the Greenland icesheet. The analysis was challenged by another eminent scientist, Hans Schellnhuber, who argued that the claim that we cannot avoid at least 2.4°C of warming depends on two pivotal assumptions: that the world will not be able to reduce global greenhouse gas concentrations below 2005 levels, and that developing countries will implement the sorts of 'clean air' policies the West has used to reduce urban air pollution.[74] The latter policies are expected to reduce the 'atmospheric brown cloud' made up of aerosols that mask the effect of warming. When the skies are cleared of the particles that create global dimming, the full effects of the enhanced greenhouse effect will be felt. Schellnhuber believes that global greenhouse gas emissions can be halved by 2050. This depends, however, on assuming that developing countries do not move too quickly to clean up air pollution, for if they do temperatures would indeed shoot up close to 2.4°C before coming down to perhaps below 2°C a century or so later. Schellnhuber's argument asks us to be optimistic about policies to reduce greenhouse gas emissions and pessimistic about the implementation of policies to reduce air pollution. Even he concedes that the possibility of keeping temperatures at or below 2°C depends vitally on the world ensuring that emissions peak in the period 2015–2020.

The adaptation myth

The new understanding of the climate system and the likely influence of tipping points induced by human intervention also forces us to reconsider one of the other foundations of international negotiations and national climate strategies, the belief in our ability to adapt. From the outset of the global warming debate some have argued that as much emphasis should be placed on adapting to climate change as on mitigating it. As the setting and meeting of targets appears more difficult, more people began talking about the need to adapt.

Underlying the discussion of adaptation is an unspoken belief that one way or another we (in rich countries) will be able to adapt in a way that broadly preserves our way of life because global warming will change things slowly, predictably and manageably. Wealthy countries can easily afford to build flood defences to shield roads and shopping centres from storm surges, and we can 'climate-proof' homes against the effects of frequent heatwaves. Yet if our belief in our ability to stabilise the Earth's climate is misconceived then so is our belief in our ability to adapt easily to climate change. If instead of a smooth transition to a new, albeit less pleasant, climate warming sets off a runaway process, adaptation will be a never-ending labour. If warming rises above three or four degrees the chances of severe and abrupt change become high. A harsh and prolonged drought can wipe out an entire region's food production. Fertile plains can turn to dust bowls. A week of temperatures above 40°C can kill tens of thousands of people.

Of course, for people in poor countries adaptation means something entirely different. The effects of warming will be more cruel and their ability to adapt is much more limited. The melting of Himalayan glaciers would stop water flowing to vast areas for the length of a dry season, leading to famine. Adaptation strategies then become severely circumscribed: the choice becomes migrate or die. The governments of low-lying island states such as Tuvalu and Maldives are already planning to shift their entire populations. All of these have implications for national security, as waves of environmental refugees seek new places to live.[75]

Of course, all of the above takes an anthropocentric stance: humans may be able to adapt to significant climate change, but other species and ecosystems will have a much harder time of it. This is a huge topic, and here is not the place to canvass it. Suffice to say that across a broad range of ecosystems certain species will prevail (including feral animals and weeds), while others will be driven out and die.[76] In the type of scenario I have described, mass extinctions are likely.

In sum, the most important assumptions on which international negotiations and national policies are founded—that we can stabilise the climate at some level, that we can overshoot our target concentration then return to it, and that we can accommodate two or more degrees of warming by adapting to it—have no foundation in the way in which the Earth's climate system actually behaves. We moderns have become accustomed to the idea that we can modify our environment to suit our needs and have acted accordingly for some 300 years. We are now discovering that our intoxicating belief that we can conquer all has come up against a greater force, the Earth itself. The prospect of runaway climate change challenges our technological hubris, our Enlightenment faith in reason and the whole modernist project. The Earth may soon demonstrate that, ultimately, it cannot be tamed and that the human urge to master nature has only roused a slumbering beast.

Chapter 2

Growth fetishism

The growth fetish

Twenty-five September 2009 was World Overshoot Day, also known as Ecological Debt Day, the day on which humanity used up all of the resources generated by nature in that year and began living off the Earth's capital.[1] In that year humans used about 40 per cent more resources than the ecosystems of the Earth could generate, equivalent to a household spending more than its income by taking out a loan. Put another way, we would need 1.4 planets like Earth to be able to sustain our consumption levels, assuming economies grew no more. Of course, except during temporary recessions, the world's economies will continue to grow, sucking up resources and pouring out wastes without any prospect of surcease. Economic growth continues to be vital for bringing people in developing countries out of poverty, but in rich countries the preoccupation with growth has long surpassed its relation with need and has become fetishised.

When we fetishise an object, we attribute to it magical or supernatural powers. The object in question protects the owner from evil or is vested with divine power. Fetish objects are usually associated with 'primitive' peoples, although it is hard to differentiate between the powers of a bone held by a shaman and the powers of a consecrated cross held by a priest. More to the point, in affluent societies religious value seems now to be invested in the most profane object, growth of the economy, which at the individual level takes the form of the accumulation of material goods. Our political leaders and commentators believe that it has magical powers that provide the answer to every problem. Growth alone will save the poor. If inequality causes concern, a rising tide lifts all boats. Growth will solve unemployment. If we want better schools and more hospitals then economic growth will provide. And if the environment is in decline then higher growth will generate the means to fix it. Whatever the social problem, the answer is always more growth.

Where once nations boasted about their great cultural achievements, their advanced state of knowledge or their military conquests, now the measure of a nation is the level of its gross domestic product or GDP per person, which can be raised by only one means, more growth. A nation whose economy is in the doldrums suffers a blow to its national pride. Among the richest countries, to fall out of the top ten of GDP per person is a cause of national soul-searching, political point-scoring and a resolve to raise productivity so that the nation can hold its head high once again. The most important number a national statistical agency produces is the one that measures annual GDP growth. Keenly anticipated and the subject of endless speculation, announcements are greeted with jubilation or dismay. The markets react, business confidence surges or plunges. If the number is good the government rejoices; if it is below expectations the opposition is secretly jubilant but grimly tells the world that the country has lost its way.

Like cargo cultists Westerners invest supernatural powers in material goods, and are convinced that acquisition of a sufficient number of them will bring about a paradise on Earth. The fetishisation of material goods takes on sublime form in the universal equivalent of those goods—money. The magical power of money has long been a subject of anthropological and sociological analysis. Far from being a mere convenient means of exchange and store of value, money has become a vital force. People will engage in the most irrational behaviour to gain access to its powers. Those who are rich beyond the ability to spend nevertheless seek more of it.

Progress itself is now measured by GDP growth; to question growth is to oppose progress and those who do are immediately accused of wanting to take us back to the stone age, as if living in a mansion or a cave were the only options, as if the only alternative to the pursuit of opulence is living in squalor.

To accuse one's opponents of religious zeal is a well-worn debating trick, one frequently used by conservatives to ridicule those calling for radical action on global warming. Yet the attribution of religious connotations to our society's preoccupation with economic growth is not far-fetched. When asked in 2001 if President Bush would be urging Americans to restrain their energy use, his spokesman, Ari Fleischer, replied: [2]

> That's a big no. The President believes that it's an American way of life, and that it should be the goal of policy makers to protect the American way of life. The American way of life is a blessed one. And we have a bounty of resources in this country.

Of course, most political leaders would scoff at the claim that the energy-profligate American way of life is blessed and that bounteous resources were given by God for human benefit; yet in a way George W. Bush's spokesman was guilty only of a lack of guile. The association in both progressive and conservative thinking between economic growth and progress is so deeply entrenched and vigorously defended that it cannot rest solely on any empirical association between higher material consumption and greater national happiness.

The 'end of ideology' in the 1980s saw the major political parties in the West converge on the belief that unfettered markets are the best way to promote growth. Eschewing their previous emphasis on inequality and exploitation, the parties of the left accepted that the road to electoral success is paved with fiscal rectitude and the confidence of the stock market. Doubts about the way the free market promotes individualism at the expense of social cohesion were dismissed. In what might be called the Thatcher–Clinton doctrine, the political *zeitgeist* was captured perfectly by the two emblematic observations of the neo-liberal era: 'There is no such thing as society; it's the economy, stupid.'

From the outset, the fetish with economic growth has provided the principal obstacle to coming to grips with the threat of global warming. The battle lines had been defined some decades previously. When, in her 1962 classic *Silent Spring*, Rachel Carson documented the effects of pesticide use on wildlife in rural America, the response from the chemical industry and the government was instant and ferocious. Carson was confronting the technological hubris of American capitalism and the attitude to the natural world on which it was constructed. Carson, a highly qualified and careful scientist, was characterised by her opponents as a 'hysterical woman'. The defenders of the status quo dismissed the book as 'subversive'. Their instincts were right: calling on humans to live in harmony with the natural world rather than treating it as a resource ripe for exploitation subverted the most powerful people as well as the most entrenched assumptions on which the system had been built—that all growth is good and technology is a boon to our wellbeing.[3]

A decade later, a group of thinkers known as the Club of Rome commissioned scientists at the Massachusetts Institute of Technology to prepare a report on the effects of continued economic and population growth on resource availability and pollution. So extreme was the response to their report, *The Limits to Growth*, from the defenders of the status quo that it was apparent it had struck a hidden nerve. Orthodox economists led the attack; after all, hadn't the free market always provided a timely response to any shortage? Prominent Yale economist Henry Wallich dismissed it as 'irresponsible nonsense',[4] and over the years the attacks escalated until today critics of any environmental warning need do no more than intone 'Club of Rome' to summon guffaws from conservatives. Environmentalism had quickly become the enemy of all the conservatives held dear. In 1985 arch defender of American capitalism Ronald Reagan declared: 'There are no great limits to growth when men and women are free to follow their dreams.'[5] Taken literally the statement is nonsensical; but Reagan was saying that environmentalism is a threat to free enterprise because it requires people to act collectively to restrain the self-interested behaviour of others.

Despite its demonisation, the principal conclusion of *The Limits to Growth* was remarkably moderate: [6]

> If the present growth trends in world population, industrialization, pollution, food production, and resource depletion continue unchanged, the limits to growth on this planet will be reached sometime in the next one hundred years.

Although the fierce criticisms that the book has been subjected to have all been aimed at the projections about when certain resources might run out—with critics confusing model projections of what *could* happen with predictions of what *will* happen[7]—the real cause of outrage lay in the second main conclusion reached by the MIT analysts. They argued that technological solutions may for a time disguise and delay the pressures of feedbacks so that growth can continue,[8] but in the long run the momentum of growth will overwhelm technological progress. We must consider another response, one that 'has almost never been acknowledged as legitimate by any modern society': to moderate growth of both the economy and population and aim for a condition of ecological and economic stability through a 'controlled, orderly transition from growth to global equilibrium'.[9]

Perhaps dimly aware of the firestorm their book would spark, the authors acknowledged that such a suggestion would strike many people as 'unnatural and unimaginable'.[10] Yet the report's authors, being scientists, had an almost touching faith in the power of reason to bring about the changes needed to avoid collapse. If calling for an end to growth was incendiary in 1972, the free-market revolution of the next two decades saw economic growth become politically untouchable.

We begin to suspect that the deeper source of outrage over the arguments of *Silent Spring* and *The Limits to Growth* is that they challenge the most deeply held assumptions of Western civilisation—that the Earth's resources are infinite and that humans have a right to exploit them without restraint for their own benefit. As we will see, this attitude to the Earth is a recent development in human history, but it lies at the very heart of the climate crisis. While ostensibly scientific in intention and method, the two books, perhaps unwittingly, called on humans to reconsider their very nature. Decades on, the evidence of damage to the natural world due to human activity continues to mount. To be sure, there have been important successes and breakthroughs. Citizen demands led governments to legislate to clean up urban air quality; national parks have helped protect some endangered species and ecosystems; and an international treaty seems to have stopped the thinning of the ozone layer. These have been important victories of environmentalism and popular activism driven by science. Oddly, the improvements have enabled critics like Bjorn Lomborg to attack environmentalists as redundant, using their victories as proof that they are superfluous.[11]

Growth as the solution

All of the arguments for the sanctity of growth have been marshalled to counter the clamour for measures to reduce greenhouse gas emissions. While global warming deniers have been effective in their aim of sowing doubt in the public mind, the most powerful argument used over and over against proposals to cut emissions has been the economic one. I could present pages of examples where the appeal to the effects on growth has been used to resist or water down measures to cut carbon emissions—including wild but uncontested claims of economic ruin and collapse—but so pervasive is the truth of this that the reader will need no convincing. Nevertheless, let me give just two.

In June 1997, in the lead-up to the Kyoto Conference, the US Senate passed by 95 votes to zero the famous Byrd–Hagel resolution which declared that the United States should not adopt any international treaty to reduce greenhouse gas emissions that 'would result in serious harm to the economy of the United States'. That was during the Clinton presidency. By 2001 President Bush's opposition to acting on global warming was so determined that he felt the need to issue a reassurance to the world: 'The earth's well-being is also an issue important to America', intuiting that perhaps the world had come to believe otherwise, even though, a few months earlier, he had tried to dispel doubts by declaring, 'I know the human being and fish can coexist peacefully'. Explaining his refusal to move on Kyoto he went on to state: 'We must always act to ensure continued economic growth and prosperity for our citizens and for citizens throughout the world.'[12]

Rather than being the cause of environmental decline, growth is everywhere touted as the *solution* to it. The arguments stretch credulity among unbiased observers but exercise a powerful sway over our political leaders and opinion-makers. It is claimed that higher national income due to more growth provides more resources to devote to environmental protection. Of course, this does not answer the question of whether those resources *will* in fact be devoted to climate protection or spent by households upgrading their home entertainment systems. As people become wealthier do they become more benevolent or more greedy? Do they place a higher value on environmental amenity? Economists have tried to demonstrate that they do through a device known as the Environmental Kuznets Curve, which purports to show that as a country industrialises and incomes rise the quality of the environment initially deteriorates but then improves. Setting aside worries about how the natural world is characterised as a commodity that becomes more desirable as incomes rise—a so-called 'luxury good' like a Lincoln Town Car or a Mercedes-Benz—if such a relationship is robust then there is no case for the government to intervene; the market will solve its own problems.

The relationship proves to be wobbly, particularly in the case of global problems like climate change. It is true that middle-class people often acquire enough money and political influence to isolate themselves from the foul emanations of slums and factories, but if we must wait until consumers feel rich enough to reduce spontaneously and dramatically their greenhouse gas emissions we are surely doomed. While a case can be made that impoverished people in developing countries are 'too poor to be green', an idea promulgated in the 1987 Brundtland Report on sustainable development,[13] there is little evidence that growth makes people 'too rich to be brown'. That developing countries are too poor to be green and should not be expected to be anything else naturally appeals to the bastion of free-market economics, the World Bank, which declared in its 1992 World Development Report: 'As incomes rise, the demand for improvements in environmental quality will increase, as will the resources available for investment.'[14] Economist Wilfred Beckerman, author of books titled *Small is Stupid* and *In Defence of Economic Growth*, was blunter: 'there is clear evidence that, although economic growth usually leads to environmental degradation in the early stages of the process, in the end the best—and probably the only—way to attain a decent environment in most countries is to become rich.'[15] More recently, the environmental sceptic Bjorn Lomborg makes the same claim: 'only when we get sufficiently rich can we afford the relative luxury of caring about the environment'.[16]

Recognising that growth fetishism stands as an immovable obstacle to action on climate, environmentalists soon capitulated and began to argue that we can have the best of both worlds, a healthy atmosphere and robust economic growth, and indeed that promoting renewable energy in place of fossil energy would accelerate economic growth. I myself undertook economic modelling studies that showed there could be a 'double dividend' from policies to cut emissions. It is quite possible to tweak economic models to show that if the revenue is used to reduce other taxes (such as payroll taxes) the imposition of a carbon tax will actually *increase* GDP growth and employment. In the climate policy debate these studies ought to be the coup de grâce, but inexplicably they are ignored. This fact suggests that, beneath the surface, objections to emission-reduction measures may not be about growth after all, an idea to which I will return.

Nevertheless, in making these arguments environmentalists have conceded that protecting the atmosphere can at best be the second most important goal. Acceptance of this 'both-ism'—growth and climate protection—imposes an enormous burden on technology. We have reached the point in international efforts where technology alone holds the possibility of reconciling continued economic expansion with a livable planet. In particular, in the minds of our political and corporate decision-makers, the future of the world has come to depend on one factor above all others, the successful development and deployment of carbon capture and storage, a technology to save the coal industry that even its most avid supporters concede will take decades to commercialise fully (as explained in Chapter 6). Yet the anxiety generated by this contradiction is less than that flowing from the thought that radical social change is necessary to preserve a habitable Earth. So, can technology save us?

Can technology save us?

One of the symptoms of growth fetishism is tunnel vision, a condition that prevents those affected from seeing any solution to the greenhouse problem other than a technological one. We can understand the burden this places on technology using the famous IPAT equation.

$$I = P \times A \times T$$

This identity simply says that the level of environmental Impact depends on the Population, the level of Affluence (measured by GDP per person) and Technology.

Before considering faith in technology, it's worth noting that some people focus on population growth as the chief culprit. It is indisputable that, other things being equal, faster population growth will make the task more difficult. There is also no question that the enormous expansion of the global population over the last several decades has left us much more vulnerable. But when we consider the task ahead of us we should remind ourselves that it is the proliferation of people with high levels of emissions that has given us the climate crisis. This is shown to devastating effect by two North American researchers, Paul Murtaugh and Michael Schlax, who have estimated the 'carbon legacies' of reproductive decisions.[17] It is obvious that our consumption decisions affect the amount of greenhouse gas emissions for which we are responsible; but so do our reproductive decisions. The researchers assign to a person responsibility for their own carbon emissions and that of their descendants, since those emissions are contingent on that person's reproductive choices. They assume that a mother is accountable for half of the emissions of her offspring and a father is accountable for the other half. Each is then responsible for a quarter of the emissions of their grandchildren, and so on.

Making a number of reasonable assumptions for various countries about fertility rates and future per capita carbon emissions, the researchers estimate that the carbon legacy of the average female in the United States is 18,500 tonnes of CO_2 while that of a Bangladeshi woman is only 136 tonnes. In other words, the future stream of carbon emissions following a decision by an American couple to have an extra child is 130 times greater than that of a decision by a Bangladeshi couple. Put another way, to have the same impact on future global carbon emissions, a decision by one American couple not to have a child would have to be matched by 130 Bangladeshi couples. So population policies should be targeted now at the United States and the larger European countries (including Russia) rather than poor but populous nations like Bangladesh, India and Nigeria. The US–Bangladesh comparison is the most extreme case, but even comparing the carbon legacies of parents in the United States and China gives a factor of nearly five.[18] For India the factor is nearly 50. In short, it makes no sense to single out population growth without linking people to their expected consumption.

Recognising that it is affluence rather than population growth that is mainly responsible for the climate crisis allows us to recast the famous Malthusian theory. In his 1798 *Essay on the Principle of Population*, Thomas Malthus argued that there is a natural tendency for unchecked population growth to outstrip the capacity of agriculture to increase food production, so that famine, pestilence and war tend to bring the supply of people back into balance with the supply of food. Parson Malthus attributed the tendency of population to grow at a geometric rate to 'the vice of promiscuous intercourse among the inferior classes'.[19] Yet I think it must now be admitted that the situation we face has arisen not from the old working-class vice of excessive copulation but the modern middle-class vice of excessive consumption. And just as in later editions of his essay Malthus recognised that the natural checks of famine and war could be avoided by 'moral restraint' in the form of postponement of marriage and abstinence, so the answer to the climate crisis lies in disinterring the middle-class virtues of moderation and frugality.

Returning to our IPAT equation, what can it tell us about the task of preventing catastrophic climate change? A country's CO_2 emissions depend on its population, its GDP per person and the technology that determines the amount of CO_2 emitted per unit of GDP. So each year

$$CO_2 = P \times \frac{GDP}{P} \times \frac{CO_2}{GDP}$$

The right-hand side cancels out to give the left-hand side, so the identity must be true.

Changing the demographic structure of a country takes a long time so a world population of close to 9.2 billion by 2050 seems unavoidable, although if we are lucky a decline in fertility rates may see growth limited to around 8 billion.[20] What about A, affluence, which is increased by faster economic growth? To suggest to a politician in a rich country that economic growth should be halved is unthinkable; to suggest it to the leaders of poor countries would be madness.

Although a change in the mix of what we consume (reflected in a shift in the composition of GDP towards more services) can moderate rises in emissions, the burden of constraining emissions falls on technological change, which must work harder and harder to offset increases in population and, especially, GDP growth. According to one study, over the 15 years to 1997 CO_2 emissions in rich countries rose by around 20 per cent due, roughly speaking, to a 10 per cent increase in the number of people and a 40 per cent increase in affluence, offset by a 30 per cent fall in carbon emissions per unit of economic output produced.[21]

Although carbon emissions are growing under the combined effect of affluence and population growth, all of the world's hopes and efforts have been loaded onto technology. But can technology carry such a burden in the face of relentless growth of affluence and population? Tim Jackson of the University of Surrey has done a simple calculation that shows what it would take.[22] In 2005 there were 6.6 billion humans (P) and their average level of income or affluence (A) was $5900 per annum (very unequally distributed, of course).[23] The technology factor (T) is 0.76 tonnes of CO_2 per thousand dollars of GDP. This gives rise to global annual CO_2 emissions of just under 30 billion tonnes = 6.6 billion × 5.9 × 0.76, an average of around 4.5 tonnes per person.

If we aim at stabilising the concentration of greenhouse gases in the atmosphere at 450 ppm (a level now recognised as too high), then we must reduce annual CO_2 emissions from 30 to around 4 billion tonnes a year by 2050.[24] Achieving this reduction requires that global emissions decline at 5 per cent a year starting now, a rate of fall that, as we saw in the last chapter, has occurred only in Russia in the 1990s when its economy was more than halved in size. If population and affluence continue to grow as expected, all the burden rests on technology. Let us say that energy technologies are transformed so that emissions per unit of output are cut by 80 per cent, so our T factor falls from 0.76 to 0.15 tonnes of CO_2 per thousand dollars of GDP in 2050.

Where will that leave global emissions? The United Nations' best estimate of the world's population in 2050 is 9.2 billion, an annual rate of increase of around 0.75 per cent.[25] But GDP for each person will rise much faster, perhaps at around 1.75 per cent a year (less in rich countries, quite a lot more in China and India).[26] At that rate, with technology cutting emissions by 80 per cent per unit of GDP, total global CO_2 emissions would fall from 30 to 17 billion tonnes in 2050. If our target is 4 billion tonnes, that would be catastrophic for the climate. What if there is a technological revolution that cuts emissions per unit of output by 90 per cent so T falls from 0.76 to 0.076 tonnes of CO_2 per thousand dollars of GDP? That cuts emissions in 2050 to less than 9 billion tonnes, still double the 'safe' level. And, of course, the economy will continue to expand after 2050, if nature permits. The only way out is to completely decarbonise well before 2050, and even that is probably not enough.

In the 2008 animated film *WALL-E* American consumerism has reached its zenith in a future community of grossly obese, physically incapable and mentally vacant consumers locked on a never-ending luxury cruise in space. A long time beforehand, they had taken to their giant spaceship after making the Earth uninhabitable. They left behind a devastated environment and a small garbage compacting robot, WALL-E, who is programmed to nibble at the edges of a vast pile of rubble, a civilisation lying in ruins. The surviving human community can float endlessly in space because of its technological mastery. Content in its lotus-eating utopia, it has no desire to return to life on Earth. Technology has wholly replaced nature and the bloated consumers have become less than human because they have forgotten what it means to be part of a natural world.

If divorcing technologically sophisticated human beings entirely from the natural world seems a bizarre scenario, there are many, like David Keith, a professor of energy and environment at the University of Calgary, who believe that while global warming may result in the 'loss of the natural world we care about', civilisation is not at stake. For him, technology allows civilisation and nature to occupy separate realms. 'Humans are amazingly adaptable and have amazing powers of isolating themselves from the environment by their technology', so that it is likely that we will end up in the business of 'planetary management' where what remains of the natural world will be managed like a garden.[27] In such a situation it would be a matter of indifference if civilised humanity inhabited a regulated Earth or a drifting spaceship. Indeed, life in a self-contained, wholly controlled environment is regarded as not just possible but preferable by the surprisingly large membership of the National Space Society, an organisation whose vision is: 'People living and working in thriving communities beyond the Earth'. The society's 'positive future for humanity' is now being trialled here on Earth with the trend towards integrated retail malls in which humans can live as well as shop and entertain themselves. Cropping up all over the United States, they are 'the wave of the future' according to the Urban Land Institute.[28] Boston's Natick Shopping Mall has twelve stories of condominiums attached to the enclosed mall; for those residents who might worry about being overwhelmed by artificiality, the developers have thoughtfully included 'a 1.2-acre park with wandering, leafy paths on the mall's roof'. It's the sort of 'integrated lifestyle' captured perfectly by the animators who created *WALL-E.*

Labouring away faithfully back on Earth, WALL-E comes across something peculiar, a green seedling, the last remnant of living Nature. By convoluted means the seedling arrives on the spaceship. Its presence sparks something hidden deeply in the humans, a vestigial memory of the meaning of Nature which stimulates a desire to rediscover authentic life. At least, that desire flickers in the ship's corpulent captain, who decides to set a course for Earth. He discovers, to his dismay, that the spaceship's computers have long ago assumed control and he has been merely going through the motions of being in charge. The vessel's computer system has developed its own objective and has no interest in returning to Earth; perhaps it senses that Nature and human free will are threats to its supremacy. A struggle to the death ensues in which the remnant humanness of the bloated consumers and their captain triumphs. They return to Earth and begin to rebuild a living authentic home from the last green shoot.

I tell this story because it is an allegory of the way in which the growth machine, which we thought we had built to enhance our own ends, has taken on a life of its own, and resists fiercely the slow awakening to its perils of the humans it is supposed to serve. The growth machine has, over time, created the types of people who are perfectly suited to its own perpetuation—docile, seduced by its promises and unable to think beyond the boundaries it sets. The closer some get to the levers of the machine the more they must be committed to its goals. It is hard to imagine that anyone who believes that economic growth is part of the problem would ever be allowed near those levers. More likely they would be ridiculed in the newspapers and denounced in the parliaments. Ordinary people may at times question the wisdom of relentless growth and conclude that it cannot go on forever, yet they are soon bounced out of their subversive reverie by the inducements to go shopping. The system has created the type of people who are perfectly suited to what it needs, unending expansion.

In this way the growth system governs itself. We think we have power, but the growth system awards power only to those who will advance its objective. We internalise the discourse (as Michel Foucault would say) so that we begin to articulate the interests of the system and govern ourselves according to its rules. So in our consumption behaviour we conduct ourselves in ways that perpetuate the system, and in our public behaviour we are implicated in political structures that also serve the needs of the growth machine. Our political leaders tend to be those who have internalised the goals of the system most faithfully and are therefore most immune to arguments and evidence that might challenge it. The state itself, which once represented the interests of the people, even if those interests were often thwarted by the power of business, has been reshaped since the 1970s to serve the interests of the Economy.

How much would it cost?

Given the fear of economic damage from measures to reduce greenhouse gas emissions—anxieties ceaselessly stoked by newspaper headlines emphasising the financial burden of tackling climate change—we would expect that economic analysis aimed at estimating those costs would generate some scary numbers. Yet—and this is perhaps the most astonishing fact about the debate over what to do about global warming—the opposite is the case. Economic analysis has repeatedly concluded that the costs would be tiny. What is going on?

In 2007 the IPCC updated its assessment of the economic costs of emission abatement by bringing together and assessing the results of a wide range of economic models.[29] What did it show? To be fair, let's consider the worst case for the economy, which is usually the best case for the climate. The most stringent target assessed involves cutting emissions to ensure that greenhouse gases in the atmosphere are stabilised at 450 ppm CO_2-e in 2050. The economic model showing the highest cost of reaching this target estimates that pursuing it would cause a reduction of global GDP of 5.5 per cent in 2050.[30] Most models show lower costs. At first blush—and most politicians and journalists never get beyond first blush—this might seem like a sizeable number. In fact, it is minuscule. It means that aiming for 450 ppm would decrease global GDP by 5.5 per cent below the level it would otherwise reach in 2050.[31] The average annual growth rate of global GDP between 1950 and 2000 was 3.9 per cent.[32] Once the world recovers from the current recession, it is expected to average around 2.5 per cent over the next decades.[33] At that rate, real global GDP will increase 2.9 times, from US$54.3 trillion in 2007 to US$157 trillion in 2050.[34] If the world aimed to stabilise emissions at 450 ppm then the model indicates that global GDP in 2050 would be 5.5 per cent lower and would 'only' reach US$150 trillion.

Bearing in mind that world income will be very unevenly

distributed, what would that mean to the typical individual? Global population is expected to increase from 6.7 billion people in 2007 to 9.2 billion in 2050.[35] If incomes grow at the anticipated 1.75 per cent each year, average incomes will double by 2047. If we took stringent measures to restrict greenhouse gas emissions so that they stabilise at 450 ppm then, according to the models that show the greatest economic damage, at most the effect on the world economy would be such that the doubling of average incomes would be held up until 2050, a delay of three years. I have selected the most pessimistic numbers. A more typical estimate of the cost to GDP is 2 per cent, which would mean the loss of only one year's income growth between now and 2050. A one-year delay in the doubling of average incomes is the basis for the belief that pursuing a safe level of climate protection would be too expensive.

The Stern intervention

Since the early 1990s all economists who modelled the costs of cutting emissions showed that continued growth and climate protection are quite consistent.[36] In 2005 Britain's then Chancellor of the Exchequer, Gordon Brown, commissioned Nicholas Stern, previously chief economist at the World Bank, to prepare a report on the economics of climate change that would consider both the costs of reducing emissions and the costs of climate change if emissions were to grow unchecked. The Blair Government was keen to disprove the argument put by the governments of the United States and Australia that ratifying the Kyoto Protocol would be economically 'ruinous'. Stern's report was a signal intervention in the global debate mainly because it put forward officially a powerful economic case for deep cuts, arguing that it will be more costly economically if we do not act. Declaring that the world does not need to choose between averting dangerous climate change and promoting economic growth, the report concluded that the cost of unchecked global warming will amount to 5–20 per cent of global GDP by the middle of the century, whereas the cost of reducing emissions to avoid the worst effects of warming would be around 1 per cent of global GDP by 2050.[37] Not only is reducing atmospheric carbon not an obstacle to continued economic growth, it is the only way to ensure it is sustained.[38]

The Stern report created a sensation around the world. But no matter how robust the economic analysis, it was never going to shift President Bush and Prime Minister Howard from their staunch opposition. The strategy of the Blair Government of undermining the economic case against taking action was based on a naive understanding of the influence of economics and economic growth on the recalcitrance of the US and Australian governments and the fossil fuel lobby. If growth is a fetish then faith in it is only superficially rooted in its ostensible purpose of raising living standards. If it can be shown that, over time, living standards will be higher by reducing greenhouse gas emissions, this destabilises but does not destroy faith in the magical powers attributed to economic growth and the place of the free market in providing it.

If, as I will argue in later chapters, we must transform our consumption behaviour and rethink our attitude to Nature in order to respond to warming, then the Stern report had the unfortunate effect of further entrenching growth fetishism and the legitimacy of the conventional economic approach to climate change. The Blair Government wanted to make economics the solution to the climate change logjam but could not see that, at a deeper level, the economic way of thinking is the problem.

Stern claimed to offer a new ethical framework for thinking about climate change; but, apart from using certain ethical arguments to justify the use of a low discount rate (considered below), he did not step outside of, or even consider, an alternative moral universe. After all, the Stern review begins with the claim that 'human-induced climate change is at its most basic level an externality',[39] that is, an effect on a third party not involved in a market transaction. Although it seems natural to orthodox economists, to characterise human-induced climate change as an 'externality' is a highly tendentious claim, for if it is so 'at its most basic level' then global warming cannot be due to our alienation from Nature, the rapacity of the growth machine, over-consumption by the affluent or the failure of governments to rein in powerful corporate interests. It is caused by a glitch in the operation of an otherwise perfect market, one that arises because those who are responsible for greenhouse pollution 'do not face directly, neither via markets nor in other ways, the full consequences of the costs of their actions'. Global warming is not a human failure but a market failure, a technical problem rather than a social or moral one. The solution, then, is to perfect the market.

The debate that followed the publication of the Stern report, which included vigorous attacks on its 'radicalism' from more conservative economists, never questioned Stern's way of framing the problem as 'the greatest market failure the world has ever seen'.[40] Even environmentalists welcomed it. The absence of any challenge reflected the total victory of free-market economics over the previous three decades. Even in the 1960s, to characterise climate change as an imperfection of the market would have seemed an odd way of understanding the relationship of human beings with the natural world. The problem is, says Stern, that the climate is 'a public good' and those who refuse to pay up for using it to dump their wastes cannot easily be excluded from access to it. Of course, this implies that the natural and manageable state of affairs is one of private goods, ones that are well defined, privately owned and able to be bought and sold. This claim naturally provokes alarm about the privatisation of the environment but beneath it lies a prior conception in which humans are conceived as radically separated from the world around them and can therefore regard it as a realm that provides goods and services for human benefit. In a later chapter I consider the philosophical transition that led to this type of consciousness; here we should simply note that most economists and the political leaders in their thrall regard it as puzzling even to question this conception. This is just how the world is, isn't it?

Stern's review of the economics of climate change concluded that aiming for 500–550 ppm CO_2-e would reduce global GDP by a mere 1 per cent by 2050,[41] so that the level of output that would be reached in January 2050 without any policy intervention would not be reached until perhaps May 2050 with intervention. In Nicholas Stern's judgment this level of costs is acceptable. However, he argues strongly against adopting a more ambitious target of 450 ppm because it would increase the costs at least three-fold.[42] But three times a tiny cost is still a tiny cost. It is acceptable, according to Stern, to ask people to wait an extra five months for their incomes to double but it is too much to ask them to wait a little more than a year.

In advising the British Government that pursuing a 450 ppm target would be too ambitious because it would be 'very costly' and difficult[43] Stern was backed by Sir David King, the government's chief scientist, whom one would have thought would stick to scientific advice rather than making political judgments about what is 'realistic'.[44] The same conclusion has been reached by Australia's Stern, the economist and former ambassador to China Ross Garnaut, who set out the disastrous consequences of warming then urged the government to adopt a 550 ppm CO_2-e global target.[45] Pursuing a 550 ppm target would shave a little more than 0.1 per cent from annual GNP growth (the same as Stern's estimate) through to 2050, while a 450 ppm target would cost a little more. Yet the implications for the world of a 450 ppm *versus* a 550 ppm target are enormous. The Garnaut report itself notes that a 550 ppm world would be expected to see the destruction of the Great Barrier Reef and a near-doubling of species extinctions.[46] Garnaut carefully weighs up all of the factors and concludes that 'it is worth paying less than an additional 1 per cent of GNP as a premium in order to achieve a 450 result'.[47] However, he did not think the rest of the world would make the same judgment and therefore recommended that the Australian Government adopt a 550 target.

Yet when we consider what is at stake this seems unhinged. The Stern report describes the vast increase in damage associated with a 550 ppm target compared to the 450 ppm target. For instance, the number of people at risk from hunger rises from 25 per cent to 60 per cent (tell them that 450 ppm is 'too ambitious'), the risk of ecological collapse of the Amazon rainforest rises from very low to high, and the onset of irreversible melting of the Greenland icesheet goes from quite likely to virtually certain.[48] Aiming at 550 ppm is very likely to cause irreversible changes to the global climate so that the question of how much we would be willing to sacrifice to preserve the climate would no longer be one we would need to agonise over.

What is apparent deep within the political judgments of these economists, and one chief scientist, is that economic growth is sacrosanct; even in the face of a catastrophic transformation of the conditions of life on Earth it seems legitimate to quibble over whether we should accept a decline in the economic growth rate of 0.2 per cent rather than 0.1 per cent. This existential calculus leaves one to wonder whether, if the numbers of the economic models had turned out differently so that sharply reducing emissions *would* significantly damage economic growth, the governments of the world would indeed sacrifice the planet to the supreme god of growth. The depressing fact is that the outcome of the Copenhagen Conference in December 2009 proved that the prophecies of the Sterns, the Kings and the Garnauts turned out to be right—the world is unwilling to make the trade-off.

The backlash

Despite its failings, the Stern report's great merit was its acknowledgment that ethical judgments always underpin economic analysis. In doing so it opened up a small crack in the intellectual monolith, albeit one that never threatened to bring it down. Even so, the report created intense controversy in the economics profession because it was seen by influential conservatives as advocating a 'radical' and 'extremist' response to global warming. Although praised by some less dogmatic stars of the profession, among its higher echelons the Stern report was seen as a threat. 'Fear-mongering', 'patently absurd' and 'destructive' were some of the epithets used. It's worth exploring the main line of attack for what it reveals about the world we have created.

The backlash was led by Yale University economist William Nordhaus. Nordhaus carved out much of his reputation by developing one of the earliest economic models to evaluate climate change policy and has become perhaps the most influential economist in the United States working in the area. When in 1997 some progressive economists prepared a statement urging the United States to take global warming more seriously, securing Nordhaus's endorsement was considered vital and the text was watered down to accommodate his opinions.

The Stern report represented a direct challenge to the softly softly approach advocated by the Yale guru. A few months after its publication Nordhaus wrote a splenetic critique that allowed the conservative segments of the profession to dismiss Stern's arguments.[49] Nordhaus accused Stern of abandoning accepted economic principles, writing a 'political' document, making 'extreme assumptions' and reaching 'extreme findings'. The barely suppressed hysteria of Nordhaus's response to Stern's challenge to orthodoxy spills over in suggestions that in commissioning the report the Blair Government was 'perhaps stoking the dying embers of the British Empire', and that the British Government is as fallible in its report on global warming as it was in its white paper on weapons of mass destruction that led to the invasion of Iraq.[50]

While carried out as a technical dispute over where to set the discount rate—the rate at which future costs and benefits are discounted to make them equivalent to current money values—the underlying argument between Stern and Nordhaus was over the ethical status of private markets. Like all committed neoclassical or free-market economists, Nordhaus believes implicitly that our private behaviour in the marketplace always represents our true preferences so that whatever the market generates is value-free and untouchable. Thus in considering the long-term impacts of policy we must use the interest rate determined by our behaviour in private markets, even if that means the interests of generations more than 50 years hence disappear from the analysis.

The belief that the market is value-free is one that many economists cling to as proof of their 'rigour'. But the determination to create a conceptual system in which real humans—with all of their foibles, biases and irrationalities, not to mention their power relations and political and social institutions—are expunged tells us something important about the character of the economists. It is not that they have driven all emotion from their work but that one particular emotion triumphed, the craving for scientific detachment.[51] Commenting on reactions to the Stern report, Julie Nelson refers to the 'hypervaluation of detachment' and points to the way in which economists like Nordhaus are captives of a self-conception characterised by emotional distance, autonomy, 'hard' knowledge, rationality and disinterestedness.[52] These were the signal characteristics of the new science that emerged in the seventeenth century and can be captured in a particular term used unashamedly at the time to describe the new worldview—'masculine'. It explains economists' penchant for mathematical formalisation, and the way in which the profession rewards those who are most adept and devoted to that form of analysis. The method has been called objectivism, 'a romantic belief in the possibility of connection-free knowledge from an outside-of-nature, perspective-free viewpoint'.[53] More informally, it's known as physics envy. In the 1980s the renowned institutional economists Wassily Leontief and John Kenneth Galbraith wrote that 'departments of economics are graduating a generation of *idiots savants*, brilliant at esoteric mathematics yet innocent of actual economic life'.[54]

Of course, accepting a discount rate generated by private-market behaviour means endorsing as somehow natural and therefore unchallengeable the prevailing distribution of income and wealth. This is an ethical judgment, yet Nordhaus actually compares the prevailing distribution of incomes with 'the eating habits of marine organisms',[55] suggesting the level of inequality in any society follows from some biological law rather than policies and social structures, as if there were no alternative to the kind of Wall Street rapacity and dishonesty that caused the 2008 market crash. This sort of social ignorance is not only philosophically naive but reflects the intellectual imperialism of mainstream economics; it just happens to provide a trenchant defence of the status quo, even though that status quo has created the climate crisis we now confront.

Arguing that we may have social preferences that stand above our market behaviour is described as 'paternalism' by free-market economists, when in truth it is the democratic process at work. Right-wing economists like Richard Tol—who said that if a student had handed in the Stern report he would probably have given it an 'f' for fail, depending on his mood[56]—believe that it is not up to 'philosophers' like Stern to speculate on the appropriate discount rate because the preferences of the people are expressed in the marketplace every day. The only preferences that Tol regards as legitimate are those expressed by consumers in the supermarket and never those expressed by citizens at the ballot box. This is perhaps the ultimate conceit of mainstream economics, the equation of market behaviour with democracy itself.

Nordhaus has his own economic model (called DICE) designed to provide an answer to the question of how much we should aim to reduce global greenhouse gas emissions.[57] It claims to incorporate the effects of climate change on various market activities, like changes in crop yields, and some 'non-market effects', such as species extinction, and converts them into a stream of dollar values which can then be compared with the costs of limiting emissions. The Earth's climate system is treated as a type of capital, like office buildings or industrial machinery, the stock of which contributes more or less to aggregate human welfare. Like all forms of capital we must decide to invest in improving it or allow it to deteriorate, which means deciding how much greenhouse gas to allow into the atmosphere to optimise its value. Comparing the costs and benefits of emission reductions over time—where the benefits are some of the avoided costs of climate change—allows Nordhaus to describe an 'optimal' path for dealing with global warming.

As this suggests, for him the warming of the globe due to the enhanced greenhouse effect is a technical problem requiring a carefully calibrated response. The more we reduce emissions the lower will be the damage due to climate change but the higher will be the cost of abatement, so there is a trade-off. Nordhaus uses his model to find the magic number.

If we do nothing, he shows, global temperatures will rise to 3.1°C by the end of the century (and 5.3°C by the end of the next), and the cost of damage will amount to $23 trillion in lost consumption.[58] We can reduce those damages by reducing greenhouse gas emissions, but only if we pay the cost of abatement policies. The task is to find the optimal outcome, the one that minimises the sum of the costs of climate damage and the cost of reducing emissions. The model spits out the answer, the 'optimal policy': it is the policy that moderates greenhouse gas emissions so that by 2100 the global temperature reaches only 2.6°C above pre-industrial levels, instead of 3.1°C. Climate damages are reduced from $23 trillion[59] to $18 trillion but we must add to that the costs of abatement, which amount to $2 trillion, so that the net cost is $20 trillion, thereby saving the world $3 trillion compared to doing nothing about warming.

So Nordhaus says the best course for the world is to set the global thermostat at 2.6°C for the end of this century, rising to 3.5°C by 2200 despite universal agreement among scientists that this would bring catastrophe beyond measure. In other words we should let atmospheric concentrations rise to 600 or 700 ppm of CO_2, at which point we stabilise and get used to a hotter world.[60]

Any attempt to keep the global temperature below the optimal level of 2.6°C would be a bad mistake, insists Nordhaus. If the world were foolish enough to listen to Nicholas Stern the economic losses would be huge—$37 trillion.[61] Stern may have his heart in the right place but Professor Nordhaus's DICE model has proven that adopting his proposals would be *worse* than doing nothing about global warming.[62] If the world would be unwise to listen to Stern it would be downright crazy to listen to Al Gore, because his proposals would have a net cost of $44 trillion. We would be better off, Nordhaus concludes, to just put up with a hotter world; the extra income will more than compensate, even if it means it's eventually 5.3°C hotter.

By any reasonable criterion Nordhaus's analysis is mad. He behaves like the ultimate economic technocrat with his hand on the global thermostat, checking his modelling results and fiddling with the knob, checking again and adjusting further, all so that the planet's atmospheric layer may be tuned optimally to suit the majority of human inhabitants. Apart from the supreme arrogance of the idea that humans should assume the role of planetary regulator, the DICE model is based on a profoundly flawed understanding of climate science. The Earth's climate system is not like a central heating system that can be smoothly adjusted to a desired temperature.[63] It is, in the words of eminent geoscientist Wallace Broecker, more like an angry beast. 'If you're living with an angry beast, you shouldn't poke it with a sharp stick,' he has said.[64] Nordhaus believes humans have tamed it, but Broecker warns: [65]

> The inhabitants of Earth are quietly conducting a gigantic experiment. So vast and sweeping will be the consequences that were it brought before any responsible council for approval, it would be firmly rejected.

The meaning of growth

I began by suggesting that the obsession with economic growth has been the principal obstacle to effective global warming policies. The implication is that if the growth obstacle can be removed then the world will act. We have seen that all economic analysis concludes that the growth impediment ranges from small to extremely small; according to the models it is not so much a mountain to climb as a barely noticeable speed bump for the global economy. The Stern report only confirmed what dozens of economic modelling studies had concluded, that the cost of cutting emissions would be tiny. Even Nordhaus's dismal DICE model cannot conjure up the big numbers that would justify claims of economic ruin flowing from rapid emission-cutting. The criticisms of conservatives, whose own figures show the costs of abatement to be a fraction larger than tiny, prompt thoughts of fairies and pinheads.

Yet there is another fact that renders the unwillingness to act almost too baffling. Arguments about the economic impact of greenhouse policies are built on a vital assumption that is never mentioned, the assumption that higher incomes are worth pursuing because they improve people's wellbeing. In rich countries—and the models are always conducted in rich countries and interpreted as applying to rich countries by decision-makers in those countries—there is virtually no relationship between increasing GDP and national wellbeing. Above a certain threshold, more money does not make people happier.[66] To argue, as the economists implicitly do, that Americans will be measurably less happy if they have to wait until 2055 instead of 2050 to be twice as rich is absurd. Even the statisticians who compile the figures acknowledge that GDP is not a measure of the nation's wellbeing; it merely measures the value of final goods and services produced in a year. As is well known, GDP takes no account of the contribution of unpaid household work to our wellbeing or of how growth is distributed. An extra $1 billion of GDP adds the same amount to national wellbeing irrespective of whether it ends up in Bill Gates' bank account or the pockets of homeless people. Moreover, GDP often counts 'bads' as 'goods'. A murder adds around $1 million to GDP when account is taken of the damage to all those involved and the costs incurred by the police, the courts and the prison system. Murder is good for the economy. So is environmental destruction. When pressed, even the most orthodox economist will concede that GDP growth bears only an indirect relation to improvements in national wellbeing.

So if cutting emissions would have only a tiny effect on growth, and in rich countries higher growth will have no appreciable effect on our wellbeing, we are compelled to ask whether a reduction in growth really is the obstacle to action on climate change. I think the answer is that the obstacle to taking resolute action is not economic growth as such but the *fixation* with economic growth, the growth fetish, the *unreasoning* obsession that arises because growth is believed to have magical powers. When political leaders and commentators say we cannot cut emissions, or must do so only slowly, because of the effects on growth, it is the *symbolism* of growth rather than growth itself that they are driven to defend. If asked, some politicians will wax lyrical about how GDP does not measure our wit or our compassion, nor the joy of our children's play. Quite so; but it is another thing entirely to ask them to put a stick in the spokes of the growth machine.

So what is the symbolic meaning of growth in affluent countries? Whereas the early economists like John Stuart Mill and John Maynard Keynes believed the value of growth lay in its ability to improve living standards, economic growth has become much more. It is the mark of vitality, the bearer of dynamism, the symbol of life itself. It is what vivifies a nation, gives reality to dreams of prosperity and confers cultural superiority. If humans are naturally optimistic creatures, their hopes have become vested in economic growth. Growth is the vehicle that delivers nations and peoples from backwardness into modernity. A nation whose economy is not growing is seen to be a moribund nation, a 'basket case'. Modernity has become inseparable from high incomes generated by sustained growth; yet the fetishisation of growth is a form of pre-modern totemism. At its core, the preoccupation with growth is a religious urge, but one displaced from the genuinely sacred to the nominally profane. There are few more noble goals than to lift people out of poverty and for this reason the preoccupation of poor countries with growth is defensible. But in China and India the process involves the creation of a vast army of middle-class consumers who quickly become moulded in the image of their counterparts in the West—unreflective materialists whose desires are insatiable.

Any challenge to the pre-eminence of growth is met with howls of outrage and suggestions that the alternative is to regress, to undo all we have achieved, to return to the caves. It is useless to argue that we can have rich lives instead of lives of riches; as I will argue in the next chapter, growth provides the raw material from which we increasingly construct our sense of who we are, and to ask us to pursue goals other than growth is to ask us to repudiate the human being created by three centuries of industrialism, consumerism and modernity.

Chapter 3

The consumer self

Growth fetishism is mirrored in the individual. Just as a nation's sense of itself has become bound up with how it grows, so our individual sense of self has become bound up with how we consume. The transformation of consumption from a means of meeting needs into a way of acquiring an identity has been underway for some decades, but shifted into a new and more intense phase from the early 1990s.[1] Although much more recent and not yet fully understood, the consumer revolution may prove to have restructured our consciousness as much as the Industrial Revolution. I will argue in this chapter that the shift from a production society to a consumption society makes the task of persuading citizens of affluent countries to change their behaviour in response to the climate crisis more intractable because of the psychological meaning of the consumption process. The shift has been reflected in a change in the nature of firms and a change in the nature of the consumer.

The new firm

In the production society, economic growth was dependent above all on investor confidence, or what John Maynard Keynes called animal spirits; today in the consumption society growth is determined more by consumer confidence, which in the 1990s became heavily influenced by the availability of consumer credit. Previously, corporations manufactured largely standardised products and competed with each other through the efficiency of their production processes, with phases including 'scientific management' (also known as Taylorisation) and mass production. Today, differentiation rather than standardisation characterises goods and services so that production decisions now respond to the enormously variegated and constantly changing demands of consumers. Marketing creativity has replaced production efficiency as the key to competitiveness and corporate success.

Whereas prices for standardised products were once the focus of both consumers and producers, for most goods and services today price is a secondary consideration. The cost of investing goods with often-intangible qualities that contribute nothing to their practical usefulness now frequently exceeds the cost of actually manufacturing the items. The emblematic case is the $200 pair of sneakers that costs only $20 to produce in China, with much of the difference made up by marketing expenses such as payments to sports stars and sponsorship of events. In the production society, marketing, including advertising, was a subsidiary aspect of business organisation; in today's consumption society marketing departments dominate production departments within firms.

Advertising long ago discarded the practice of selling a product on the merits of its useful features and began building symbolic associations between the product and the psychological states of potential consumers.[2] The task of the advertising industry became to uncover the complex set of feelings that might be associated with particular products and to design marketing campaigns to appeal to those feelings. Thousands of the most creative individuals now devote their lives to helping corporations persuade people to buy more of their brand of car, margarine or running shoes at the expense of another corporation selling a product that is essentially the same. It is virtually impossible today to buy any product that is not invested with certain symbols of identity acquired by the buyer knowingly or otherwise.

While once the wealthy elite were alone preoccupied with consumption as a marker of status, in the 1990s luxury consumption broke out of the world of the rich to reach down to all consumer groups, a phenomenon known as 'luxury fever'.[3] It led manufacturers of prestige products to put their brands on a broader range of items including 'entry-level products' accessible to all. Thus Gucci and Armani attached their brands to sunglasses bought by people who could not otherwise afford to buy clothes or accessories with such prestigious labels. Other brands tried to keep their prestige status while selling to ordinary consumers—the 'democratisation of luxury'—thereby providing the latter with the opportunity to emulate the lifestyles of the rich. Car-makers such as Mercedes now manufacture entry-level models that those on modest incomes can afford. The Mercedes A-Class, launched in 1997 and updated in 2004, was promoted to the masses by aging celebrity fashion designer Giorgio Armani, superannuated tennis champion Boris Becker and down-market pop singer Christina Aguilera. The tag-line linked to these icons of conventional culture was 'Learn the rules, and break them'.

Consumption today is now inseparable from profligacy. Bathrooms are no longer seen as functional places but new spaces for displays of excess, with computer-assisted design tools now used to create new taps, baths, showers and lighting. It is not unusual for American homes to have a bathroom attached to each bedroom. Nor is it unusual, even for households with modest incomes, to own five or six television sets, so that many family homes resemble a cluster of self-contained flats. In addition to having several bathrooms, each is more likely to sport two basins, perhaps with gold-plated fittings. While the cost of an average bath in the United Kingdom is around £300, luxury models retail for up to £8000. Whirlpool offers a gold-plated designer toilet seat—'A stunning addition to any bathroom, this toilet seat has been completely plated in a luxurious shade of gold to bring a touch of sparkle and splendour to your cloakroom or bathroom.' In the era of hyper-consumerism the urge to satisfy any desire has reached sublime levels. It is now possible to buy capsules filled with 24-carat gold leaf which, when swallowed, make your excrement sparkle. Created by New York designer Tobias Wong, the gold pills are promoted as a signifier of excess and a means of 'increasing your self-worth'—although presumably for only as long as the digestion process takes. At $425 each they are the ultimate confirmation of the ancient association, often noted by anthropologists, between gold and excrement, a conjugation reflected in a favourite piece of Latin American graffiti: 'If shit turned to gold, the poor would be born without arses.'

The new consumer

None of the trends I have identified could have occurred unless the consumer too had changed in some essential way. In the production society consumers were seen to have given tastes and the task of advertising was to persuade them that the product would satisfy their needs. In the consumption society marketers are now engaged in an endless process of creating and transforming, as well as responding to, consumer desires. Those desires are no longer merely the expressions of particular urges but grow out of the need to find and express a sense of self. The reinvention of the consumer has occurred in the context of broader social changes. The new social movements of the 1960s and 1970s ushered in the era of 'individualisation'. In place of societies in which people living in largely homogeneous neighbourhoods and communities formed their sense of self by unconsciously absorbing the cultural norms and behaviours of those around them, we became free to create our own selves, to 'write our own biographies' instead of having them more or less drafted by the circumstances of our birth.[4] In a society saturated with the outpourings of the mass media, the symbols of achievement and the characters worthy of emulation appear on the screen and the magazine pages rather than in the local community or in handed-down stories of the saintly and the stoic. Individualisation created the social conditions for the flourishing of modern consumerism by providing the opportunity for the marketers of goods to step in and satisfy the desire to find and express a self.[5] The desire for an authentic sense of self was pursued increasingly by way of substitute gratifications—external rewards and, especially, money and material consumption. Indeed, it is well established that those people with a more materialistic goal-orientation are more likely to engage in consumption for identity-related and emotional motives.[6]

The problem is that these substitute gratifications can never provide what we really need; one cannot find an authentic identity in a supermarket or department store. Yet this unbridgeable gap is precisely what the latest phase of consumer capitalism needed, a constant feeling of dissatisfaction to sustain spending. While economic growth is said to be the process whereby people's wants are satisfied so that they become happier, in the consumption society economic growth can be sustained only as long as people remain discontented. Economic growth no longer creates happiness: unhappiness sustains economic growth.

The perceived gap between what we had and what we desired is the only explanation for the unprecedented consumer debt binge of the 15 or so years leading to the crash in 2008. In particular, the housing bubble—described by *Economist* magazine as the biggest bubble in history[7]—was driven by escalating desire, with buyers willing to commit larger shares of their future incomes to acquiring the houses of their dreams. In the United States, along with ballooning mortgages, the sizes of new houses also grew—55 per cent since 1970—at the same time as the number of people in them fell—by 13 per cent.[8] The same phenomenon occurred in Britain and Australia.[9] Before the crash, among younger American home buyers, a third said that having a home theatre in their house was 'important' or 'very important' in choosing a house.

Of course, bigger houses must be carpeted, curtained, heated, cooled and filled with furniture. The supply of larger houses stimulated the demand for more stuff. But the link between bigger houses and more stuff has worked the other way as well. Despite the inflation in house sizes, the accumulation of stuff outgrew the capacity of houses and apartments to accommodate it. As a result, a new industry sprang up. Over the last two decades the fastest growing segment of US commercial real estate has been the self-storage industry.[10] Driven more by residential than commercial demand, the number of self-storage facilities around the country grew by 81 per cent in the six years to 2006.[11] (In Australia it grew by 10 per cent a year through the boom years, and in Britain by an astonishing 35 per cent annually.[12]) Nearly one in ten American households now rents self-storage space to accommodate the stuff spilling out of their homes.

Over-consumption also has psychological costs. One study found that four in ten people 'feel anxious, guilty or depressed about the clutter in their homes'.[13] They say they feel overwhelmed and disorganised; some feel trapped by their possessions. Six out of ten women say there is a room in their house they are too embarrassed for visitors to see. The desire for more stuff has been so relentless that the market has responded by throwing up another new industry—home organisers, specialists who provide advice on how to organise our homes so that we are no longer oppressed by the clutter. Googling 'de-clutter your home' yields 36,000 responses, including links to books with titles like *Put Your House on a Diet*, *Making Peace With the Things in Your Life* and *Does This Clutter Make My Butt Look Fat?* Perhaps in the hothouse world of the next century an underground museum will display copies of these books as symbols of the world of excess that led to a transformed climate.

In the 1990s and 2000s spending more than you earn became almost a patriotic duty. In 2004 the *Wall Street Journal* lamented the unwillingness of Europeans to spend unnecessarily and their penchant for electing governments that introduced laws to restrict retail hours and limit the use of credit cards: 'Western Europe has only 0.27 credit cards per person compared with 2.23 in the US', the *Journal* complained. 'Moreover, many affluent Europeans just do not want to spend their free time shopping.'[14] Those interviewed for the story said they preferred playing with their children, meeting friends and reading books. The *Journal* was dismayed that French television regularly warned viewers about the dangers of over-indebtedness. It even blamed European thriftiness for the US trade deficit. Whereas once debt was disreputable, by the 1990s in the United States *refusing* to shop on credit was a sign of poor character. Prudence had become uncool.

As a result of easy credit and escalating mortgages, the US household savings rate—the difference between household income and household spending—saw a dramatic decline from over 10 per cent in the mid-1980s to zero in the mid-2000s.[15] (In Australia the decline was even sharper; net savings became negative in the 2000s.[16]) This was matched by a huge increase in consumer debt, from $10 billion a month in the mid-1980s to $25 billion in the mid-2000s.[17] Throughout the 1950s, 1960s and 1970s, US household debt as a proportion of annual income was stable at around 60 per cent. In the mid- to late 1980s it began to rise, accelerating in the late 1990s until it reached over 130 per cent in 2005.[18]

The huge increase in indebtedness was not for the most part the result of poorer households being forced to borrow to cover living expenses; it was the result of wealthier households splashing out on luxuries. In 2004 US households in the lowest income group had a little over 3 per cent of the income and a little over 3 per cent of the debt. Those in the middle 20 per cent of the population had a little over 12 per cent of the income but held 15 per cent of the debt, while the second richest 20 per cent of households had 19.5 per cent of the income but 24 per cent of the debt.[19] Only the richest 10 per cent had a higher share of income than of debt.

The collapse in national savings and the blow-out in debt reflected an upheaval in the values that had defined the post-war era. Norms of moderation and thrift were replaced in the 1990s by a culture of impulsiveness. We wanted it now and once we had it we soon began to think about replacing it. Where once we took pride in making things last in order to get full value from them, now we have an urge for constant renewal. It was the era of the makeover. One study found that some iPhone shoppers are turned off by advertisements that emphasise the generous five-year warranty because it signals that buyers should commit to the gadget for a long time, when they would rather replace it in a year or two.[20] Similarly, we don't hear much nowadays about the emblematic consumer complaint of the 1960s, planned obsolescence, because consumers often tire of a product well before it physically expires.

The point of all of this for climate change is evident. When we ask affluent consumers to change their consumption behaviour we are asking of them much more than we realise. The purpose of the shift in marketing from promoting the qualities, real or imagined, of a product to promoting brands as a lifestyle choice was to exploit the modern need to construct a sense of self. If we have constructed a personal identity in large part through our consumption activity, and consuming is how we sustain ourselves psychologically from day to day, a demand to change what we consume becomes a demand to change who we are. If, in order to solve climate change, we are asked to change the way we consume, then we are being asked to give up our identities—to experience a sort of death. So firmly do many of us cling to our manufactured selves that we unconsciously fear relinquishing them more than we fear the consequences of climate change. So the campaign to maintain a livable climate is in this sense a war against our own sense of who we are.

Wasteful consumption

The transformation of the consumer gives rise to two phenomena that bear directly on the question of how consumption has become a barrier to tackling climate change—wasteful consumption and green consumerism.

The idea that in affluent countries much of our consumption behaviour is driven by an urge for 'self-completion' rather than any real material need is reinforced by the evidence on wasteful consumption, that is, spending on goods and services that we do not in fact consume.[21] If our desire knows no bounds, our capacity to use things is nevertheless limited: there is only so much we can eat, wear and watch, and a house has only so many rooms that can be usefully occupied. The difference between what we buy and what we use is waste.

A study of the extent of wasteful consumption in Australia revealed that virtually all households admit to wasting money by buying things they never use—food, clothes, shoes, CDs, books, exercise bikes, cosmetics, kitchen appliances, and much more. They admit to spending a total of $10.5 billion every year on goods they do not use, an average of $1200 for each household, more than total government spending on universities or roads. These numbers do not account for spending on houses that are too big, holiday homes that are not used and automobiles that rarely leave the garage. If they did, the figures would probably double.

The problem of wasteful consumption will worsen. The study

revealed that richer households waste more than households with low and moderate incomes. That is to be expected. When asked if they feel guilty about buying things they do not use, wealthy people are less likely than poorer people to express remorse. (Close to half of people in low-income households say they feel 'very guilty' compared to around 30 per cent of those in high-income households.) In addition, despite two decades of environmental education, young people are both more likely to engage in wasteful consumption and less likely to feel guilty about it.

In the case of greenhouse pollution, wasteful consumption is related to the idea of 'luxury emissions', those emissions associated with consumption above a subsistence level. According to some, the moral status of a tonne of luxury emissions is not the same as a tonne of emissions that allows someone to survive. The difference between luxury and subsistence emissions is not the same as the economist's idea of the diminishing contribution of each extra tonne of emissions to our wellbeing as we become richer. It is a qualitative rather than a quantitative difference. As ethicist James Garvey has written: [22]

> Not all emissions have the same moral standing. Some emissions have more or different value, even if the quantity of emissions is just the same. The emissions resulting from an African farmer's efforts to feed his family are not on a par with the emissions resulting from an American dermatologist's efforts to get to Vegas for the weekend.

What can we say about the moral standing of emissions associated with the purchase of consumer goods that are not consumed but simply thrown away? While the American dermatologist's

Vegas emissions may have some form of moral standing because they at least impart some benefit to him, the emissions from wasteful consumption—including those associated with houses with unused rooms and holiday homes that are not visited—must have 'negative' moral standing because they are emitted for no benefit yet cause damage to others. While persuasive, these arguments neglect the purpose of modern consumption whose benefits often lie in the act of acquisition and ownership, rather than the act of consuming. Shopping confers psychic benefits. From a utilitarian point of view, the philosophical standpoint of free-market economics, that is enough. But who would want to have to explain the psychic benefits of shopping to the African farmer who must struggle to feed his family?

The truth is that US consumers, who currently account for around 23 tonnes of CO_2 equivalent each year, could live reasonably comfortable, healthy and safe lives with emissions of a quarter or a fifth of that amount even without any change in the way energy is supplied. French emissions stand at nine tonnes per person. In 1970 air travel by passengers from affluent countries was 10–20 per cent of current levels. Were we miserable then? Would our quality of life collapse if we were required to return to those levels, so that travelling by plane was restricted to essential journeys? Of course not, yet the psychological resistance to such a change would be almost insuperable.

Green consumerism

For many years governments, businesses and environmental organisations have been sending us a powerful message: we can make a difference if we change how we use energy in our daily lives. The environment sections of bookstores are stuffed with cheerful volumes describing all the things we can do to cut our greenhouse gas emissions—change our light bulbs, walk to the store, boil only as much water as we need, make sure we have a full load to put in to the washing machine and dry the clothes outside. WWF lists them under 'What you can do to fight climate change', and under the heading 'Ten Personal Solutions to Global Warming' the Union of Concerned Scientists declares: 'Individual choices can have an impact on global climate change. Reducing your family's heat-trapping emissions does not mean forgoing modern conveniences.'[23]

The idea that individuals can solve global warming infects the academic literature as well as popular culture. One study designed to test the belief that lack of public concern can be explained by a lack of knowledge about global warming found the opposite: those who are more knowledgeable about global warming feel less responsible for it. The authors treat this as a contradiction that needs resolution, yet perhaps the more one understands about the causes of warming the more one recognises that changing individual behaviour can have relatively little effect and that only collective action will work.[24] While some of us understandably want to reduce our own contribution to global warming, green consumerism is effective only to the extent it fosters political mobilisation.

Nevertheless, the message of green consumerism is seductive: if I am worried about climate change then I should try to do something about it, and the one thing I can control is my own behaviour. The danger of green consumerism is that it transfers responsibility from the corporations mostly accountable for the pollution, and the governments that should be restraining them, onto the shoulders of private consumers. As Michael Maniates has written: 'A privatization and individualization of responsibility for environmental problems shifts blame from state elites and powerful producer groups to more amorphous culprits like "human nature" or "all of us".'[25] Instead of being understood as a set of problems endemic to our economic and social structures, we are told that we each have to accept liability for our personal contribution to every problem. Websites that allow us to calculate our own 'ecological footprint' reinforce the personalising of responsibility.

In practice, green consumerism has failed to induce significant inroads into the unsustainable nature of consumption and production, and is unlikely ever to do so. For example, in those countries where green power (renewable electricity) has been made available to households and businesses, take-up rates have been low despite heavy promotion. In Australia, after a decade of promotion, by 2008 only 9 per cent of householders had picked up the phone to ask their electricity retailer to switch them over.[26] And despite the fanfare, buying carbon offsets has to date had no appreciable impact on the growth of greenhouse gases, nor is it likely to. Climate change is a collective problem that demands collective solutions. In other words, it needs good, strong policies enforced by governments.

Green consumerism is advocated by some who are less well-meaning than green groups. Governments and corporations often want to show how concerned they are about the environment and divert attention from their own role. Few are as blatant as E.ON, the owner of coal-fired power plants, which tells its customers: 'It's easy to blame industry and transport for environmental crime. But who decides what to produce and what to ship to different parts of the world? Isn't it you as a consumer?'[27] It's not our coal-fired power plants that bear the guilt but you, our customers, who are the environmental criminals.

The trend to individualise environmental problems has far-reaching implications for the nature of democracy too. When environmental problems become individualised the nature of public debate is no longer about the institutions that perpetuate and reinforce environmental degradation; it's about our personal behaviour. As Maniates argues, when citizens concerned about the environment are told to express their concern through their purchasing decisions, social conscience becomes a commodity.[28] The environment becomes depoliticised so that the major parties can share a common vision without getting into a potentially damaging bidding war over who will better look after the environment. The ethical conversation is also changed: instead of understanding the systemic factors that are the cause of and solution to the environmental problem, it becomes a question of personal morality. We are encouraged or shamed into buying eco-friendly products, insulating our homes and recycling our waste. While these activities do not deserve to be criticised in themselves—engaging in them reduces our personal responsibility—when they are promoted as the solution to environmental decline they may actually block the real solutions.

While advanced as a way of harnessing the power of consumers, green consumerism can actually disempower us because it denies our agency as citizens or political actors instead of consumers. It is important to stress that the failure of consumers to take up greenpower or recycle everything does not mean that they don't care and nothing should be done. This confuses the role of the self-interested consumer with the role of the responsible citizen. Despite attempts to turn us all into rational economic calculators, consumers are not the same as citizens; supermarket behaviour is not the same as ballot box behaviour. There is a wealth of evidence to show that people think and act quite differently in the two roles.[29] Thus it is not inconsistent for consumers to decline to take up green power when it is offered but to vote for a party that promises to require everyone to buy green power.

One of the striking features of the campaign to persuade us to change how we use energy is the way the various organisations stress that we do not have to give up any of our comforts.[30] The slogan 'It's easy being green' is built on the assumption that if it's hard people won't go green. A television program with that name is promoted as 'an entertaining, fun and upbeat look at the growing "green" lifestyle ... But it's not about throwing away everything you have and changing your lifestyle dramatically'.[31] No one wants to ask us to change our lifestyles because to do so may challenge much more than our energy use; it may ask us to confront our sometimes fragile sense of self. Indeed, the consumption of 'green' consumer goods has itself become a method of self-creation through consumption practices (albeit a sometimes far less damaging one). By shifting responsibility on to individuals and reinforcing the sacrosanct nature of consumer lifestyles, green consumerism threatens to entrench the very attitudes and behaviours that have given us global warming.

Greenwash

The counterpart of voluntary action by consumers is voluntary action by producers. In response to criticism, corporations will typically try to change public perceptions of what they do before they change what they do. It's cheaper. Thus rising public alarm about global warming has seen firms respond with a rich variety of dissimulation, of which greenwash has become the highest form. Greenwash has been defined as a strategy in which corporations 'put more money, time and energy into slick PR campaigns aimed at promoting their eco-friendly images, than they do to actually protecting the environment'.[32] In responding to concern over their role in global warming, energy companies have been especially creative. Shell decided to describe its Canadian tar sands operations—in greenhouse terms by far the worst way to produce energy—as 'sustainable'. When challenged, the company displayed astonishing brio in defending its use of the word by invoking the authority of the Brundtland Report. Shell interpreted Brundtland's celebrated definition of sustainable development—'development which meets the needs of the present generation without compromising the ability of future generations to meet their own needs'—to mean anything that helps to meet the world's growing energy needs, including tar sands. Although found guilty of misleading advertising by the UK Advertising Standards Authority,[33] Shell is an organisation that seems unable to experience shame, and subsequently ran newspaper advertisements depicting its oil refinery chimneys emitting flowers instead of smoke. In a similar move, E.ON, the owner of the Ratcliffe-on-Soar coal-fired power plant, the third largest single source of carbon dioxide in Britain, installed solar panels on the roof of its administration block then issued a media release proclaiming: 'This is one of the cleanest coal fired power stations in the UK, and, by fitting this array, it just goes to show how committed we are to improving our environmental performance even further.'[34] It was estimated that the panels reduced carbon emissions from the plant by less than one millionth.[35]

A large part of the resources of the global marketing and PR industries are now devoted to trying to convince the public that fossil fuel emissions are good for us. In one of the most creative tactics in advertising history, the coal industry is now trying to persuade us that coal-fuelled electricity is an 'environmentally sound' form of energy.[36] To do so they have deployed the intentionally misleading term 'clean coal'. The phrase is used in the climate change debate to give the impression that coal is or can be benign because of the possibility that carbon emissions might be captured and stored underground.[37] In truth, as we will see in Chapter 6, carbon capture and storage for coal-fired power plants is a technology still on the drawing board that will not have any effect on emissions for at least 20 years, if at all. When pressed on the point the industry claims that it has 'invested more than $50 billion in emission-reducing technology over the past 30 years'.[38] The emissions reductions in question have nothing to do with climate change but are a response to government regulations requiring reductions in air pollutants like sulphur dioxide and nitrous oxide. The deception has been compared by Sheldon Rampton to the 'bait-and-switch' tactic used by fraudulent retailers and unscrupulous real estate agents in which customers lured by attractive offers are presented with a different and more expensive substitute.[39] Note too that after fiercely resisting for decades the imposition of regulations to clean up air pollution from coal-fired power plants the industry now claims the results as proof of its commitment to the environment.

It's hard to imagine corporate spin being more cynical, but examples can be found. In the United States growing sales of SUVs and pick-up trucks—between 1999 and 2007 they exceeded sales of cars[40]—generated public ire. Concerned at the strident criticisms, General Motors—maker of the Hummer—decided to act. But rather than changing what it manufactured it created a magazine advertisement showing an SUV placed on an icefloe surrounded by inquisitive polar bears, penguins and whales. It was as if GM wanted both to assuage any concerns in the minds of potential buyers and incense environmentalists at the same time. Although disguised as its opposite, GM displayed the same contempt for its customers that Henry Ford did in his famous retort that those who complain about restricted choice for the Model T could have any colour they want, 'so long as it is black'. After all, as late as 2008 the vice-chairman of GM, Bob Lutz, was telling journalists that global warming was a 'crock of shit'.[41] It was perhaps poetic justice that the single-minded focus on SUVs and pick-up trucks took GM to the point of bankruptcy in 2009. In January, as the company staved off collapse through a government bail-out, Bob Lutz complained: 'I have to stand in line at the Northwest counter. I've never quite experienced this before.'[42]

Saved by the crash?

The recession that arrived in 2008 seemed to some to herald a change in direction in the West, a return to more balanced and healthy ways of living. Certainly, people began to borrow less and save more. In some respects this was a welcome, if unsurprising, development. However, higher savings rates are not the answer to climate change. Although they reduce consumption in the short to medium term, in the long term higher savings will only make the problem worse. Higher savings facilitate more investment and more investment fuels faster economic growth. Looked at another way, saving just means deferring consumption, and deferring consumption means more consumption later because savings earn interest. The answer lies in consuming less now and forever.

There is some evidence that Western consumers reacted to the recession by abandoning their profligate ways and returning to older values of thrift and moderation. Certainly, 2009 saw many stories about new community groups, books and websites telling us how to save money by economising, making things at home and buying second hand. Even Rupert Murdoch's *Wall Street Journal* began telling its readers how to have a 'want-free month', how to use the internet to barter for goods and how to cut off financial support to adult children.[43]

The new frugality takes various forms, including cutting back, bartering, buying second hand, making things last and downshifting—the voluntary decision to reduce income and consumption. Their common feature is that they represent a partial withdrawal from the market. The irony is that if these trends were to have an appreciable impact on consumer behaviour the recession would be prolonged because it is their opposites that make GDP grow. Prudence, moderation, delaying gratification—all of these behaviours, although of proven benefit to our wellbeing, are inimical to economic growth. The big question is whether they are a sign of a permanent return to earlier values of parsimony and restraint, or whether we will soon be overtaken by the hyper-consumerist values that defined the last boom. Certainly, the return to frugality would reflect a yearning in the West that has always run deeper than the desire for more stuff. A poll in 2004 found that most Americans believe that their society's priorities are all wrong. More than nine in ten (93 per cent) believe that Americans are too focused on working and making money, and not enough on family and community.[44] Remarkably, nine in ten (88 per cent) also believe that American society is too materialistic, with too much emphasis on shopping. And at the height of the biggest consumption binge in history, 90 per cent said that excessive materialism meant people were living beyond their means and ending up in debt.

In a 1930 essay titled 'Economic Possibilities for Our Grandchildren', John Maynard Keynes imagined what life would be like after another century of economic growth, a state now reached by most people in affluent nations. For the first time, he wrote, humans will be able to choose to live 'wisely and agreeably and well'. 'It will be those people, who can keep alive, and cultivate to a fuller perfection, the art of life itself and do not sell themselves for the means of life, who will be able to enjoy the abundance when it comes.'[45] Is it possible to imagine a society in which we live up to Keynes' vision, one in which we are no longer obsessed with growth and consumption and instead cultivate the art of life? It would be a society in which we nurture the things that really do improve our wellbeing, rather than dreaming evermore of the things that only money can buy. In a way the recipe for such a society is simple. Sooner or later, we spend what we earn. So if we want to consume less we must earn less, and if we want to earn less we must work less. At least, we must perform less paid work. If that sounds shocking today, it is nothing more than a call to resume the great historical trend of declining working hours. Until the trend was disrupted in the 1980s, falling working hours were regarded as the surest sign of social progress. A return to the downward trend would mean a social choice to take less of the gains from productivity growth in money income and more in free time. Society could be just as vibrant and technologically innovative; the difference would be that we would have much more time for activities other than paid work, including caring for others, education, community work, hobbies and leisure. One of the most effective long-term policies that Western governments could adopt to tackle growing greenhouse gas emissions would be to redefine progress so that falling working hours became its foremost indicator. For that to happen we would first need to redefine ourselves.

So will the recession be an opportunity for new values to become entrenched, ones that will rule out a repeat of the rampant materialism and debt-fuelled consumption that marked the 1990s and 2000s? The depressing answer must be 'no', for in the course of the last long boom the marketers planted a poison pill deep within affluent society—a generation of children consciously moulded into hyper-consumers. Figures for the United States tell a frightening story of the results of the sustained campaign by marketers, beginning in the early 1990s, to target children. In 1983 companies spent $100 million annually advertising to children. By the end of the boom they were spending more than $17 billion. Each year children aged two to eleven see more than 25,000 television advertisements.[46] Susan Lynn, Associate Director of the Harvard University-affiliated Media Center for Children, reinforces the message: [47]

> This generation of children is marketed to as never before. Kids are being marketed to through brand licensing, through product placement, marketing in schools, through stealth

> marketing, through viral marketing. There are DVDs, there are video games, there's the Internet, there are iPods, there are cell phones. There are so many more ways of reaching children, so that there's a brand in front of a child's face every moment of every day.

Children now begin to recognise corporate logos when they are as young as six months. A British study found that for one in four children the first recognisable word they utter is a brand name.[48] A generation of children, now reaching their late teens, has grown up in an unrelenting barrage of commercial messages, all with one underlying theme: that the path to happiness is through consumption. The marketers do not apologise for this; they brag about it. A professor of marketing speaks for them when he declares: [49]

> The positive effect I see is that they are able to function in the marketplace at an earlier age. And in a full-blown developed, industrialized society, that's where we satisfy most of our needs—in the marketplace.

This captive generation of children, whose minds have been shaped by marketing, will be the powerhouse that drives the next consumer boom. Their capacity to moderate their desires has been systematically dismantled from birth, and this weakness will naturally be exploited by companies everywhere. Who is going to stop them?

The China syndrome

Everything I have written so far in this chapter applies to rich countries. However, we must also consider, if only briefly, the growth of consumption in developing countries, especially China. This is not an exercise in blame-shifting, for rich countries are responsible for around 75 per cent of the increased greenhouse gases in the atmosphere now.[50] Although China's annual greenhouse gas emissions have recently surpassed those of the United States (each now accounts for nearly 20 per cent of global emissions), it will be some decades before developing countries account for half of the increased concentrations of greenhouse gases in the atmosphere. Moreover, it is true that the largest part of emissions from rich countries are luxury emissions because they are associated with producing and consuming goods and services that are not necessary to live a comfortable life.

While the profligate lifestyles of affluent nations must be the first target of emission-reduction policies, the gains of those policies will be more than offset over the next decades unless large developing nations—China, India, Brazil and a few others—begin soon to rein in their emissions. So it is worth considering the forces in play in those nations, and particularly in China, whose 1.3 billion people comprise a fifth of the world's population.

The growth of China's economy since the early 1980s has been extraordinary, averaging 9.5 per cent and accelerating to 11 per cent in 2006 before slowing to around 8 per cent in 2008.[51] We saw in Chapter 1 that China's fossil fuel emissions grew at 11–12 per cent each year in the first years of this century.[52] Typically, growth rates like these slow considerably after two decades or so once the country makes the industrial transition. Even so China's carbon dioxide emissions are expected to more than double by 2030, from a little over 5 billion metric tonnes in 2005 to just under 12 billion in 2030.[53] Its greenhouse gas emissions are expected to account for one third of global emissions by that time.[54]

It is sometimes said that much of the growth in China's emissions is really the responsibility of Western consumers because they have provided the demand for much of China's output. This is true up to a point; in 2005 around one third of China's carbon dioxide emissions were attributable to production of exports,[55] although these should be offset against the carbon emissions in other countries due to China's imports. However, as the economy matures this share due to exports is likely to decline. The corollary is that a larger and larger share of output in China will be consumed at home so that efforts to constrain emissions will have to focus on Chinese consumers, particularly urban households. Population growth will contribute a very small amount and energy efficiency and renewables will offset the impacts of consumption growth to a significant degree; but that will still leave a huge increase in China's carbon emissions driven mainly by domestic consumption.[56] Perhaps most worryingly, there seems to be nothing that can prevent a massive increase in China's emissions. According to one study, if we make the extremely optimistic assumption that from now on *all* new coal-fired power plants include carbon capture and storage technology, cutting their emissions by 85 per cent, the nation's carbon emissions would still increase by about 80 per cent by 2030.[57]

When the Communist Party decided to open up China's economy in 1979 official concern about the flow of Western cultural influences was met, in the early 1980s, with the Socialist Spiritual Civilization campaign, aimed at cultivating frugal living and rejection of materialism and the idea that consumption is the path to happiness.[58] The campaign was bolstered by a rehabilitation of Chinese history, previously condemned as the root of the evils that made the revolution necessary. Chinese civilisation became a source of national pride. Confucius, once the subject of mass criticism and a target of the Cultural Revolution, was rehabilitated as a means of resisting Western decadence and providing a focus for national cohesion threatened by political turbulence. Unsurprisingly, the essentially ecological sensibility of Confucian thought[59] was not allowed to stand in the way of a rapacious industrialisation drive.

However, a manufactured official ideology cannot counter the lure of consumption among deprived people, and through the 1980s the socialist preoccupation with production gave way to an emphasis on consumption. Elisabeth Croll argues that the government turned increasingly to consumption for its legitimacy, particularly to overcome the unpopularity of the one-child policy and unrest as expressed in events like Tiananmen.[60] One China expert has wondered: 'Will the fruits of a growing economy and the passion for consumption be the distraction, the narcotic that postpones the day of political reckoning for the still dominant Communist party?'[61]

The transition 'from comrades to consumers' telescoped into one decade a process that in the West took several, sparking a period of 'consumer madness' perhaps best encapsulated in the department store maxim 'the consumer is god'.[62] Although the volume of consumer spending fell short of expectations, shopping became a favourite form of recreation, in the process transforming the desires and life goals of ordinary Chinese city-dwellers. China now has a vast class of middle-class consumers with a seemingly unquenchable taste for Western-style consumer goods. In 2005 they accounted for 12 per cent of global luxury goods purchases, not far behind US consumers, who bought 17 per cent.[63] For a period, blue jeans came to signify for young people the mood of 'difference and defiance' that was the antithesis of the Mao suits that symbolised the dull conformity of their parents' generation. Western brands came to represent aspirations of modernity, sophistication and cosmopolitanism. They filled the gap left by the vanishing legitimacy of the socialist program of revolution. Croll writes of a study she undertook to investigate children's perceptions in which she asked kindergarten children to draw pictures of their families: [64]

> Many not only featured televisions and fashionably bright-green refrigerators prominently placed. Life-sized but also life-like, these goods were given their own faces and legs, suggesting that, perhaps, in the absence of siblings, significant things vied with significant persons in defining the single-child's sense of self or family.

Many middle-class Chinese saw the ability to consume as liberation from Maoist uniformity. At the same time, they confess that their purchasing is driven in part by competitiveness, its own variety of social compliance. According to Fu Hongchun, a business professor at Shanghai's East China Normal University, 'If one resident in a community buys a new TV, all residents in the same community will update their TVs'.[65] While there is no gainsaying the material benefits of escaping poverty, the 'Mao-inspired conformity' of earlier generations has been replaced by the consumer-style conformity and brand worship of the present one.

The cultural dangers of a rush to embrace consumer capitalism—materialism, selfishness, money worship and moral decay—were recognised early by Chinese intellectuals, authors and artists, as well as the government. The Communist Party's 'capitalism with Chinese characteristics' was a bold slogan, but the desire for a distinct type of capitalism could hardly withstand the force of Western brand culture. Chinese people often say they want to become 'modern' rather than Westernised, but the distinction is a fine one. Thus one Western advertising company that markets Nike sportswear in China 'puts a Confucian spin' on its ads, stressing Western individualism while maintaining 'it's never outside the group'.[66] In truth, the only Chinese characteristic in the Nike brand is the location of the factories.

Curiously, in China consumerist values spread more rapidly than consumption itself. Except among the wealthiest, the people did not abandon financial caution in the way Western consumers did in the 1990s. They spent more but they also continued to save. The reluctance to abandon frugality altogether became a source of frustration in the United States. In October 2005 US Treasury Secretary John W. Snow travelled to a village in Sichuan to promote 'financial modernisation'. According to the *New York Times* correspondent accompanying him, Mr Snow 'urged China ... to take lessons from the United States on how to spend more, borrow more and save less'.[67] He told his hosts that they badly needed to emulate the sophistication of American banks and financial institutions. At the time China's leaders were more alert to the mounting dangers of sub-prime loans in the United States than the Bush Administration or its Treasury secretary and were wary of importing America's deregulated financial system with the alacrity they had imported its retail malls. Their caution could not have been vindicated in more spectacular fashion three years later.

The point of this brief commentary on the rise of Chinese consumerism is to emphasise the rapidity and irreversibility of the transition to a consumer culture in that vast nation. The fact that a large part of the country remains impoverished while another large part has come to define itself by its access to Western consumer goods vitiates any attempt to reduce carbon emissions that may jeopardise growth. Despite the government's recognition of the dangers of global warming, it would sacrifice its political legitimacy if it pushed through the sorts of measures required by the science. The only way out is for rich countries to make large financial transfers to China, India, Brazil and a handful of other developing nations. The history of foreign aid in the West does not augur well.

Chapter 4

Many forms of denial

Cognitive dissonance

In the early 1950s a woman in Minneapolis began to receive communications from an extraterrestrial being named Sananda. Marian Keech, as she was pseudonymously known, heard that a great flood would cleanse the world of earthlings at midnight on 21 December 1954. Only those who believed in Sananda would be saved; they would be taken to another planet in a spaceship that would arrive just before the flood.

A cult formed around Ms Keech. Apart from a single press release, it shunned publicity. Members quit their jobs, sold their houses and left their families. On the day of judgment they gathered in Keech's house to await the arrival of the spaceship. The media gathered on the front lawn. The clock ticked down to midnight, but neither the spaceship nor the flood arrived. Inside the house some cult members wept; others stared at the ceiling.

The cult had been infiltrated by a young psychologist, Leon Festinger, who was intrigued by how the members would accommodate the prophecy's failure. As it dawned on them that the world would not be ending that night, how would they react?

The rational response would be to face up to the truth that they had been duped, and sink into deep despondency because they had made enormous sacrifices for nothing.

In fact, the opposite occurred. The cult members became excited, throwing open the curtains and inviting the television cameras in. They were told that Marian Keech had just received an urgent message from a high-density being, telling her that the world had been spared the flood because the group had spread so much light that God had saved the world from destruction. Over the next days Keech and other cult members told as many media outlets as they could that their devotion was not in vain, for through it they had saved the world.

These counterintuitive events stimulated Festinger to develop the theory of cognitive dissonance, which describes the uncomfortable feeling we have when we begin to understand that something we believe to be true is contradicted by evidence.[1] Festinger hypothesised that those whose firmly held views are repudiated by the emergence of facts often begin to proselytise even more fervently after the facts become incontrovertible. He wrote that we spend our lives paying attention to information that is consonant with our beliefs and avoiding that which is not. We surround ourselves with people who think as we do and avoid those who make us feel uncomfortable.

Festinger's analysis helps us understand the phenomenon of climate change 'scepticism' or, more accurately, denial. If humans are rational creatures, we would expect that as the scientific evidence confirming human-induced global warming has become overwhelming, the deniers would adjust their beliefs to accommodate the facts. Yet they have become more vehement in their attacks on climate scientists, environmentalists and anyone who accepts the evidence for global warming. They have ways of explaining away the facts: scientists have distorted their results to obtain more research funding; other scientists in possession of the truth have been silenced; governments have caved in to pressure from environmentalists who are hell-bent on destroying the free-market system.

Wherever there is uncertainty in the body of scientific evidence, the deniers insert a crowbar into the chink and try to open up a crack that will bring the edifice down. They proselytise about the disastrous consequences if the world fails to listen to them, with predictions of economic collapse if governments are foolish enough to try to cut greenhouse gas emissions. As evidence of global warming accumulates, the deniers cling ever more firmly to their contrarian views. They bombard newspapers with angry letters and express outrage in blogs and online forums, where they vilify those who do not share their beliefs. They meet together at their own conferences where they engage in mutual reinforcement, convinced that they possess a special knowledge that the rest of the world needs urgently to hear. The truth has been revealed to them because they are more rational than others and are therefore able to see through the distortions of the mainstream climate scientists.

The denialists are masters of what C.S. Lewis termed 'bulverism', a method of argument that avoids the need to prove that someone is wrong by first *assuming* their claim is wrong and then explaining why the person could hold such a fallacious view. The argument has the following structure: you scientists say there is human-induced global warming, but you make this claim because you want more research funding, or because you are caught up in herd behaviour, or because you are environmentalists; therefore, there is no such thing as global warming. Lewis wrote of the fictitious coiner of the term: 'Ezekiel Bulver, whose destiny was determined at the age of five when he heard his mother say to his father—who had been maintaining that two sides of a triangle were together greater than a third—"Oh you say that *because you are a man*."'[2] Why, it is reasonable to ask, do climate sceptics who declare themselves loyal allies of science repudiate the accumulated evidence when it becomes inconvenient? Why do they *want* the science to be wrong? Of course, in posing these questions I could be guilty of bulverism myself, except for the overwhelming weight of evidence in favour of human-induced global warming. Beginning with the facts makes analysis of the motives of those who reject them fair game.

Roots of climate scepticism

If we search for the roots of climate denial it soon becomes apparent that they lie in the reaction of American conservatism to the fall of the Berlin Wall in 1989 and the collapse of the Soviet Union in 1991. As the threat of the 'red menace' receded, the energy conservatives had put into opposing communism sought other outlets. Islamism had for some time been building as a threat, as it seemed to challenge the achievements of the West and the inevitable march of its influence. But there was an internal enemy too. Since the 1970s 'neo-conservatism' had set itself against the influence of the 'new class' of liberal intellectuals who had betrayed the Western tradition with a sustained critique of its assumptions and achievements. Feminism, multi-culturalism and anti-colonialism not only sought to correct injustices, but uncovered oppressive structures buried deep within the foundations of Western civilisation.

Environmentalism posed a particular threat because it called into question the benign nature of the system not from the perspective of an oppressed group but from the perspective of science, the very basis of Western civilisation. In the emergence of the 'green scare' the Rio Earth Summit in 1992 was a critical moment, one that brought to a head three decades of rising environmental concerns around the world.[3] Attended by 108 heads of state or government, it put environmentalism at the centre of global action and, among other important agreements, adopted the Framework Convention on Climate Change which to this day provides the architecture for international negotiations on climate change. The Earth Summit not only highlighted the growing body of science that identified environmental decline but signalled a marked shift in values.

President George Bush senior was well aware of the political dangers of the Rio Summit and instructed the US delegation to water down or block most diplomatic initiatives, including the Framework Convention.[4] Bush and fellow conservatives recognised that after the Cold War a new threat to their worldview had emerged. Germany's environment minister remarked at the time: 'I am afraid that conservatives in the United States are picking "ecologism" as their new enemy.'[5]

From the outset, environmentalism was seen as a threat to US national sovereignty. Before Rio, a senior Bush Administration official had expressed it this way: 'Americans did not fight and win the wars of the twentieth century to make the world safe for green vegetables.'[6] This nationalistic framing of the issue has had a powerful and enduring impact in the United States. In his 2008 presidential campaign Barack Obama's climate policy emphasised greater energy efficiency in order to free the United States from the influence of 'foreign oil'. In defending the expansion of nuclear power, climate sceptic Frederick Seitz had put it more bluntly: 'We have more control over the cost of nuclear power. The Muslims can raise the price of oil to any level they want.'[7]

Among the 17,000 people attending the Rio Summit was Dixie Lee Ray, an influential conservative activist. A marine biologist with a doctorate from Stanford on the nervous system of a type of lanternfish, in 1973 Ray was appointed by President Nixon to chair the Atomic Energy Commission and was subsequently elected governor of Washington State. She co-authored *Environmental Overkill*, a 1994 book critical of environmentalism, and was closely associated with the heads of two right-wing think tanks, the Heritage Foundation and the Competitive Enterprise Institute, both active in denying climate science. At Rio Ray expressed alarm because the summit was sponsored by UN officials who, she said, were members of the 'International Socialist Party'. She saw the summit's Agenda 21 as designed to impose 'world government under the UN, [so] that essentially all governments give up their sovereignty, and that nations will be, as they said quite openly, frightened or coerced into doing that by threats of environmental damage'.[8]

Ray was expressing one of the deepest fears of US conservatives, but their anxiety over national sovereignty was matched by the disquiet they felt at environmentalism's destabilisation of the idea of progress and mastery of nature. For conservatives, these beliefs define modernity itself. Their refrain that environmentalists want to take us back to living in caves reflects not just an inability to imagine a third path other than affluence and poverty, but their unquestioned identification of progress with unfettered growth. Any challenge to growth could only mean the end of progress, of civilisation and of the American way of life.

Yet within the collection of core ideas that defined conservative belief a contradiction had emerged. Science itself seemed to be saying that continued human advancement was inconsistent with endless growth and the desire to master the natural world. The easiest resolution of the cognitive dissonance this generated was to reject the science that causes the discomfort. For some, the creationists, this was not difficult as a prior decision had been made to accept science conditional on its consistency with deeper beliefs. For more sophisticated conservatives, those who led the movement and privileged science over biblical literalism, the solution was not to reject science per se but to reinterpret some scientific practice with the claim that its objectivity had been corrupted by biases introduced by scientists themselves, those who had become infected by the values of liberalism that spread in the 1960s and 1970s.

These sentiments help explain why a handful of scientists with genuine climate science credentials broke from the bulk of their colleagues and joined the anti-environment movement in the 1980s. Myanna Lahsen has studied in detail the life experiences and beliefs of three prominent physicists who have participated in the conservative backlash against climate science.[9] In the post-war decades Frederick Seitz, Robert Jastrow and William Nierenberg were physicists at the pinnacle of the profession, where they enjoyed the respect of society and the patronage of governments who understood scientific endeavour as the source of national power and prestige. Part of the nuclear science establishment with links to the defence effort, their influence reached a peak in the

1970s, just as the environment and peace movements began to challenge the benefits of nuclear technology and the undue power of the 'military–industrial complex'.

The social benefits of science and technology were no longer accepted uncritically and these challenges found expression in political demands for independent evaluation of science and technology. The scientific power and privilege of the elite went into decline. Lahsen reports that Seitz himself wrote of his depression over the new political environment and its attacks on the modernist program of progress through technological advance. 'Their discourses generally', writes Lahsen, 'reveal a pre-reflexive modernist ethos characterized by strong trust in science and technology as providers of solutions to problems ... an understanding of science and progress that prevailed during the first half of the twentieth century'.[10] They do not see nature as fragile and they believe in the right of humans to use technology to exert mastery, and it is in respect to this supreme ability of humans that elite scientists such as themselves have a unique entitlement to shape opinion. They express outrage at those who challenge this view of science and progress, experiencing it as a personal affront, as a 'sense of violated entitlement'.[11] Their intolerance of scientific ignorance can perhaps be forgiven, but how do they respond to those better informed? When asked why most scientists reject his sceptical views on global warming, Seitz (who has been president of the US National Academy of Sciences) opined: 'Most scientists are Democrats ... I think it's as simple as that.'[12]

Among the characteristics of elite physicists like the trio is an intellectual arrogance that leads them to believe, as one close observer put it, that global environmental problems are 'trivia that can be handled by a good physicist on a Friday afternoon over a beer'.[13] Being the stars of the sciences, with a rigour others want to emulate, gives them a sense of intellectual superiority and permission to be contrarian. This conceit allowed the 2009 intervention of Freeman Dyson in the global warming debate. Dyson, a revered physicist who made his name in the 1960s, freely admits he knows almost nothing about climate science. But that was no impediment to his attack in the *New York Times* on global warming science as grossly exaggerated.[14] He believes it is humankind's duty to transform nature in our own interests. That Dyson's views should have any currency reflects the modern cult of the big brain, our reverence for sheer cleverness even when it is disconnected from knowledge.[15]

Defending themselves against the perceived attack on their privileged place and on the ideas of modernity built on science[16] was only one manifestation of a broader conservative resistance to the social and cultural transformations brought by the 1960s. On the trio of climate science-denying physicists, Lahsen observes: [17]

> Their engagement in US climate politics can be understood as part of a struggle to preserve their particular culturally and historically charged understandings of scientific and environmental reality, and an associated, particular normative order.

In 1984 Seitz, Jastrow and Nierenberg founded the George C. Marshall Institute, a Washington think tank initially devoted to defending President Ronald Reagan's embattled Strategic Defense Initiative, or 'Star Wars' program, panned by most experts as unworkable and a massive waste.[18] Although still campaigning on missile defence, in the 1990s the Marshall Institute's foremost activity became attacking climate change science. It is no surprise to find that Exxon began providing funding.[19] Claiming its purpose is to counter the politicisation of science 'by providing policymakers with rigorous, clearly written and unbiased technical analyses',[20] every paper on the subject of climate science it publishes or links to on its website aims to debunk the science.

The way in which conservative think tanks amplified the message of sympathetic scientists is well documented.[21] The handful of qualified scientific sceptics found a welcoming political environment during the presidency of George W. Bush (2000–2008), and the Republican dominance of Congress. The 'Republican war on science', in which think tanks like the Marshall Institute played a vital role, is also well documented.[22] Given their status as a very small minority, it is a sign of their effectiveness that, in appearances before congressional hearings on climate change, representatives of conservative think tanks achieved virtual parity with scientists representing the consensus view.[23]

Climate scepticism grew directly out of the conservative counter-movement against environmentalism. Its first task was to erode confidence in the science on which environmental concerns were based by arguing that the scientists had become politicised and were using their research, or allowing it to be used, to advance an anti-corporate political agenda. An analogy is sometimes drawn between those who have resisted the tide of scientific evidence on the dangers of climate change and those who once questioned the link between smoking and lung cancer in the face of overwhelming medical evidence. It turns out that the links between denialists in the climate change and smoking controversies go much deeper than mere analogy. In response to the 1992 report of the US Environmental Protection Agency linking passive smoking with cancer, Philip Morris hired a public relations company named APCO to develop a counter-strategy.[24] Acknowledging that the views of tobacco companies lacked credibility, APCO proposed a strategy of 'astroturfing', the formation and funding of apparently independent front groups to give the impression of a popular movement opposed to 'overregulation' and in support of individual freedom. Foremost among the fake citizens' groups was The Advancement of Sound Science Coalition (TASSC). According to secret documents uncovered in a court case, and reported by George Monbiot, it was to be[25]

> a national coalition intended to educate the media, public officials and the public about the dangers of 'junk science' ... Upon formation of Coalition, key leaders will begin media outreach, e.g. editorial board tours, opinion articles, and brief elected officials in selected states.

The strategy was to link concerns about passive smoking with a range of other popular anxieties, including global warming, nuclear waste disposal and biotechnology, in order to suggest that these were all part of an unjustified social panic, so that calls for government intervention in people's lives were unwarranted. It set out to cast doubt on the science, to link the scare against smoking with other 'unfounded fears' and to contrast the 'junk science' of their opponents with the 'sound science' they promoted. As one tobacco-company memo noted:[26] 'Doubt is our product since it is the best means of competing with the "body of fact" that exists in the mind of the general public. It is also the means of establishing a controversy.'

As the 1990s progressed and the rear-guard action against restrictions on smoking faded, The Advancement of Sound

Science Coalition started receiving funds from Exxon (among other oil companies) and its 'junk science' website began to carry material attacking climate change science. Monbiot wrote that this website 'has been the main entrepôt for almost every kind of climate-change denial that has found its way into the mainstream press'. Having been set up by Philip Morris, TASSC 'was the first and most important of the corporate-funded organisations denying that climate change is taking place. It has done more damage to the campaign to halt it than any other body.'[27]

So the tactics, personnel and organisations mobilised to serve the interests of the tobacco lobby in the 1980s were seamlessly transferred to serve the interests of the fossil fuel lobby in the 1990s. Frederick Seitz had in the 1980s served as principal scientific adviser for cigarette-maker R.J. Reynolds, from which position he challenged the link between tobacco smoke and cancer.[28] The task of the climate sceptics in the think tanks and PR companies hired by fossil fuel companies was to engage in 'consciousness lowering activities', to 'de-problematise' global warming by characterising it as a form of politically driven panic-mongering.[29] As a result, climate denial and political conservatism have become, at least in the United States, entwined. Although some evangelical churches now encourage action to avert global warming as an expression of good stewardship of God's Earth, climate scepticism has become part of the worldview of some Christian fundamentalists. This stew of paranoia finds expression in figures such as Republican Congresswoman Michele Bachmann, who attacked House Speaker Nancy Pelosi for her 'global warming fanaticism ... She has said that she's just trying to save the planet. We all know that someone did that over 2,000 years ago.'[30] And in March 2009 Bachmann called on her Minnesota constituents to take up arms to resist the Obama Administration's energy plans.[31]

Values determine beliefs

Many environmentalists believe that big business is responsible for the worst forms of environmental damage, that, left alone, the free market cannot fix the problems and that government intervention is essential. In the case of global warming they also believe that only international cooperation, including legally binding obligations on the major polluters, can solve the problem. In these views environmentalists are perhaps not far from the views of most citizens of developed countries, including US citizens.[32] Others go further to argue that the system itself is at fault, tracing ecological decline to uninhibited corporate power, the structural compulsion to grow, technological determinism and the allure of the consumer life.

So neo-conservatives were right to identify environmentalism, and its hold on the public imagination, as a threat to their worldview and political aspirations. Peter Jacques and colleagues argue that this challenge to conservative values generated 'a sustained anti-environmental counter-movement' in the United States that soon became 'institutionalised in a network of influential conservative think tanks funded by wealthy conservative foundations and corporations'.[33] In the United States, if not elsewhere, the effectiveness of associating global warming advocates with a view of the world hostile to conservative values has served to polarise the debate and break down the broad public consensus on climate science. The campaign by the Clinton Administration in the fall of 1997 to build public support for an agreement at the upcoming Kyoto conference saw the global warming issue drawn into a bitter process of political polarisation, one that caused Republican and conservative citizens to adopt or harden a belief against human-induced climate change.[34]

In 1997 there was little difference between Republican and Democrat voters in views on global warming. But by 2008 a wide gulf had opened up. For example, in 1997 52 per cent of Democrats believed that the effects of warming had already begun, and 48 per cent of Republicans agreed. Reflecting the accumulation of stronger scientific evidence, by 2008 the proportion of Democrats taking this view had risen from 52 to 76 per cent, while the proportion of Republicans agreeing had fallen from 48 to 42 per cent.[35] A 4 per cent gap had become a 34 per cent gap. By 2008, 59 per cent of Republicans believed that the seriousness of global warming is generally exaggerated in the news, up from 37 per cent in 1997. Among Democrats, only 17 per cent held this belief in 2008, down from 27 per cent in 1997.

In an era of intense ideological division, rejection of global warming had for some Americans become a means of consolidating and signalling their cultural identity, in the way that beliefs about patriotism, welfare and musical tastes do. A recent study by Edward Maibach, Connie Roser-Renouf and Anthony Leiserowitz used statistical techniques to divide Americans into six distinct groups or global warming audiences—the Alarmed (18 per cent of the population), Concerned (33 per cent), Cautious (19 per cent), Disengaged (12 per cent), Doubtful (11 per cent) and Dismissive (7 per cent).[36]

Although mostly indistinguishable by demographic criteria, the groups differ markedly in their values and political and religious beliefs. In sum:

> The segments that are more concerned about global warming tend to be more politically liberal and to hold strong egalitarian and environmental values. The less concerned segments are more politically conservative, hold anti-egalitarian and strongly individualistic values, and are more likely to be evangelical with strongly traditional religious beliefs.[37]

Among the Alarmed—defined as those most convinced warming is real and a serious threat and who worry about it a fair amount or a great deal—48 per cent regard themselves as politically liberal and only 14 per cent conservative, with the rest (38 per cent) 'moderate'. At the other end of the spectrum, among the Dismissive—who do not accept that warming is real and who regard themselves as being well informed about it but wholly unconcerned—76 per cent say they are conservative and only 3 per cent liberal. The correspondence in beliefs is shown in the figure (from which 'moderates' are excluded).[38] The way in which concern about global warming declines consistently as political views shift to the right is striking.

The strong association between political ideology and responses to global warming is reflected in attitudes to issues that typically divide left and right in the United States. The Alarmed group is much more likely than the Dismissive group to believe that the world would be more peaceful if wealth were more equally divided among nations (62 per cent versus 12 per cent); they are more likely to support government programs to get rid of poverty (85 per cent versus 30 per cent); and they are less likely to believe that government regulation of business usually does more harm than good (31 per cent versus 87 per cent).[39] Predictably, the Alarmed are much more likely to favour environmental

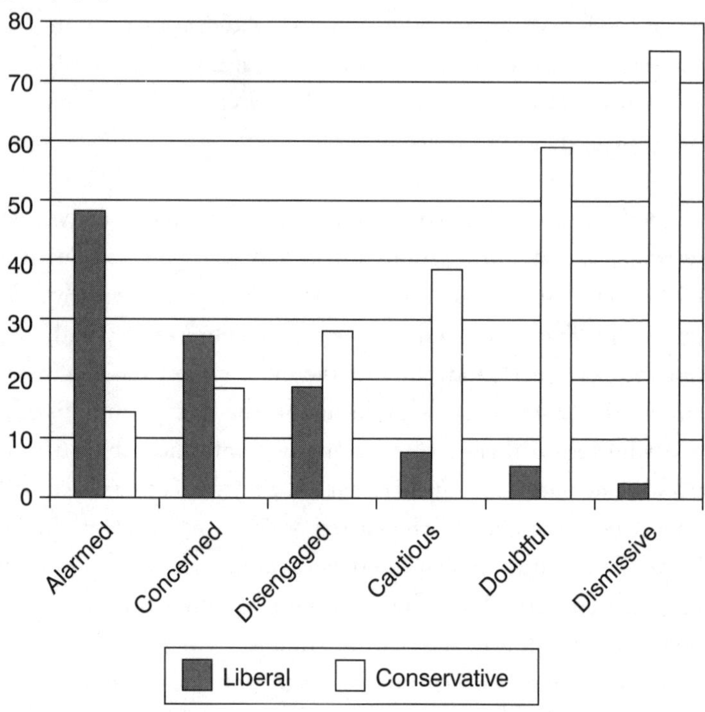

Source: Based on Table 20 in Edward Maibach, Connie Roser-Renouf and Anthony Leiserowitz, *Global Warmings 'Six Americas' 2009*

Note: 'Moderates' are not shown

protection over economic growth even if it costs jobs (89 per cent take this view) where the Dismissive support economic growth even if it leads to environmental problems (90 per cent).[40] The views of each of the other four groups lie close to a straight line diagonally connecting these two positions.

The Alarmed are much more likely to watch the news on the mainstream networks (63 per cent) while the Dismissive are much more likely to watch Fox News (62 per cent) and listen to right-wing radio host Rush Limbaugh (47 per cent).[41] (While the proliferation of competing sources of information is usually regarded as good for democracy, the erosion of the domination of the major television networks and newspapers by the rise of cable television, talk radio and the internet has meant that people can more easily go to news sources that confirm their own biases and avoid information that challenges them.)

The data from the *Six Americas* study reinforce the suspicion that, for many Americans, the position one takes on global warming depends on one's prior political values, although this is truer on the right. On most issues that divide left and right—such as the proper role of government, the extent of welfare, national sovereignty, rights versus responsibilities—there are legitimate differences of values that can be mobilised to support either position, although 'facts' are often selected to support each position. In the case of global warming facts concerning its existence, severity and likely impacts are not questions of values but of scientific evidence. The facts are filtered through an opaque ideological lens.

The strong association between political ideology and beliefs about global warming is a peculiarly American phenomenon, although it spills over into Australia where scepticism is also strong and is promoted by a number of conservative think tanks with links to counterparts in the United States.[42] In Europe the alignment of conservatism and climate scepticism is much weaker. In Britain the Conservative Party under David Cameron is highly critical of the Labour Government for not going far enough, and some 58 per cent of Tory voters say he takes a 'welcome and courageous stand on the environment'.[43] Germany's Angela Merkel takes at least as strong a position as her Social Democratic predecessor. A similar situation prevails in France, but not in Italy where Prime Minister Berlusconi's politics are well to the right of his northerly conservative counterparts and include climate scepticism. In Canada the conservative government of British Columbia in 2008 introduced a small carbon tax, only to be attacked by the left-leaning New Democratic Party that sought government with an 'axe the tax' campaign aimed at 'protecting consumers'.[44]

The political colouring of the global warming debate in the United States helps explain why there is a comparatively lower level of concern in that country, despite high levels of awareness of the issue. (Although it should be noted that a 2003 survey found that 47 per cent of Americans believe, erroneously, that global warming is caused primarily by damage to the ozone layer.[45]) The *Six Americas* study found that 54 per cent of Americans believe that the world was created literally in six days 'as the Bible says',[46] reflecting a widespread willingness to disregard scientific evidence when it conflicts with deeper values. When asked in 2006 how serious a problem they consider global warming to be, fewer than 50 per cent of Americans rated it 'very serious'.[47] In part due to their more secular character western Europeans are less resistant to the scientific evidence, with more than 65 per cent of citizens regarding warming as 'very serious'.[48] A better measure than the level of concern about climate change is the extent to which people worry about it, because worry is an active emotional state.[49] When citizens of fifteen nations were asked in 2006 how much they personally worry about global warming those in the

United States ranked last, with only 18 per cent saying they worry 'a great deal' (with another 35 per cent saying they worry a fair amount).[50] Japanese people are the most anxious, with nearly two thirds worrying a great deal. Europeans range from high levels of worry in Spain and France (with around half worrying a great deal) to the phlegmatic British (25 per cent), although this may reflect not so much different appreciations of the evidence as differences in national neuroticism (French people are among the most neurotic and Britons the least).[51]

Left-wing scepticism

It was not only those on the right-hand end of the ideological spectrum who saw environmentalism as a political threat. From the 1970s some small groups on the far left derided the rise of environmentalism as a middle-class fad that was a distraction from the true causes of poverty and exploitation. Even among traditional social welfare organisations and centre-left parties environmentalism was often resented because, more glamorous than homelessness and wage disputes, it drew the oxygen away from traditional progressive concerns. Among those who scorned environmentalism was a Trotskyist splinter group in the United Kingdom known as the Revolutionary Communist Party. In the 1990s the RCP published a controversialist journal titled *Living Marxism* (later *LM Magazine*) that frequently ran bitter attacks on environmentalism, describing it as a middle-class indulgence and a neo-colonial smokescreen. Repudiating the environmentalism of Dixie Lee Ray's mythical International Socialist Party, the Marxist journal carried articles with titles like 'Red and green won't go', 'Animals have no rights' and 'Environmental imperialism'. The successor to *LM* lives on in cyberspace in the form of *Spiked*, a lively online mix of ultra-libertarianism and 'left-wing' opinion, much of it devoted to attacking what its editor calls 'the ugly elitism and end-of-days mania of the environmentalist movement'.[52] (For aficionados of the left, *Spiked* hints at its Trotskyist origins by claiming in its 'tongue-in-cheek' blurb that it would be endorsed by Marx but hated by Stalin.)

The initial intellectual force behind the RCP was British academic Frank Furedi (who earlier wrote under the pseudonym Frank Richards), now a professor of sociology at the University of Kent and frequent contributor to *Spiked*. Furedi has written a number of books that explore and denounce the excessive emphasis in Western societies on risk and danger, suggesting that Westerners have become oversensitive to small risks and are prone to overreact to threats such as global warming, which he describes as a 'moral crusade' against humanity. In a reprise of Dixie Lee Ray, Furedi cleaves to the first principle of modernism, that it is the duty of humans to control the Earth: 'Instead of bowing to the divine authority of the planet, we ought to uphold the age-long project of humanising the planet.'[53] In doing so he abandons the second principle of modernism, an absolute faith in science.[54]

This background is germane because activists associated with the Revolutionary Communist Party were responsible for the 2007 documentary *The Great Global Warming Swindle*. Initially given the working title *Apocalypse My Arse*, the film describes the idea of man-made climate change as 'a lie ... the biggest scam of modern times'.[55] It was directed by Martin Durkin, whose links with leaders of the RCP go back many years. Immediately after it was broadcast, *Spiked* editor Brendan O'Neill wrote a vigorous defense of Durkin and *Swindle*, an endorsement of the film's anti-environmental claims veiled by appeals to the right to dissent.[56] A few years earlier, Durkin had made an equally inflammatory documentary called *Against Nature* which, according to the publicity material, characterised 'environmentalist ideology as unscientific, irrational and anti-humanist'.[57] It created a furore after it was broadcast in Britain, not least for its extraordinary claims that modern environmentalism has its roots in Nazi Germany (Hitler was a vegetarian—get it?) and that self-interested environmentalists are responsible for enormous suffering in the Third World. It combined images of Third World children dying of horrible illnesses with commentary on how environmentalists oppose dams that would bring clean water and electricity, portraying them as callous fanatics.

Although criticised by media regulators for its devious editorial devices and attacked by bodies such as the Royal Society for its crude distortion of scientific facts, *Swindle* was lauded by sceptics groups around the world—like *Against Nature*, it did after all feature some of denialism's most prominent names.[58] It is not the first time that those representing 'workers' and 'capitalists' have united to defend their common worldview, including periodic alliances between trade unions and business organisations formed to head off or water down greenhouse gas abatement policies. The accord between some elements of the far left and far right is grounded in their shared beliefs in the priority of material consumption in human wellbeing, their defence of human domination of nature, and their anti-authoritarian commitment to individual rights. While conservatives saw environmentalism as a threat to capitalism and the American way of life, some on the far left saw environmentalism as a threat to their objective of overthrowing capitalism because it was a distraction from the main game. Speaking on behalf of the forgotten working class, *Spiked* editor Brendan O'Neill wrote that the environmental elites 'cannot comprehend, indeed are "baffled" by, *our* everyday behaviour, *our* desire to have families, *our* resistance to hectoring, *our* dream of being wealthier, better travelled, *our* hopes of living life to the full'.[59] *Swindle* traced the origins of global warming science to Margaret Thatcher's attacks on the working class, viz. her desire to destroy the British mining unions by promoting nuclear power in place of coal. Needing a reason to deprecate coal, the prime minister invested public funds in global warming science and the scientists dutifully responded by coming up with the evidence.

As if the political alignments caused by global warming were not already weird enough, the conservative counter-movement has implicitly allied itself with the post-modern challenge to the idea of truth advanced by mainly French, post-structuralist intellectuals.[60] Neo-conservatives have for years fulminated against the influence of post-modernism in university campuses and schools, with its pernicious promotion of 'moral relativism'. They see themselves as defending objective truth after decades of leftist challenge to the Western canon. Yet in the case of climate change the conservative counter-movement has actively promoted those who challenge the established science. Sceptical commentators like Charles Krauthammer in the United States, Melanie Phillips in Britain,[61] Mark Steyn in Canada and Michael Duffy in Australia not only dismiss the science but repeatedly attempt to 'deconstruct' the motives of the scientists who carry it out.[62] They are always on the lookout for biases and prejudices that could lie behind the scientific facts on global warming, explaining away the vast accumulation of evidence by impugning the motives of those who collect it. In their view, scientific truth is malleable, contingent and contestable. Like the creationists who believe that victory requires them to destroy the theory of evolution, they promote a form of anti-scientific fundamentalism that has less regard for scientific method than the most committed constructivist on any university campus. Modernism now finds itself under siege from both the dwindling band of academic post-modernists and resurgent neo-conservatives. Both reject the claims of science to objective truth. For the former the truth of modernism was socially constructed and the real truth is always contestable; the latter never accepted the elevation of matters of fact over matters of belief. For the sceptics and their patrons loyalty to belief is paramount and every piece of evidence that challenges their convictions represents a threat to their worldview and must be destroyed.

It is for this reason that climate sceptics are not true sceptics, that is, those who suspend credulity in order to subject accepted beliefs to rigorous questioning. Climate sceptics do not carefully assess the claims of climate science in order to establish those that are credible and those that are not. They reject all claims of climate science and search for reasons to justify their rejection. Thus in 2009 Australian 'sceptic' and geologist Ian Plimer published a book, *Heaven and Earth*, which he claimed would 'knock out every single argument we hear about climate change'.[63] It would not cast doubt on *some* aspects of global warming science, or focus attention on the uncertainties, it would disprove *every* piece of evidence generated by hundreds of scientists over the last twenty or more years in support of human-induced climate change. This is not so much the agnosticism of the sceptic but the zealotry of the fanatic who believes himself to possess the Truth.

Coping strategies

I wrote in the Preface that the most immediate reason we now face climate disruption lies in the political power of the fossil fuel lobby, which has set out to sow doubt in the public mind and has resisted attempts to curb the carbon emissions of the companies it represents. The story of their power and influence has been told several times;[64] the more perplexing question is why they have been allowed to get away with it. To this point I have tried to account for the unwillingness to override the interests of the fossil fuel lobby by pointing to the ways in which growth fetishism and consumerism are embodied in our institutions and embedded in our understanding of the world. As Tim Kasser and colleagues argue, institutions create and reinforce ideologies and together they encourage individuals to behave in ways that ensure the reproduction of the system,[65] an argument also made in Chapter 2 of this book.

In addition to institutional factors we must consider the ways in which the human psyche has prevented or slowed recognition of the existential threat we now confront. As much as anything else, the objective of industrial society has been to isolate ourselves from the effects of the weather. Against the dream of the scientific–technological revolution, global warming reminds us that Nature is untamable and fractious. The return of chaos is a particular challenge to those who fear uncertainty and believe the environment can be controlled by application of rationality. For sceptics (many of whom are engineers) the return of chaotic nature seems to harbour a special fear. They are scornful of climate models because they cannot predict the future with certainty, thereby attributing the irreducible uncertainty of climate systems to the personal failings of the scientists who try to model them. Ian Langford reminds us that one of the main defences against death anxiety is belief in personal specialness derived from a superior ability to reason and understand.[66] This is the heroic pose adopted by climate sceptics.

While the sceptics' denial has succeeded in muddying the waters of public understanding, the strategies routinely used by the public to avoid or downplay the scientific warnings have been a more powerful factor in the reluctance of governments to do what is needed. The truth of this has leaked into popular culture. In an episode of *The Simpsons* Lisa's school project on 'what Springfield will look like in 50 years' time' leads her to investigate the effects of global warming on her town. Her presentation terrifies her classmates so Homer and Marge take her to a psychiatrist who prescribes 'Ignorital', a sure-fire cure for gloominess. Lisa enters a drug-induced fantasy world where, among other things, the toxic plume from an industrial chimney becomes a cloud of smiley faces (much like the Shell advertisement depicting flowers wafting from the company's oil refinery smokestacks). Lisa's trance state is interrupted only when Marge recognises the dangers of disconnection from reality.

One hurdle to recognising the threat posed by global warming is the fact that humans have evolved to assess and respond to risk through immediate feelings rather than cognitive processing. Most discussion of reactions to climate change assumes a consequentialist model of risk; that is, we hear the scientific warnings, form a judgment about the likely effects on our wellbeing, and change our behaviour accordingly. However, it is now well established that immediate instinctive reactions (such as fear, anxiety and dread) are more powerful influences on assessment of risk.[67] George Lowenstein and co-authors suggest this explains why we react fearfully to events that are (now) objectively harmless, such as seeing a tarantula in a glass box or climbing to the observation deck of a sky-scraper, but show little fear in the presence of genuinely dangerous objects like guns and cars.[68] As the effects of warming are delayed, a proportionate response requires us to anticipate emotions we may feel many years hence; anticipation of feelings is a weak stimulus compared to pressing anxieties we may have about job losses or higher taxes. In other words, if humans evolved to survive by assessing risks through instant visceral reactions we are at a loss when confronted with global warming which requires us to rely heavily on cognitive processing. We can sometimes use our reason to conquer our fears, but in the case of global warming we need to use our reason to stimulate our fears. Yet when we do succeed in conjuring up the emotions that the science warns of, we are superbly equipped with strategies to defend against them.

Superficially, most people accept the message of the climate scientists. In the United States, where scepticism is strongest, among the 92 per cent of the population who have heard of global warming, 90 per cent believe that the United States should reduce its greenhouse gas emissions, with 76 per cent wanting this to happen regardless of what other countries do.[69] However, for most US citizens concern about climate change does not run deep.[70] It is not strong enough to make them change their behaviour, especially their voting behaviour. This may be changing, although a poll in January 2009 saw Americans rank global warming last of a list of 20 priorities.[71]

Those who do understand the threat posed by global warming—the Alarmed and perhaps some of the Concerned in the study of 'Six Americas'—naturally feel worried, anxious and stressed. Yet it is in the nature of climate change that individuals, as individuals, can do nothing to prevent it happening and little to protect themselves from its effects. Particularly for those most alarmed about the future of a warming world, the situation can induce a chronic state of anxiety. Psychologists are beginning to identify a range of coping strategies used to manage the unpleasant feelings that follow when we open ourselves to the message of climate science.[72] These coping strategies may be adaptive or maladaptive.[73] Maladaptive coping strategies admit some of the facts and allow some of the emotions, but do so in distorted form. Adaptive coping strategies are positive behaviours based on full acceptance of the facts and experience of the emotions. I consider adaptive strategies in the last chapter and devote the rest of this chapter to the maladaptive ones. These early insights have been built on by Tom Crompton and Tim Kasser in an important intervention by WWF-UK to develop an innovative campaigning strategy in a world of 'greenhouse fatigue'.[74]

Reinterpreting the threat

Maladaptive strategies are akin to the various 'defence mechanisms'—identified by Sigmund Freud and, more so, his daughter Anna—we use to shield ourselves from distressing features of the world.[75] In recent years, psychologists have developed and applied these ideas to the way we accommodate ourselves emotionally to environmental threats.

Distraction is an everyday form of denial.[76] When reading a newspaper or watching the news, if global warming comes up we frequently just 'switch off' because the information is too disconcerting. We shift our attention to something less upsetting because the alternative is to follow it through and dwell on what it means for our own future, that of our children and the world more broadly. Accepting the reality of global warming takes emotional fortitude and could overwhelm us. I know I sometimes make a conscious decision not to take notice of some unfolding disaster that I find particularly distressing. I tell myself that there are too many terrible things in the world to cope with, that I am not being callous because I do allow myself to be affected by other events, and it is therefore morally defensible to ignore the suffering of people somewhere in the world. I am conscious that I am engaged in a rationalisation in order to avoid feeling upset or depressed, but it usually works. Engaging in this type of suppression is maladaptive only when it amounts to a sustained refusal to acknowledge the facts.

Another common maladaptive strategy for coping with the threat of global warming is to change the appraisal of the threat, to 'de-problematise' it. The threat is diminished by deploying inner narratives such as 'humans have solved these sorts of problems before', 'the scientists are probably exaggerating' or 'if it were that big a threat the government would be doing something about it'.[77] Minimising the threat in this way reduces the anxiety that would follow acknowledging it.

Similarly, 'distancing' emphasises the time lapse before we feel the consequences of warming—'It's a long way off so we have time to find solutions'. It is a form of "wishful thinking" because, by putting the problem well into the future, we are hoping that something will come along to resolve it before we have to act. Nations, as well as individuals, usually pass through this phase, or become stuck in it. In 2006, after a thorough review of public attitudes, Anthony Leiserowitz concluded that 'as a whole, the American public is currently in a "wishful thinking" stage of opinion formation, in which they hope the problem can be solved by someone else … without changes in their own priorities, decision making or behavior'.[78]

Governments pursue similar strategies. For several years governments in most OECD countries have adopted a target of cutting emissions by 60–80 per cent by 2050. It is easy being green in the remote future. Indeed, research shows that higher-level values govern intended actions when those actions are expected to occur in the distant future, but more pragmatic considerations dominate when actions are expected in the near future.[79] Policy goals 40–50 years in advance are at best meaningless because they express only an intention; at worst, they are a substitute for immediate measures to cut emissions. They allow governments, and their publics, to feel good because their intentions reflect their values without committing to the difficult and dissonant task of putting those values into practice.

Pleasure-seeking

I have already referred to what might be dubbed casual scepticism, a form of denial in which ordinary people allow themselves to be persuaded by hard-line 'sceptics' into believing that the scientists can't make up their minds. An extreme version of this might be called 'hairy-chested denialism', a form best illustrated by Jeremy

Clarkson, host of the popular British television program *Top Gear*. *Top Gear* is about thrills, escapism, laddish humour and smashing things up. In other words, it is a teenage boy's dream. Clarkson's anti-environmentalism can be thought of as an adolescent refusal to hear anything that might spoil the fun. Like the old left activists at *Spiked*, Clarkson sees himself as 'the champion of the ordinary people' (although he has also been described by the *Economist* as a 'skillful propagandist for the motoring lobby').[80] He has become notorious for green-baiting, deriding public transport, promising to run down cyclists and declaring: 'What's wrong with global warming? We might lose Holland but there are other places to go on holiday.'[81] It's an opinion, or rather a sentiment, that has instant appeal to the segment of the population that feels cheated of its enjoyment by climate doom-mongering, particularly when combined with state nannyism. In this way, Clarkson transforms climate transgressors into victims of political correctness. For some, it validates their resistance to behavioural change, justifying their reluctance to take the bus, buy a smaller car or recycle waste.

Ridiculing environmentalism has become an advertising technique in its own right. It is a strategy pitched mainly at older Anglo men building on what is known as the 'white male effect', the well-established tendency for white men to be less concerned about the environment than women and minorities.[82] A magazine ad for a Porsche shows a sleek sports car above the tag-line: 'Save the males. Oh ... and the planet.' The text adds that the car's CO_2 emissions are 15 per cent lower—although, in a classic dangling comparative, it does not say what they are lower than. Nevertheless it claims this fact makes driving the Porsche 'guilt-free' (as if an embezzler could be rendered innocent by stealing 15 per cent less). If Porsche takes a jocular approach to global warming the tourist industry has resorted to chirpiness to gloss over the awfulness of climate change. Thus tourist operators now urge us to take the trip of our lives to see the natural wonders of the world before they melt or disappear under rising seas. The grim truth is buried by the airy enthusiasm of the advertising, as if there will be plenty more fun destinations after these have vanished.[83]

Whereas most people associate driving with a range of emotions, *Top Gear*'s team celebrates only one—power. Why shouldn't I be allowed to drive at 100 mph on the motorway, Clarkson wants to know. One does not need to be a petrolhead or into pimping one's motor vehicle to enjoy *Top Gear*'s fantasies. For some, it is not inconsistent to enjoy an evening watching Clarkson do donuts in a Mack truck and drive to work in a Prius the next day. But for Clarkson, driving a hulking SUV itself becomes a form of rebellion, a rejection of the wearying limitations on his liberty and a way to stick it to the greenies and the politicians who want us to conform. Howls of outrage at Clarkson's provocations only validate the sense of cultural identity derived from these anti-green sentiments. Clarkson's caricature of greenies as half-crazed hippies is a means of defining an 'other' in opposition to which his fans can solidify their own sense of identity. (In a similar way, caricaturing those who try to reduce their emissions as 'carbo-rexic' is a reassuring means of 'othering' that allows us to devalue their behaviour.) So pleasure-seeking can also become a means of in-group reinforcement of values. The technique works: some 50,000 people signed a petition to make Clarkson, the kid who never grew up, prime minster of the United Kingdom. Clarkson's ridiculing of climate science and the social limits it demands has provided large numbers of Britons with a rationale for switching off from the warnings and, for some, actively rebuffing them. For those who want a reason to disbelieve, Clarkson provides it.

But there is another dimension to Clarkson's scoffing at global warming through the celebration of powerful cars driven at speed. Pleasure-seeking is recognised as a way of escaping from reality in itself,[84] and there is a perverse redoubling of the effect when the pleasure is derived not just from driving high-performance vehicles but also from the wilful transgression of the social prohibitions against climate-damaging activities. It is almost as if *Top Gear* represents a last wild fling before we all crash and burn.

Blame-shifting

In her study of a small environmentally conscious community in Norway, Kari Marie Norgaard notes that it is widely assumed by researchers that people fail to respond to the threat of global warming because they are poorly informed, greedy, self-focused or have faulty cognitive processes. Yet she observes that the people she spoke with[85]

> expressed feelings of deep concern and caring and a significant degree of ambivalence about the issue of global warming … Community members described fears of loss of ontological security, feelings of helplessness, guilt, and the associated emotion of fear of 'being a bad person'.

So what do we do with these feelings? Norgaard identified blame-shifting as an effective method of managing troublesome emotions. As citizens of a small country, many of her Norwegian subjects were quick to blame 'Amerika' and mentioned the Bush Administration's repudiation of the Kyoto Protocol. When they were reminded that Norway is the world's second-largest exporter of oil, attention shifted to the fact that Norway is not seen as important geopolitically.

Blame-shifting is a useful, if often indefensible, means of denying guilt. It is a form of moral disengagement whereby we disavow our responsibility for the problem or the solution. Throughout the world over the last few years, there has been a strong push to scapegoat China. That China 'builds a new coal-fired power plant every week' and 'China is now the world's biggest emitter' have been used by conservatives in Australia, for example, to argue there is no point cutting emissions until China does. Blame-shifting reached a sublime level in 2008 when the president of the powerful American National Mining Association defended the US coal industry in the following terms: 'Reducing U.S. emissions will not have any meaningful impact on atmospheric greenhouse gas concentrations when emissions from China and India already surpass our own.'[86] In their analysis of coping strategies Tom Crompton and Tim Kasser suggest that blame-shifting can take the form of denigration of outgroups.[87] Studies show that derogation of outsiders is enhanced when people are reminded of their mortality.

A related strategy is to shift responsibility for the problem to a higher power, thereby making us the instrument of forces beyond our control. This strategy is adopted by some people with a religious outlook and some with a scientific outlook. In the Rapture movement of certain fundamentalist Christians God rather than humanity is responsible for climate calamity, an aspect of the 'tribulation' that is understood as divine retribution for human sin. 'The rapture is a way to escape the terrible things that will come after it.'[88] The 'pre-wrath' return of Jesus to rescue the faithful before the tribulation is a reprise of the beliefs of

Mrs Keech's 1954 sect, who were convinced that a flood would destroy the Earth, sparing only those who committed themselves to God through Keech. In keeping with millenarian tradition, the Rapture sees the coming tribulation as a cleansing of the Earth.[89] As such, human-induced climate change is reframed as the will of God and therefore a good thing, or at least a necessary thing.

Closely related to the Rapture is another form of defence favoured by some who would be aghast at ever being mentioned in the same breath. It involves a kind of intellectual distancing through characterising global warming and its impact on the world as 'natural' within a larger frame that views humans as just another form of life. This intellectualisation is the preferred coping mechanism adopted by James Lovelock, who argues that Gaia, like the God of Rapture, is indifferent to the fate of humans who are, after all, only one species among many.[90] The fact that the elimination of that species would involve death and suffering on a scale unparalleled is abstracted from by a process of mental withdrawal to a vantage point somewhere in outer space or lodged in universal time from which the cries of the dying cannot be heard. In a similar way, Alan Weissman's 2008 book *The World Without Us* plots the relentless revegetation and reclamation of the Earth after humans have suddenly vanished from its surface. The imagery celebrates Nature's power and majesty and invites us to take an unsentimental view of human extinction by focusing on forces beyond our control.

The mendacity of hope

Every serious discussion of climate change is haunted by the idea of hope. In the Greek myth, Pandora ignored Zeus's warning to keep the lid on her box.[91] All the evils of mankind escaped, except for one item that remained—hope. Explanations conflict; some see hope as the consolation, for in the face of all evils we can always rely on it (although not if it remains locked in the box). For others, what remains in Pandora's Box is another evil, false hope which deludes us with dreams of being saved, intensifying the torment of the evils that escaped.[92]

Nevertheless, the need to remain hopeful seems axiomatic. Environment organisations insist that campaigning must always hold out hope, believing the alternative to be capitulation to despair and apathy. While usually understood as the absence of feeling, apathy can reflect a suppression of feeling that may serve a useful psychological function. Renée Lertzman argues that inaction does not mean the absence of caring, but may be a strategy to defend ourselves from the anxiety and distress that follow from allowing ourselves to care too much.[93] If I don't care, I won't feel bad. The temptation to practise apathy is particularly strong in the case of global warming because of the feelings of helplessness that grow as we find out more about the nature and scale of the threat. Nevertheless, it is a maladaptive strategy, not least because the refusal to feel can exact a heavy emotional toll.[94]

In many countries the need to be optimistic is a powerful emotional norm. Norgaard quotes a Norwegian teacher who felt that his own doubts and feelings of powerlessness about global warming must be suppressed so as to give his charges a sense of hope.[95] Optimism as a social norm is particularly strong in the United States, where the culture of self-help and self-improvement reigns.[96] Programs teach primary school children how to be more optimistic. Optimism is closely tied to the norm of individualism, because it is believed that hopes are realised through personal accomplishments.[97] Although a caricature, it is sometimes said that in the United States a homeless person is just a millionaire temporarily down on his luck.

Although we generally think of a willingness to face up to reality as a sign of mental health, a strong case can be made that the normal human mind interprets events in ways that promote 'benign fictions' about oneself, the world and the future. This is the argument of psychologist Shelley Taylor in her important book *Positive Illusions*.[98] 'The ability of the mind to construe benefit from tragedy and to prevent a person from becoming overwhelmed by the stress and pain of life is a remarkable achievement.'[99] Cultivating these benign fictions is in fact an adaptive response to an often unfriendly world in which one's self-belief is constantly at risk of a battering, as many young people discover when they enter talent shows and as academics learn when they receive devastating referees' reports on papers submitted for publication. Self-aggrandising fictions help us maintain control over our situations. Feeling that we have control over events in our lives has been shown repeatedly to be essential to effective functioning. It is well-established that holding a positive view of the future enhances mental health, and that chronic pessimism is associated with anxiety and depression. One study concluded that resignation can indeed induce passivity, including a reluctance to engage in pro-environmental behaviour.[100] Another study found that those who belong to fundamentalist religious groups (such as hard-line Calvinists, some Muslims and Orthodox Jews), who have a surer view of the world and their place in it, are more optimistic than those who belong to moderate religions, and the moderates are in turn more optimistic than members of the most liberal religious communities (such as Unitarians, Reformed Jews and members of the Uniting Church).[101]

Taylor defines 'unrealistic optimism' as a proclivity that leads us to predict what we would prefer to see happen rather than what is objectively most likely.[102] Surveys show that most people believe their life at present is an improvement on the past and that the future will be better still.[103] While they have a rosy view of their own future they may simultaneously believe that the state of the world is in decline. Although it causes us to filter out or downplay incoming evidence that could contradict our expectations, the truth is that unrealistic optimism has been shown to be associated with 'higher motivation, greater persistence at tasks, more effective performance, and, ultimately, greater success'.[104] So while pessimism, especially if it morphs into depression, is likely to lead to passivity and brooding, optimism is more likely to lead to action. Indeed, one of the simplest and most effective treatments for depression is to turn this around so that instead of mood determining behaviour, behaviour determines mood. Acting in response to depression works from the 'outside-in'.[105]

Yet within the phenomenon of unrealistic optimism it is vital to distinguish between illusion and delusion. Illusions respond and adapt to reality as it forces itself on us, while delusions are held despite the evidence of the outside world. 'Delusions are false beliefs that persist despite the facts', writes Taylor. 'Illusions accommodate them, though perhaps reluctantly.'[106] Martin Seligman, the guru of 'learned optimism' and 'learned helplessness', also recognises that cultivating optimism is helpful only when the future can be changed by positive thinking; when that is not the case 'we must have the courage to endure pessimism',[107] although after a period of feeling pessimistic it is usual for buoyancy built on a new understanding of the world to return.

In this book I am arguing that the evidence that large-scale climate change is unavoidable has now become so strong that healthy illusion is becoming unhealthy delusion. Hoping that a major disruption to the Earth's climate can be avoided is a delusion. Optimism sustained against the facts, including unfounded beliefs in the power of consumer action or in technological rescue, risks turning hopes into fantasies. Sooner or later the constant striving to control events must come up against the reality. How long will it be before well-meaning people who have accepted the message of green consumerism—that we can all make a difference by changing our personal behaviour—begin to say to themselves, 'I have been doing the right thing for years, but the news about global warming just keeps getting worse'? How long before our political leaders allow their enormous emotional investment in carbon capture and storage to be confronted by the fact that, even if it proves technically and economically feasible, it will not be deployed until after it is too late?

Unthinking optimism about the ability of humanity to avoid climate change is misplaced. But once we have faced up to the reality of a world under global warming, with all of its horrors, we can perhaps begin to make plans and take actions built on the new reality (a theme I will return to in the last chapter). It is true that this is a judgment call and that maintaining the fiction that it is not too late to prevent dangerous global warming may improve the chances that strong action will be taken in the next few years, thereby at least postponing the inevitable. Yet it seems to me that the observations of climate change have taken such an alarming turn in the last few years, and global action remains so inadequate, that maintaining optimism seems more and more like a disconnection from reality. This is the only explanation for the launch of the bizarre campaign to 'rebrand' the 2009 Copenhagen Conference 'Hopenhagen', a concept developed by some of the world's biggest advertising agencies and centred on creating a 'popular movement' that will 'empower global citizens' who can, through the website, send 'messages of hope to UN delegates'.[108] The advertising corporations behind the Hopenhagen campaign included Ogilvy & Mather which, when not saving the planet from climate change, is persuading us to buy more petrol from BP and cars from Ford. They are joined by Colle + McVoy, which promotes petrochemicals for DuPont, and Ketchum, which wants us to fly more on Delta Airlines. Like Lisa Simpson's Ignorital, 'Hopenhagen' functions as an emotional tranquilliser. Enforced optimism becomes a means of disengaging from a reality that contradicts our deeply held belief that everything will work out in the end.

Chapter 5

Disconnection from Nature

There is persuasive evidence that our concerns about the environment, as well as our attitudes and values, are influenced by the extent to which we feel ourselves to be part of the natural world.[1] On a continuum of connectedness with Nature, some people experience themselves as wholly separate and have an ego-centred self-concept, while others experience themselves as inseparable from the natural world so that their sense of self expands to encompass the biosphere and beyond. Cultures vary. Reviewing some of the evidence, Wesley Schultz and colleagues conclude:[2]

> In essence, respondents from the United States and Western Europe tend to be less biospheric and more egoistic in their approach to environmental issues, while respondents from Central America and South America tend to be more biospheric.

On the other hand, the rise of Western environmentalism since the 1960s, stimulated by the works of writers such as Aldo Leopold, Henry David Thoreau and Arne Naess, can be understood as an attempt to persuade us to reconnect.

The modern concept of 'progress' embodies the idea of separating ourselves from Nature both physically and psychologically. The processes of urbanisation and technological advance have been aimed at isolating humans from the effects of nature, and especially the weather. The distancing has not necessarily meant we have become hostile to the natural; it is possible that our distance from the natural environment makes it easier to adopt an idealised or even romantic view of Nature, one that we can sustain because we can engage with it in our own time and on our own terms. That would explain the popularity of eco-tourism, camping, bushwalking and widespread support for wilderness protection across Western countries over the last few decades.

While these activities can be motivated by the aesthetic appeal of unspoiled landscapes, for some there has always been a deeper urge. Encounters with nature can re-establish or reaffirm the sense of connectedness, a re-linking that can induce a shift from self-focused to biospheric value-orientation.[3] Even so, while contact with nature can have a transformative effect, our attitudes to the natural world are often complex and contradictory. Some people actively dislike wild places and avoid them. A study of children required to encounter wilderness on school excursions found that for many nature is 'scary, disgusting and uncomfortable'.[4] They are afraid of forests, insects, snakes and wild animals, disgusted by the perceived dirtiness of the environment and discomforted by exposure to the elements. This recoil may have evolutionary roots, but they are reinforced by peers, parents and the media, including 'nature nasties', a documentary style popularised by crocodile-wrangler Steve Irwin, in which the excitement of interacting with and provoking animals to extreme behaviour takes the place of the respect and wonder elicited by more traditional observational nature documentaries such as those featuring David Attenborough.

Disconnection from nature is a modern phenomenon. Before the advent of the scientific and industrial revolutions Europeans had a conception of the self radically different from that typical today. Indeed, those revolutions were at heart the remaking of consciousness that began with the arrival of the so-called mechanical philosophy at the end of the seventeenth century. If in order to respond to global warming we need a new consciousness, a fruitful way to understand the prospects for such a shift is to study the last major revolution in consciousness. In other words, if we can understand how we became radically disconnected from nature, this should help us understand what it would take for us to become reconnected once more. The intellectual and social history of the rise of the mechanical philosophy is complex and contentious and a full account would take a book in itself, so the argument I give here should be understood as no more than a stylised outline of a much more detailed story.[5]

The death of Nature

Prior to the second half of the seventeenth century the dominant philosophy of Nature outside of the Church was Hermeticism. In the Hermetic philosophy the world was understood organically, that is, as akin to a living organism. The modern distinction between animate and inanimate objects was not recognised; rocks, metals and the elements were not seen as passive but animated by an internal principle.[6] So, for example, metals grow in the earth according to their own principle rather than due to the influence of external force. The original conception is often attributed to Plato, who wrote in the fourth century BCE:

> Therefore, we may consequently state that: this world is indeed a living being endowed with a soul and intelligence ... a single visible living entity containing all other living entities, which by their nature are all related.[7]

To separate the spiritual and the physical was the first objective of the new mechanical philosophy of the seventeenth century. Particularly in the second half of the century, natural philosophers were drawn to the new worldview closely associated with the name of René Descartes. Descartes saw the world as comprising no more than matter and motion, with matter itself defined solely by the space it occupies, ruling out any inner essence or form. By taking the machine as a metaphor for the cosmos he denied it any life force or inner motive. In the mechanical philosophy, the progressive dissection of the material world yielded only finer particles, an atomistic conception from which the spirit was banished. In this conception the Earth was rendered dead. Today we take a dead Earth as given yet, as Mircea Eliade pointed out, experience of a radically desacralised nature is a recent discovery.[8]

The romantic movement of the early decades of the nineteenth century was a reaction against the denial by mechanical science and industrial practice that matter had any inner essence or vivifying force. Francis Bacon had shockingly likened scientific experimentation to torture, in which Nature is placed on the rack by the scientific inquisitor and forced to yield up its secrets. For Wordsworth the new science meant the death of the world he loved:[9]

Sweet is the lore which Nature brings;
Our meddling intellect
Mis-shapes the beauteous forms of things:–
We murder to dissect.

A decade later, in Germany, Goethe expressed the same sentiment:[10]

To docket living things past any doubt
You cancel first the living spirit out:
The parts lie in the hollow of your hand,
You only lack the living link you banned.

Descartes' intervention was in fact the culmination of a philosophical break that occurred some three centuries earlier within the dominant theological school of Scholasticism.[11] Prior to this the prevailing view, inherited from the Greeks and formalised by Thomas Aquinas, understood reality as possessing a mysterious aspect beyond human comprehension. In the thirteenth century some began to argue that there is nothing essentially inexpressible about the divine or the inner essence of things, and indeed we can talk about God in the same way we can talk about other beings. If there is nothing inherently mysterious then the human intellect can attain certainty about all things. In other words, the world, reality, is characterised by clarity and distinctness, and so has to be graspable by the human intellect. It was this prior shift that allowed Descartes to reduce the world to matter and motion.

To the modern mind the presumption that existence can only be conceived as clear and intelligible seems obvious, almost banal, yet the argument that existence must be graspable by the human mind was a momentous shift. In sharp contrast with Thomas Aquinas's notion of being as 'something with unknowable and unanalysable depth',[12] reality has no deeper quality. The unknowable becomes that which is not yet known, so knowledge is confined to the rational, conceptual and empirical. As this view took hold, the Earth was emptied of any powers other than those identifiable by mechanical science.[13]

The new science's presumption of the knowability of reality seems indisputable today—the alternative is characterised as superstitious—yet it met resistance from poets, philosophers and ordinary people. Wordsworth wrote of 'a sense sublime, of something far more deeply interfused', and the enduring appeal of the romantic poets (and perhaps French impressionist paintings) speaks to the popular recognition of something beyond the superficial appearances of everyday life. In the new science, 'life' no longer had something mysterious at its core but became graspable in biological terms, which killed any idea of a living Earth. Still, it took some time for the old idea of a living Earth to be expelled from the public realm. In 1817 the philosopher Hegel wrote that 'the earth is a living whole or an individual organism because it is the totality of all of its own chemical processes ...'.[14] Goethe, too, referred to the Earth as 'a living earthly body',[15] and in 1851 Thoreau penned these words: 'The earth I tread on is not a dead inert mass. It is a body—has a spirit—is organic ... It is the most living of creatures.'[16]

In resisting the Cartesian division between the human and the non-human the romantic poets and philosophers stood before a tide of history that would soon wash over them. This was a pity because their conception has been vindicated now that Nature has struck back, reminding us that the separation and elevation of humans was all along a conceit and that the 'master' was no more than a servant who stole onto the throne while the monarch slept.

Modern science's separation of the knower and the known needed vigorous promotion and there was no proselytiser more committed than the father of modern chemistry, Robert Boyle, who laid down the rules for experimentation endorsed by the Royal Society in the seventeenth century.[17] In his 1686 book *A Free Enquiry into the Vulgarly Received Notion of Nature*, Boyle imagined the world to be like a puppet moved by a divine force that can overrule any mechanical processes that may be present.[18] In the new conception the world is like 'a rare clock' which, once constructed, is set ticking so that 'all things proceed according to the artificer's first design' without any subsequent intervention by God, the clockmaker.[19] The new conception, according to Boyle, complied with the church's understanding of the increasingly detached role of the divine being.[20] God was being banished from the Earth to some separate realm. If at any time God should decide to overrule the operations of the clockwork mechanism, which knows nothing more than matter and motion, then the result is properly understood as a miracle. Instead of a God that both transcended the world and lived within it, He became a divine outsider to a spiritually denuded world. His actions then became external interventions, in the absence of which science rules.[21]

In a remark that lends early weight to the contention that the mechanical philosophy helped release the forces that have given us the climate crisis, Boyle observed that one of the lamentable consequences of the philosophy that venerates a living natural world is that it deters men from exercising their rule over it; piety towards nature, he wrote, is 'a discouraging impediment to the empire of man over the inferior creatures of God'.[22] William Derham, who in 1711 delivered the prestigious Boyle Lecture, put it more bluntly:[23]

> We can, if need be, ransack the whole globe, penetrate into the bowels of the earth, descend to the bottom of the deep, travel to the farthest regions of this world, to acquire wealth, to increase our knowledge, or even only to please our eye and fancy.

Political science

Along with Descartes, the seminal intellectual figure in the transition from the old to the new natural philosophy was Isaac Newton, whose work, particularly the 1687 *Principia*, contributed more than any other to the revolution in consciousness. Indeed the mechanical philosophy is known interchangeably as the Newtonian or the Cartesian worldview. In his early years as a student at Cambridge Newton imbibed the mechanical philosophy, including the conceptualisation of matter as inert or inactive, unless, of course, acted upon by an external force. Yet at the same time, from his earliest days until late in life Newton was heavily engaged in the ideas and practices of alchemy, the foremost esoteric practice of those steeped in the Hermetic philosophy.[24] For years Newton collected and pored over alchemical manuscripts, transcribing, translating and absorbing them. He immersed himself in alchemical experiments, building his own laboratory in the garden outside his rooms at Trinity College and sometimes keeping the furnace alight for days at a time while he worked on his chemical transformations. He was perhaps the most theoretically knowledgeable and experimentally proficient alchemist of all time.

While it is easy today to mock Newton's efforts—one experiment optimistically began 'Take of Urin one Barrel'[25]—in fact he went about his chemical labours with the same concentrated application of systematic and careful thought and testing that marked all his work. Yet throughout his scientific career Newton never abandoned the intuition that the Earth is always engaged in incessant activity. In some respects, the idea is not too far from the truth for modern geology tells us that the Earth's crust is being constantly overturned by the process of subduction, the underthrusting or down-welling of tectonic plates into the Earth's mantle. 'For nature is a perpetuall circulatory worker', Newton wrote,[26] and in texts such as the *Principia* he forever sought to capture the Earth's ceaseless transformation with the use of verbs like condensing, fermenting, coagulating, precipitating, exhaling, vegetating, circulating and generating.[27] He understood gravity as the divine force that animates and orders the universe and which is caused by 'the direct action of God'. However antagonistic the two worldviews seem today, the mechanistic view in Newton's hands became permeated from the outset with a conception of a living Earth. He infused the mechanical philosophy with something new and distinctive, which led some at the time to criticise the *Principia* for occultism.[28]

The story of Newton's intellectual development suggests that the essential Hermetic insight of a living Earth and the rigorous practice of modern science are not, at heart, incompatible. Conceiving of the world as alive or dead is not a decision that can be taken on the basis of scientific evidence but is due to either intuition or habit. To be sure, alchemical practice—which made the mistake of interpreting the metaphysical in physical terms—could not withstand the withering force of scientific experimentation. But mechanism was never more than a metaphor, although it did not take long for the metaphor to be mistaken for the thing it represented, not least because it suited certain social and political forces to do so. The difficulty for Newton was that Hermeticism had become closely associated with political radicalism and religious enthusiasm, both of which presented a threat to the established political order and church authority in the late seventeenth century.[29] Newton's dilemma became acute in the 1690s when radical and free-thinker John Toland linked demands for social change with the implications of Newton's natural philosophy.[30] If Nature is in a constant state of transformation there is no philosophical justification for a stable human order.[31]

Whatever its intellectual force, the mechanical philosophy could not succeed on the basis of evidence or logic alone. In addition to the church—which from the Middle Ages had been retreating from its more holistic instincts and for which pantheism and enthusiasm had become threats—the mechanical worldview found its advocate in the emerging middle class, whose accumulation of pecuniary and political influence depended on a stable social order. The growth of commerce and industry also needed to overcome resistance to exploiting the Earth's resources. Since minerals were seen to have some form of vegetative life mining had to be treated cautiously, and miners often performed propitiatory rituals.[32] As Carolyn Merchant observed: 'The image of the earth as a living organism and nurturing mother had served as a cultural constraint restricting the actions of human beings. One does not readily slay a mother ...'[33] Yet there was mounting commercial pressure to expand mining. In the 90 years to 1680 the amount of coal dug from English soil increased tenfold.[34] The cloth industry and large-scale farming were other sectors growing rapidly along capitalist lines, so that 'for the first time in England the earth was seen primarily as a source of profits by an increasingly powerful sector of the economy'.[35]

Max Weber, the founder of sociology, began his great work, *The Protestant Ethic and the Spirit of Capitalism*, with the observation that the development of certain types of practical rational conduct may encounter serious inner resistance from spiritual obstacles. 'The magical and religious forces, and the ethical ideas of duty based upon them, have in the past always been among the most important formative influences on conduct.'[36] The development of the ethos of modern capitalism first had to overcome these obstacles and it was the Protestant ethic that brought to capitalism 'the change in moral standards which converted a natural frailty [acquisitiveness] into an ornament of the spirit, and canonized as the economic virtues habits which in earlier ages had been denounced as vices'.[37] Calvinists and Puritans believed God had given man dominion over the Earth and it was his duty now to exploit it.

If the natural world can be expunged of immanent purpose and intrinsic value, the world has value only to the extent of its contribution to human welfare. Weber coined the phrase 'the disenchantment of the world' to refer to the way the modern mind began to see the Earth as an inert realm 'out there', ripe for exploitation. The notion that the world is alive and in which we are intimately involved came to be seen as superstitious and disreputable. The scientific attitude of dispassionate withdrawal and non-participatory deliberation found favour with the official church as well as the rising bourgeoisie, and it was this combination that saw European industrial power come to dominate the world.

Gaia: the rebirth of Nature?

In the Greek tragedy attributed to Aeschylus, Prometheus steals fire from Zeus and gives it to humans so as to increase their power. Zeus is angry and punishes both man, by sending Pandora with her box, and Prometheus by having him chained to a rock where an eagle eats out his liver, which regenerates each night only to be devoured again the next day. Prometheus, who saw himself as the benefactor of mankind, reveals that he also taught men how to increase their powers with agriculture, metallurgy, medicine, mathematics, architecture and astronomy. Later, Hercules kills the eagle and releases Prometheus. The idea of the 'unbound Prometheus' has been interpreted in modern times as the release of the powers of technology and industry in eighteenth-century Europe.[38] But just as Zeus and Prometheus remain estranged, so the unrestrained powers of Prometheus have brought about the modern tension between 'heaven and earth'. In the myth it is only when Prometheus reveals to Zeus a secret that allows him to prevent his downfall that the two are finally reconciled.

Once set in motion it took a couple of centuries for the Promethean powers of science and technology to conquer the world, and it was not until the 1960s that the first stirrings of a political challenge emerged. I have mentioned already the outrage this impudence spurred—the hysterical reaction to Rachel Carson, the angry defensiveness of the 'trio' of physicists, the conservative counter-movement in the United States—but the tide had turned. And the cause of the turn lay in the overreach of the scientific–industrial revolution itself. Humanity is now forced to confront the question of whether a consciousness rooted in a dead Earth subjugated to our material needs can respond adequately to the climate crisis, or whether we need to rediscover some form of consciousness that recognises a living Earth yet remains scientifically credible. Clearly a return to pre-scientific animism is out of the question; we know too much. The development of the science of ecology has helped to point out the intricate interconnectedness of natural systems and our reliance on them for survival. Although ecologists themselves may be motivated by some deeper intuition, as a science ecology remains within the confines of the mechanical philosophy. The notion of 'adaptive complex systems' does not easily translate into any recognisable idea of life.

The closest tenable conception of a living Earth from an 'ecological' perspective that I have come across is from a most unexpected source. In a book published in 1926 Jan Smuts, then between periods as prime minister of South Africa but also a philosopher of note, coined the term 'holism' to describe a relationship between humans and the non-human world. Rejecting all mechanistic conceptions, Smuts wrote that it is the inner character of a whole that makes it more than the sum of its parts:[39]

> The concept of holism … dissolves the heterogeneous concepts of matter, life and mind, and then recrystallises them out as polymorphous forms of itself … We shall thus be prepared to find more of life in matter, and more of mind in life, because the hard-and-fast demarcations between them have fallen away.

Smuts seemed to have the vision but not the science to justify it.

In more recent times another idea has emerged that promises to combine the best scientific understanding with a conception of the living Earth—James Lovelock's Gaia hypothesis. While working for NASA on how to detect life on Mars, Lovelock had the intuition that the Earth is a large living organism sustained by energy from the Sun.[40] The basis for this is the hypothesis that 'the evolution of the species and the evolution of the environment are tightly coupled together as a single and inseparable process'.[41] The Gaia theory maintains that the Earth is a living system in which the biosphere interacts with other physical components of the Earth—the atmosphere, the cryosphere (the frozen parts of the Earth), the hydrosphere and the lithosphere (the Earth's crust)—to maintain conditions suitable for life. 'We live in a world that has been built by our ancestors, ancient and modern, and which is continuously maintained by all things alive today.'[42]

Life does not simply respond and adapt to the environment around it but modifies that environment for its own ends. In particular, the composition of the atmosphere, the temperature at the Earth's surface and the salinity of the oceans are influenced by the biota so that they are maintained in a stable state suited to life. In the case of temperature, Lovelock argues that the ability of life unconsciously to regulate the Earth's atmosphere has allowed it to maintain a fairly stable temperature, even though the energy provided to the Earth by the Sun has increased 25–30 per cent since life forms emerged. There is now a body of science that lends weight to the Gaia theory by identifying and measuring various feedback mechanisms.

So has Lovelock solved the conundrum of how to marry a conception of a living Earth with the methods of modern science?

Although Gaia theory maintains that the Earth is alive, this only provokes the question of what is meant by 'alive'. An adequate definition of life is notoriously elusive.[43] Biochemical definitions centre on the observations that living entities grow, metabolise, respond to stimuli, possess DNA, reproduce, die and evolve across generations. Yet these definitions reduce life to certain of its properties and seem to miss something essential. And they don't work for the idea of a living Earth because it does not do some of these things.

An alternative definition arises from the observation that life forms seem to resist, as long as they live, the second law of thermodynamics, which tells us that the universe always moves from a state of order to a state of disorder, a process known as entropy. Thus when coal is stored under the ground it forms a dense energy source in a highly useful state. When it is dug up and burned its energy is used up and its physical components are dissipated across the globe. The disorder represents the decline in useful energy after the coal is burned. Living things can forestall the effects of entropy through metabolic processes that create order and organisation within their physical boundaries; they generate order from disorder. Life then can be thought of as a process that for a time resists the relentless dissipation of energy and matter in the universe. However, while directing flows of matter and energy through themselves to defer their own decay, life forms also put waste into the outside environment, thereby accelerating entropy beyond their boundaries.

Lovelock is attracted to this explanation, writing: 'If life is defined as a self-organizing system characterized by an actively sustained low-entropy, then, viewed from outside each of these boundaries [of the living entity or system], what lies within is alive.'[44] It's a conception that seems to work for Lovelock's purposes because it fits with the claim that the Earth is a living organism. Yet on closer inspection this notion of life in Gaia theory becomes a stepping stone to rendering the Earth less than alive.

In the early years of the Gaia hypothesis, Lovelock was criticised by fellow scientists for implicitly adopting a teleological explanation, that is, the view that the Earth is evolving purposively towards some goal. To the modern scientific mind teleology is a heresy, and Lovelock was keen to distance himself from it. 'True knowledge can never be gained by attributing "purpose" to phenomena', he wrote.[45]

To prove that Gaia is not a teleological theory Lovelock developed a simple computer model consisting of a planet dominated by two plant species—white daisies and black daisies.[46] White daises reflect a lot of incoming solar radiation, while black daisies reflect little and absorb a lot. If the planet becomes too warm more white daisies grow. The white surfaces reflect more solar radiation and the planet cools. Then when it cools too much, more black daises grow.

The Daisyworld model can be used to show that a planet can be self-regulating with the 'objective' of maintaining the conditions for life. It's a feedback system that has an objective without having a purpose, just like a machine with an automatic governor. Lovelock describes it in cybernetic terms as an unconscious self-regulating system that is constantly brought back to a homoeostatic point (although that point can jump to a new equilibrium), a circulatory system that replaces the usual sequential thinking of the sciences.

It is apparent that in disowning all teleology Lovelock has returned to a mechanical world in which a 'living Earth' can be no more than a metaphor. In the end Lovelock defines Gaia as a 'control system' that 'has the capacity to regulate the temperature and the composition of the Earth's surface and to keep it comfortable for living organisms'.[47] Gaia is in truth a mechanical system into which Lovelock has smuggled life. He contrasts the idea of a living Earth with the common one of 'a dead planet bearing life as a mere passenger',[48] but Lovelock's Gaia is a dead planet with some organisms living on it, ones that unconsciously modify the lifeless components of the system.

In the end, Lovelock concedes that he talks of the Earth being alive only in a metaphorical sense, arguing that we should '*imagine* it as the largest living thing in the solar system'. 'Unless we see the Earth as a planet that behaves *as if it were alive*, at least to the extent of regulating its climate and chemistry, we will lack the will to change.'[49] Yet it is difficult to believe that we can be motivated to radically change the way we live just by imagining Gaia to be alive rather than feeling intuitively it to be so.

Lovelock is an intellectual descendent of René Descartes rather than Thomas Aquinas. For him Gaia had to conform to the universe of clarity, distinctness and knowability. If at the core of life there is something indefinable and mysterious then Lovelock's Gaia cannot be alive. Lovelock is more a product of mechanical thinking than he realises. He admits that after the publication of *The Ages of Gaia* he was mystified by the large number of letters he received from readers who saw his vision in essentially religious or transcendental terms. It is not surprising that many people should have read the book from a different standpoint, one that recognises that being is deeper than how it appears to us and intuits a mysterious foundation for life and the cosmos.

Although formally rejecting teleology, Lovelock frequently

anthropomorphises Gaia. In his hands Gaia assumes the character of an Olympian god who alternates between indifference, impatience and hostility towards the human beings who crawl over her surface. For some who care about human suffering, the temptation is strong to defend against the pain it causes by retreating to the cerebral. In his books Lovelock appears to have taken himself to a place in the future where the one million fittest humans who survived have created 'a truly sentient planet',[50] a place from which he can declare that the current inhabitants of Earth are of no importance except insofar as they provide the raw material for the evolution of 'a much better animal'.[51] It is a consoling vision for the octogenarian Lovelock, but will be of little comfort to future waves of climate refugees as they roam the oceans in search of a new home. A more emotionally honest expression of despair over environmental destruction came from the pen of the Australian poet Judith Wright.[52]

> I praise the scoring drought, the flying dust,
> the drying creek, the furious animal,
> that they oppose us still;
> that we are ruined by the thing we kill.

Although Lovelock has been unable to defend the claim that his Gaia is a living entity, his books have encouraged many readers to have more courage in their intuitive conviction that the Earth is in some sense alive and therefore has interests. His other contributions to the global warming debate have been much less helpful. He is contemptuous of environmentalism, though his reasons are hard to divine. He is implacably opposed to windfarms, especially anywhere near his dwelling in rural England, regarding protection of landscape aesthetics as more important than the promotion of renewable energy.

Self and world

The mechanical philosophy set out to create a division between humans and the non-human world, a fissure between people and Nature that allowed a growing preoccupation with the personal self. The process reached its peak with the rise of modern consumerism, and especially the phase from the early 1990s to the financial crisis of 2008. Heavy emphasis on the creation of personal identities through consumption activity reinforced the turn to the outer self. In the face of these individualising pressures many people still retain a sense of connectedness with the environment, as if three centuries of mechanical thinking, self-determination and self-creation could only cover over but not sever some primal bond with the natural world. In recent years, an extensive volume of research has codified the extent to which the modern self remains bound to the natural world.[53]

The conception of the self is not fixed but dynamic, responding over time to social, cultural and personal influences. This is implicit in the claim that the era of neo-liberalism and modern consumerism has promoted more self-focused, individualistic behaviour. In addition, systematic differences in conceptions of the self have been found across cultures, with people in Asian countries defining themselves less by their independence from others and more by their relationships with them. Indeed, these observed cultural differences stimulated psychologists initially to define two distinct forms of 'self-construal', the independent and the interdependent.[54] Those who emphasise their uniqueness and differentiation from others are said to have *independent self-construal.* Characteristic of Western individualism, this model values autonomy and emphasises self-enhancement, personal motivation and realising one's internal attributes and goals. In contrast, those with *interdependent self-construal* see the self defined through connection with others; the barrier that separates the self from others is more porous so that the interests and concerns of others also become one's own. It is not so much that a distinct personal self empathises with others, but that the self is *defined* in relation to others, so that notions of status, belonging, duty and respect are emphasised. Interdependent self-construal is not always associated with an altruistic approach to other people; it may be motivated by the desire for in-group harmony at the expense of out-groups, or by altruistic objectives in which the division between in-groups and out-groups is overcome.[55] The idea parallels Robert Putnam's distinction between *bonding* social capital, which emphasises social networks within a homogenous group (for example, gangs, ethnic enclaves and some religious groups), and *bridging* social capital, which cultivates networks between heterogeneous social groups with a view to breaking down barriers.[56]

These two well-established forms of self-concept share a vital characteristic—they are anthropocentric, that is, concerned with the interests of humans. More recently, two Canadian researchers, Mirella Stroink and Teresa DeCicco, have identified a third distinct model of self-construal.[57] *Metapersonal self-construal* describes a sense of self inseparably connected to all living things or some wider notion of the Earth or cosmos. It is the conception of an expanded self that underpins Buddhist theory and practice, but which can be found in all cultures.

Most people contain elements of all three models, although cultures tend to validate and encourage one orientation more than others. It would be fair to argue that Western consumerism actively promotes an independent self-concept while the 'deep green' stream of Western environmentalism promotes a metapersonal self-concept. Emergent Chinese consumerism (considered in Chapter 3) has promoted a shift from a more interdependent to a more independent type of self. As we will see, to a large degree how we construct ourselves determines how we think about and act towards the natural environment. Indeed, types of environmental concern and models of self-construal are well matched.[58] Specifically: the degree of independent self-construal is correlated with an egocentric form of environmental concern, that is, a concern for the effects of environmental decline on one's own welfare; interdependent self-construal is correlated with altruistic values, that is, concern for the effects of environmental quality on others; and metapersonal self-construal is associated with 'biospheric values', a concern for the whole natural environment and all living things.

It is helpful to think of the three forms of self-construal in terms of different degrees of expansion and contraction of the self. Interdependent self-construal entails an expansion of the self to encompass other humans, while metapersonal self-construal entails expansion of the self to encompass all living things and the environment as a whole. The biosphere becomes valued because it is included in the conception of the self.[59] Just as those with a strong interdependent self-construal experience the death of someone close as a disintegration of the self, those with a strong metapersonal self-construal experience the destruction of some valued natural object as the death of part of the self.

Interdependent self-construal is more limited than meta-personal self-construal, but it is not always the case that a self expanded to encompass all things entails as much altruistic feeling as an interdependent self. We have all met people who show an intense concern for the welfare of other people but little concern for the environment, and people who are intensely concerned about the state of the natural environment but show little concern for the interests of fellow humans, except in an abstract way. However, the evidence suggests that the first group is probably much bigger than the second group: those with biospheric values are more likely to be altruistic than altruistic people are likely to have biospheric concerns.[60] This seems natural since the biosphere includes humans, but humanity does not encompass the biosphere.

When government policies and NGO campaigns appeal to people's self-interest they are presupposing an independent model of self-construal, one consistent with the values of the market. Yet if those with egoistic values decide that the desired behaviours, while perhaps in the interests of other people or the biosphere, are of little value to themselves they will not act. For many previous environmental problems, appeal to egoistic values could be effective because by acting to protect themselves people were also protecting the interests of others. In the case of global warming individuals cannot act to isolate themselves from the effects, nor can individual actions alone reduce the threat significantly. Yet policies and campaigns may actually reinforce egocentric concerns, perhaps doing more harm than good. This is the basis for my critique of green consumerism in Chapter 3.

Evidence in support of this argument comes from a number of studies. In one, cooperative thoughts were first activated in the minds of subjects through a priming device such as asking them to unscramble sentences with words like 'group', 'friendships' and 'together'.[61] Subjects were then exposed to a social dilemma in which both sides benefit from acting altruistically. Those primed to think in an interdependent way placed more emphasis on outcomes for others. On the other hand, when thoughts of independence were activated with words like 'individual', 'self-contained' and 'independent', they behaved in more self-interested ways. That both altruistic and self-interested behaviour can be activated suggests that the self in all of us has some combination of independence and interdependence, and that one or both may come to the fore, temporarily or chronically, in response to the social environment.

The evidence indicates that priming is effective when it goes against the cultural norm. So when Americans, who come from a society in which independence is the norm, have interdependent thoughts activated they report more collectivist values, but when independent thoughts are primed they do not intensify individualist values.[62] The opposite happens in Hong Kong where, despite 40 years of capitalism, interdependent self-construal remains stronger than in the United States. It seems likely that in a highly individualistic country like the United States independent self-construal is chronically activated in daily life, so any additional priming has no effect. Those with a consumerist orientation—'a value structure that emphasizes the importance of material possessions and the pursuit of personal wealth'—have been shown to pay more attention to self-enhancement and less to community goals, while those with biospheric values—reflecting an expansion of the concept of the self to incorporate the interests of the natural environment—are more focused on self-transcendence than self-enhancement and engage in more environmentally responsible behaviour.[63] In addition, self-concept has been shown to correlate well with certain personality traits. One in particular emerges as the best predictor of both the degree of consumerism and the degree of environmentalism—agreeableness, a composite measure of empathy, compassion and concern for others. Those with a consumerist value structure score lower on agreeableness, while those with an environmental value structure score higher.[64] In short, environmentalists are nicer people than consumers.

The point about these studies is that they indicate that if the objective is to motivate people to act on climate change we should not be reinforcing their independent self-concept but seeking to remind them of and activate their cooperative, pro-social side. Remembering the three-way distinction between independent, interdependent and metapersonal self-construal, both the interdependent and metapersonal types are associated with more cooperation and sharing of resources, with other people and the biosphere respectively.[65] This does not mean those with an independent concept of self have no environmental concern, but their concern is largely for the effects of environmental decline on their own interests, including those of their children. For them the self is the individual. The significance of avoiding messages that appeal to personal gain is underlined by Tom Crompton and Tim Kasser who argue that, by triggering awareness of our mortality, the threat of global warming is liable to induce us to shore up our sense of self in counterproductive ways:[66]

> Given the current economic and cultural climate that frequently serves to equate an individual's worth with his or her financial status or possessions, it seems probable that, when …

reminded of their mortality, people will tend to orient towards self-enhancing, materialistic values.

Climate change is intimately linked not just to the transformative powers of the scientific–industrial revolution, or even the political and cultural forces of growth fetishism and consumerism; it arises from the reshaping of human consciousness. Disconnection from Nature led inexorably to a stronger orientation towards the personal self. The shift is by no means complete and has met resistance along the way, but its extent renders an adequate response to climate disruption much more difficult. For if we are mired in an existential crisis because Prometheus was unbound, salvation requires the shackling of Prometheus once more. The task falls not to Zeus but to the humans whom Prometheus allowed to flourish. Current trends suggest that the more likely response is to seek to counter a Promethean problem with a Promethean solution. And, as someone said,[67] if current trends continue we will not.

Chapter 6

Is there a way out?

Setting aside the grand talk of a new consciousness, surely there must be a more prosaic and immediate way to avoid climate disruption. Can we not deploy those great forces of the scientific revolution, technology and know-how? There are three big technological sources of hope—carbon capture and storage, renewable energy and nuclear power—and one bold fall-back strategy if everything else fails—geoengineering. Let us consider each.

Capturing carbon

When we dig up and burn coal the carbon dioxide flows into the atmosphere and destabilises the climate. But what if we could remove the carbon dioxide from the power station smokestack, or from the coal before it's burned, and pump it back underground where it stays put? Forever. Then we could keep burning coal to our heart's content. After all, at current usage rates known reserves of the black stuff will last for two or three hundred years.[1] Capturing carbon and disposing of it safely is the dream of the coal industry. It has set up institutes, commissioned experts, lobbied governments and developed a slick marketing campaign to resuscitate the reputation of the world's dirtiest form of energy. The marketer's euphemism for the process of capturing and storing carbon dioxide is 'clean coal', a phrase that 'harnesses the awesome power of the word clean'.[2]

Political leaders have flocked to 'clean coal' or carbon capture and storage (CCS). In the United Kingdom, Gordon Brown has said we must have it 'if we are to have any chance of meeting our global goals'.[3] US President Barack Obama's public endorsement of 'clean coal' now features in PR videos made by the American Coalition for Clean Coal Electricity, an industry lobby group.[4] His most important advisers, Steven Chu and John Holdren, are firm supporters. German Chancellor Angela Merkel is backing industry plans to build dozens of new coal-fired power plants, expecting that at some point they will be able to capture the carbon dioxide and send it to subterranean burial sites.[5] In Australia, the world's biggest coal exporter and the nation most dependent on coal for electricity, Prime Minister Kevin Rudd has declared CCS 'critical' to generating jobs and bringing down greenhouse gas emissions.[6]

The Stern report calls CCS 'crucial'.[7] Jeffrey Sachs, director of the Earth Institute, repeats the common opinion that there is no way China will stop building coal-fired power plants so the technology 'had better work or we're in such a big mess we're not going to get out of it'.[8] The Garnaut report declares upfront that the future of coal depends on its success. So confident is Ross Garnaut that it will prove feasible and be rapidly commercialised that he predicts in a carbon-constrained world that Australia's coal industry has many decades of *expansion* in front of it.[9] In words that were a balm to politicians' ears, he wrote that the success of 'clean coal' will ensure that any negative impacts of greenhouse policies on coal-dependent regions are 'many years away'.

Government leaders have put our money where their mouths are, with torrents of public funding for research. The Obama Administration's stimulus bill in early 2009 allocated $3.4 billion to support CCS, and in May 2009 the US Department of Energy announced it will provide $2.4 billion to 'expand and accelerate the commercial deployment of carbon capture and storage technology', which Energy Secretary Steven Chu said was essential to the government's strategy.[10] In the same month, the Rudd Government in Australia announced it would commit A$2.4 billion (about US$2 billion) to an industrial-scale demonstration project.[11]

We are all tempted to grasp at straws and, as straws go, 'clean coal' is a doozey. After all, which government would not seize on a promise to tackle global warming and save the coal industry at the same time? The *Economist* says 'the idea that clean coal ... will save the world from global warming has become something of an article of faith among policymakers'.[12] So reluctant have governments been to restructure their economies to cut greenhouse gas emissions that we have reached a point where the future of the world now rests on the widespread and rapid deployment of a technology that is still on the drawing boards.

So can carbon capture and storage save us? There are no coal-fired power plants capturing their carbon today, only a handful of demonstration projects, and a lot of research, mainly publicly funded. Despite its relentless hyping of the technology, the private sector is reluctant to invest in it. It's fearsomely expensive and unproven, so the risks are unacceptable. In Australia, the rich nation with the most to lose economically from ending coal mining, industry funding for CCS research is one thousandth of its revenue. By contrast, wool growers allocate 2 per cent of their sales to fund innovation.[13] Big coal thinks it's cheaper to lobby governments to provide public funding, with the result that governments are investing heavily in research into 'clean coal' while the fossil fuel industries spend up on PR campaigns and political lobbying to keep the public funds flowing and quash any thought of the need to phase out coal.

As soon as one begins to investigate the issue, one is struck by the yawning gap between the deadlines for action provided by the climate scientists and the time lapse before the technology can deliver. While climate scientists say we must begin to radically reduce emissions in rich countries inside a decade, the best estimates for 'clean coal' indicate it will not be ready for widespread adoption for at least two decades. Independent analysis suggests that full-scale commercial implementation of carbon capture and storage will not occur until 2030.[14] In Australia, economic modelling by the Treasury assumes that 'clean coal' technology will not begin reducing emissions from coal-fired power plants until 2026 at the earliest and more likely 2033.[15] Yet the International Energy Agency (IEA), long seen to be the captive of the traditional energy industries, estimates that by 2030 the world will need more than 200 power plants fully equipped with CCS if warming is to be limited to 3°C.[16] Three degrees! The IPCC estimates that by 2050 only 30–60 per cent of power generation will be technically suitable for carbon capture and storage, and the IEA's projections show the technology will deliver less than 20 per cent of the emission reductions needed by 2050 in order to stabilise concentrations close to 450 ppm.[17]

The scale of the proposed carbon capture enterprise is vast.

By 2050 some 6000 underground carbon dioxide repositories, each receiving a million tonnes of carbon dioxide a year, will need to be in operation. Carbon capture supporters frequently point to the Sleipner project as proof that the technology can work. Located over a gas and oil well in the North Sea, the Sleipner storage project separates carbon dioxide from natural gas produced from the Sleipner West gas field and injects it into a large saline formation some 800 metres below the seabed.[18] (This does not, of course, eliminate the carbon dioxide released into the atmosphere when the natural gas is later burned to generate energy.) Jeff Goodell writes:[19]

> It is an enormous engineering project deploying one of the largest offshore platforms in the world. But compared to the engineering effort that would be required to stabilise the climate, it's nothing. It would take 10 Sleipner-size carbon dioxide storage projects to offset the annual emissions of a single big coal plant.

An even more striking indication of the size of the enterprise comes from energy expert Vaclav Smil. He calculates that in order to capture just a quarter of the emissions from the world's coal-fired power plants we would need a system of pipelines that would transport a volume of fluid twice the size of the global crude-oil industry.[20]

Countering the damage caused by one technological dinosaur with another gargantuan engineering venture reflects the characteristic technological hubris of modern industrial capitalism. Capturing carbon is driven more by testosterone and wishful thinking than reason. It is true that replacing the coal industry with alternative forms of energy will also require huge engineering works, including large numbers of wind farms, biomass generators, solar collectors and so on. But at least we know they will work, will be widely dispersed and can be built now.

If it proves technically feasible, capturing and storing carbon from coal-fired power stations will be expensive. It involves extensive engineering work to attach scrubbers to power plants and then pipe the captured carbon to underground storage sites. For cost reasons the power plant must be within 100 kilometres of the underground mine or saline aquifer,[21] which rules out many potential sites. The processes of capture, compression, transport and injection of carbon dioxide are energy-intensive, so to generate the same amount of energy a power plant will need to be around a third bigger and use a third more coal.[22] It seems perverse to *accelerate* the exploitation of the world's coal reserves in order to offset the effects of burning coal. No one is too sure how much capturing and storing carbon will add to the cost of electricity from coal plants, but estimates indicate that it may be in the order of $40–90 per tonne of carbon dioxide avoided.[23] This is well above the price of a tonne of carbon dioxide expected over the next several years from existing or planned emissions trading systems. As emission caps tighten the price of emissions will rise, which could make capturing and storing carbon commercially viable, but by then the market will have brought forward several cheaper options in addition to those available now.

Bearing in mind that it has to stay put for thousands of years, leakage from transporting and storing carbon dioxide renders the technology risky. If it leaks then all the effort is wasted. We don't have much idea about the geological implications of trying to lock away millions of tonnes of compressed gas for thousands of years. The Sleipner storage project has been in operation only since 1996. Apart from the climate damage caused by leaks, the effects on any populations close to the storage site could be lethal. Carbon dioxide is 1.5 times denser than air and will settle in a valley. In August 1986 a geological disturbance occurred in Lake Nyos in the Cameroons. The lake lies in a volcanic crater and is unusual in being saturated with carbon dioxide that seeps from magma beneath. One night a cloud of carbon dioxide spilled out of the lake and spread down neighbouring valleys, asphyxiating 1700 people and 3500 cattle. In fact every animal and bird within a 25-kilometre radius died.[24]

To give free reign to the construction of new coal-fired power plants in the hope that their emissions will be neutralised in perpetuity by successful development of a highly speculative technology is folly of the highest order. The industry is unwilling to bear these risks and wants government, that is, the public, to indemnify it and to take over ownership of sites where carbon dioxide is stored.[25] Yet more subsidies for folly. No wonder the Stern report concludes: 'Public opinion needs to be won over.'[26] It does not help when prominent climate protection advocates say no new coal-fired power plants should be built 'unless they have carbon capture and storage'. Suggesting that coal can be rendered safe allows the industry and politicians to say, 'Yes, that is what we are doing; we will soon have the technology to render it safe.'

Each year around the world a hundred new large-scale coal-fired power plants are constructed, a trend that is expected to continue. In all of the reports and commentaries by political leaders this is accepted as a *fait accompli*, as if it were an unstoppable force. Given that coal plants are built to operate for 40–50 years and carbon capture and storage technology will not begin to reduce their emissions significantly for at least 20 years, climate catastrophe can be avoided only if we stop building them.

Far from being the solution to climate change, the promotion of carbon capture and storage is delaying effective responses to it. It assuages legitimate public fears that the construction of new coal-fired power plants will send carbon pollution into the atmosphere for decades to come. The promise of CCS is locking the world onto the coal track just at the time we should be getting off it. Greenpeace sums up the situation perfectly:[27]

> The urgency of the climate crisis means solutions must be ready for large-scale deployment in the short-term. CCS simply cannot deliver on time. The technology is highly speculative, risky and unlikely to be technically feasible in the next twenty years. Letting CCS be used as a smokescreen for building new coal-fired power stations is unacceptable and irresponsible.

Yet the most damning assessment of the prospects for carbon capture and storage is provided by the world's most hard-headed and respected business magazine, the *Economist*:[28]

> The world's leaders are counting on a fix for climate change that is at best uncertain and at worst unworkable ... CCS is not just a potential waste of money. It might also create a false sense of security about climate change, while depriving potentially cheaper methods of cutting emissions of cash and attention—all for the sake of placating the coal lobby.

If the coal industry, through its own research and development efforts, can develop and apply a technology that is safe, effective and ready for widespread adoption in a carbon-constrained world, few would have any objection to it. But the coal industry knows that by the time it could get to that point, 2025 at the earliest, other, much safer forms of energy will be available at cheaper cost. But it is unwilling to make its way in a free market. Paul Golby, chief executive of Britain's biggest provider of coal-fired electricity, E.ON, wants the government to pay for the capture and storage of carbon emitted from its planned new giant power plant at Kingsnorth.[29] 'If they fund it, we will fit it.' In a creative use of the language he describes providing a massive public subsidy to the dirtiest form of energy as a 'level playing field'.

The CCS boosters know that they cannot promise to build new coal-fired power plants with carbon-capture equipment installed so they promise instead to build plants that are 'capture ready'. Governments too are finding it easy to puff out their chests and declare they will not allow any new coal-fired power plants unless carbon-capture equipment can be bolted on in the future.[30] If 'capture-ready' sounds too much like 'rapture ready' perhaps the end result is not dissimilar. If the world goes ahead and builds a new generation of coal-fired power plants that are no more than capture ready, then we should all start preparing for the end of days.

Wind, sun, atom

The fact that the great hope of carbon capture and storage cannot solve the climate crisis does not mean there is no solution. We have the technological means to drastically reduce emissions, beginning immediately and at reasonable cost. Such a strategy would rely on large investments in energy efficiency, renewable energy and, in the medium term, natural gas (which has half the emissions of coal and saves even more if used in a way that captures waste heat). This is not the place to present a detailed justification of this assessment; others have done so.[31] However, a few comments are warranted.

The situation is extremely urgent. The most important period is the next 10–15 years, both because global emissions must peak soon and because, if industrialised countries were to commit to genuine emission cuts of 40 per cent by 2020, an enormous surge of inventiveness would create solutions that are currently undreamed of or are languishing in their infancy. This surge in creativity would provide the know-how to take the world to the next phases of emission reduction—cheap and effective energy technologies that can reduce global emissions by 80 per cent or more by 2050. One of the ironies of the global warming policy debate is that environmentalists have much more faith in the ability of the market to deliver what is needed than the bureaucrats, politicians, newspaper editors and business advisers who are locked into the view that the transition is too daunting to attempt.

A frequent taunt from coal's defenders is that the supply of electricity from wind and sun is intermittent, so renewables cannot provide for 'baseload' power. When Google put forward a plan, built partly on an aggressive expansion of renewable energy, to phase out coal use in the United States by 2030, the CEO of American Electric Power declared it impossible and sneered: 'If you can make the wind blow 24/7 that would be good. Maybe Google's got a plan for that.'[32]

In a modern electricity system generation never falls below

a minimum level of around 40 per cent of maximum demand.[33] This minimum constitutes what is termed baseload demand. However, to leap from this undoubted fact to the assertion that renewables cannot provide baseload power depends on a series of misconceptions and falsehoods. First, coal-fired generators are not continuous. Each is subject to unexpected stoppages. The electricity supply is maintained by having a large number of generators available and by maintaining at all times a reserve margin of unused generating capacity that can be brought into operation at short notice to cover the shortfall in supply.

All forms of electricity supply are unreliable. There's not much difference between an unexpected shutdown of a large coal-fired generator, a sudden fall in wind speed at a wind farm and a cloudy day over a solar thermal facility. In fact, the shutdown of a large coal-fired generator is a much larger problem than a dormant wind farm, which generates less power. In countries with a large land mass, wind and solar generating facilities can be spread over large areas with diverse weather patterns ensuring more continuous supply.[34] The use of tidal power can diversify further. Modelling has shown that when the share of wind in total electricity supply exceeds about 15 per cent reliability may decline, although grid operators have learned to better manage intermittent supply. Denmark already draws 21 per cent of its electricity from wind and three northern German states exceed 30 per cent from wind, so most other countries could increase their shares of wind-power dramatically.[35] It is estimated that offshore wind farms could provide a quarter of Britain's electricity needs.[36] An electricity system with a diversified supply of renewable energy could be more reliable than one dependent on a few very large coal or nuclear plants.[37]

At present some nations rely on gas-powered turbines, which can be turned up or down quickly, to respond to peak demand. They can also be used to fill gaps due to a decline in renewable supply. So intermittent supply can be overcome at relatively low cost, either by the installation of a limited amount of gas turbine generating capacity or by greater use of pumped storage. Pumped storage, in which water is pumped uphill when there is surplus power from other generators on the grid, can increase the amount of electricity on demand. 'Storage hydro' is the most responsive of all forms of electricity generation—large generators can be brought from stationary to full power in just a few minutes, allowing the generators to be run when the electricity is most needed.

The baseload power myth is also used to attack solar electricity which, of course, can only be generated during daylight hours. Solar thermal electricity produces steam to drive a turbine and generator. But the heat can be stored in fluids and used at night to generate power. A vast solar thermal array is planned for the Sahara desert and may eventually generate a sixth of Europe's energy supply.[38] California's electric utilities are required by 2020 to source 33 per cent of their power from renewable energy, with solar energy expected to be the main source.[39] In addition, solar thermal and solar electric power can easily be combined with natural gas-fuelled boilers which produce steam during the night. Solar power can also be stored in batteries. There are very good prospects for the commercialisation within a few years of several energy-storage technologies that could make this possible, including the vanadium redox and zinc-bromine batteries. Improved battery technology provides a far more promising and much less dangerous answer to carbon abatement than building an enormous new industrial infrastructure to capture and store carbon dioxide.

For other types of renewable generation, the supposed inability to supply baseload energy is simply untrue. Biomass, such as wastes from forestry and sugar cane, can be stockpiled to cover fluctuations in demand. Electricity from hot rock geothermal sources, which is likely to be commercially developed well before carbon capture and storage, will be readily available at all times. In summary, an electricity system that uses a mix of renewable and low-emission (gas-based) fossil fuel generation technologies, with some energy storage and a geographical dispersion of wind and solar generation, will have just as much ability to supply reliable baseload power as the current coal-based generation system.

However, the rapid and widespread deployment of existing low-emission energy sources cannot keep up if demand continues its rapid growth. Their deployment must be supplemented, or rather built on, the aggressive promotion of energy efficiency in homes, offices, factories and transport systems. According to a report commissioned by the European Renewable Energy Council and Greenpeace International, instead of doubling by 2050, growth in global energy demand can be limited to less than 30 per cent through the deployment of energy-efficiency measures.[40] These savings can be increased by changes in consumption patterns. The biggest gains can be had from people in rich countries travelling less or differently, eating less meat (especially lamb and beef) and buying fewer electrical appliances.[41] If these sorts of savings cannot be achieved then the task of meeting burgeoning energy demand with low and zero-emissions sources becomes impossible.

The debate over the role of nuclear power in the solution to global warming is messy and fraught, so I want to make only a few brief comments. I have no in-principle opposition to nuclear power and the more one appreciates the extraordinary threat posed by climate disruption the more one is willing to accept alternatives to coal-fired power stations even if they have serious environmental problems of their own. If the only choice were between a new wave of nuclear power plants and a new wave of coal-fired power plants, in my judgment nuclear power wins hands down. This is simply because, for all of its faults and dangers (waste storage, nuclear proliferation and nuclear terrorism), it is an established technology whose dangers can be contained, if not resolved. Compared to the threat of runaway global warming, the potential damage to the environment and human health from nuclear accidents is small.

So in my view the question comes down to the costs and timing of nuclear power compared to the alternatives. In these respects nuclear suffers from some of the drawbacks of carbon capture and storage. In countries that already have experience with nuclear power, including well-established regulatory and waste-disposal regimes, it takes at least a decade for a new nuclear power plant to be planned, approved, built and commissioned. Construction time alone now averages six years.[42] The International Energy Agency envisages a four-fold increase in the amount of electricity generated by nuclear power by 2050. This would require the construction of 32 nuclear power plants every year until then, a huge expenditure that would reduce carbon dioxide emissions from the energy sector by only 6 per cent. Wind farms could generate the same amount of power for 60 per cent of the construction cost without the continuing expense of supplying fuel and disposing of waste, and with greater emissions savings.[43] As Amory Lovins and Imran Sheikh observe: 'The more urgent it is to protect the climate, the more vital it is to spend each dollar in ways that will displace the most carbon soonest.'[44] Investing in energy efficiency and various forms of renewable energy, including storage technology, have the added advantage over nuclear power that they do not generate long-lived dangerous waste or provide materials that can be used for hostile purposes, although these risks might be sharply reduced with the successful development of so-called fourth-generation nuclear power.[45]

An emergency response over the decade to 2020 based on a huge effort to shift from fossil fuels to energy efficiency, renewable energy and natural gas is certainly feasible technically. It could also be achieved at reasonable economic cost. That is not to say it would be painless. Large numbers of workers would lose their jobs in the old energy industries, although more and better jobs would be created in the new industries. Those made redundant will need help, including extensive retraining programs. Even so, such a structural change inevitably causes turmoil in the lives of those most affected. It is also likely that in the decade or two that it takes to transform energy systems disruptions to the power supply may occur, something politicians scare us with when they warn of 'the lights going out'. But given the alternative of catastrophic climate disruption, is that too big a burden? It seems that it is. These costs loom so large in the political calculations that no government seems willing to do what is needed, which is to speak to their citizens as adults, explaining that we face an emergency, one that can be met only at some cost and inconvenience. Sadly, the national and international political institutions that must bring about the changes are too slow, too compromised and too dominated by old thinking to mandate the energy revolution we must have to guarantee our survival.

Climate engineering

In the history of environmental policy it has long been accepted that cutting pollution at its source is usually better than 'end-of-pipe' solutions aimed at moderating the damage after it has been done. In the case of greenhouse pollution, it is a lesson some want to abandon in the most dramatic way. The best definition of geoengineering is 'the deliberate large-scale manipulation of the planetary environment to counteract anthropogenic climate change'.[46] Methods fall into two types: carbon dioxide removal from the atmosphere, and solar radiation management aimed at reducing solar radiation coming in or reflecting more of it out.[47] Various schemes have been put forward to remove carbon from the atmosphere. Fertilising the oceans with iron filings is thought to promote the growth of tiny marine plants called phytoplankton, which absorb carbon dioxide as they grow and, on death, take carbon to the ocean depths. Trials have been unpromising, and it is feared the technique would create 'dead zones' in the ocean. Another scheme aimed at hastening the removal of carbon dioxide from the atmosphere is to install in the ocean a vast number of floating funnels that would draw nutrient-rich cold water from the deep to encourage algal blooms that suck carbon dioxide from the air and then take more carbon back down. This idea has met with little enthusiasm.[48] A third idea is to build thousands of devices, called sodium trees, that would extract carbon dioxide directly from the air and turn it into sodium bicarbonate from which carbon dioxide could be separated, using a method the inventors are keeping secret, before being safely disposed.[49] This too remains speculative, and it is hard to see how it would be cheaper to extract carbon dioxide from the air, where its concentration is 0.04 per cent, than from the exhaust of a coal-fired power plant.

Rather than removing surplus carbon dioxide from the atmosphere, most geoengineering schemes are aimed at cooling the planet by increasing the Earth's albedo, that is, the extent to which it reflects incoming solar radiation. Some of the ideas would be far-fetched even in a science fiction novel, such as the proposal to send ten trillion 60-centimetre reflective discs, in lots of one million every minute for thirty years, to a point in space known as L1, which is 1.5 million kilometres from Earth towards the Sun.[50] Another idea is to launch specially designed, unmanned ships to plough the oceans, sending up plumes of water vapour that increase cloud cover. Up to 1500 dedicated vessels would be needed, but they would do nothing for ocean acidification. Others have suggested converting dark-coloured forests into light-coloured grasslands. Or we could mandate the whitening of city rooftops and roads, a requirement already for some houses in California, although the creation of shining cities could offset warming only a little.[51]

The option that is taken most seriously is altogether grander in its conception and scale. The scheme proposes nothing less than the transformation of the chemical composition of the Earth's atmosphere so that humans can regulate the temperature of the planet as desired. It involves injecting sulphur dioxide gas into the stratosphere, 10–50 kilometres above the Earth's surface, to create sulphate aerosols, particles that reflect solar radiation. Currently the atmosphere reflects about 23 per cent of solar radiation back into space, and it's estimated that the injection of enough sulphate aerosols to reflect an additional 2 per cent would offset the warming effect of a doubling of atmospheric carbon dioxide.[52]

In the stratosphere sulphate particles remain in place for one or two years, unlike aerosols in the lower atmosphere that may last only a week.[53] The effect would be similar to a volcanic eruption, with analysts often pointing to the 1991 explosion of Mount Pinatubo, the sulphur and silicate ash from which cooled the Earth by around half a degree in the first year and by somewhat less for the next couple of years.[54] Another analogy is the brown haze, due largely to the burning of fossil fuels, that envelops the lower stratosphere and is concentrated over South Asia and China. By cutting the amount of incoming solar radiation, the haze keeps the Earth cooler than it would otherwise be, a process of 'global dimming' that masks the effect of global warming.[55] Air pollution laws in affluent countries have reduced smog and allowed more solar radiation to reach the Earth's surface.[56] The gains are being eroded by pollution from the expansion of global aviation. It is estimated that when all aircraft were grounded for three days after the 9/11 attack on the United States, daytime temperatures in that country rose as the skies cleared.[57]

Attempting to regulate the Earth's climate by enhanced dimming is fraught with dangers. We saw in the first chapter that the absorption of carbon dioxide by the oceans is an essential component of the carbon cycle. The oceans absorb around a third of the extra carbon dioxide in the atmosphere arising mainly from the burning of fossil fuels. The acidity of the oceans is slowly rising, dissolving corals and inhibiting shell formation by marine organisms.[58] Injecting sulphur dioxide into the stratosphere (along with other schemes aimed at enhancing the Earth's albedo) would do nothing to slow the acidification of the oceans. In other words, responding to warming by reducing the amount of solar radiation reaching the Earth's surface disregards the complexity of climate change; it is not just about the atmosphere but the entire carbon cycle that governs life on Earth.

In *Fixing Climate*, Robert Kunzig and Wallace Broecker tell the story of the eminent geoscientist Harrison Brown, who in 1954 wrote a book in which he proposed solving world hunger by increasing the carbon dioxide content of the atmosphere to stimulate plant growth.[59] Brown suggested the construction of 'huge carbon-dioxide generators pouring gas into the atmosphere', and calculated that doubling the amount in the atmosphere would require the burning of at least 500 billion tonnes of coal. Brown's book was endorsed by Albert Einstein. His wish has come true: we have huge carbon dioxide generators pouring gas into the atmosphere. They are called coal-fired power stations. Curiously, it was one of Brown's students, Charles David Keeling, who a decade later, from his measuring station on Mauna Loa in Hawaii, first alerted the world to the rising concentration of carbon dioxide in the atmosphere and its implications for the warming of the world.

Harrison Brown wanted to pump carbon dioxide into the atmosphere to improve the lot of humankind. Today there is incipient pressure to pump sulphur dioxide into the atmosphere to control the effects of pumping too much carbon dioxide into it. (There was an old woman who swallowed a fly ...) Although our understanding of the effects of climate engineering is rudimentary to say the least, one effect of it may indeed be to increase hunger. A study published in 2008 in the *Journal of Geophysical Research* used a comprehensive atmosphere–ocean circulation model to simulate the effects of the proposed injection of sulphur dioxide into the stratosphere. The authors found that it would disrupt the Asian and African summer monsoons, reducing the food supply for billions of people.[60]

Although ideas for climate engineering have been around for at least twenty years, until recently public discussion has been discouraged in the scientific community. Environmentalists and governments have been reluctant to talk about it too. The reason is simple: apart from its unknown side effects, geoengineering could become a substitute for reducing emissions. Economically it is an extremely attractive substitute because its cost would be 'trivial' compared to those of cutting carbon pollution—cheap enough for a single country easily to offset the emissions of the whole world.[61]

Most scientists at the forefront of climate research fear that broaching the subject will weaken resolve to cut emissions. Governments fear being accused of wanting to escape their responsibilities by pursuing science fiction solutions. The topic is not mentioned in the Stern report and receives only one page in the Garnaut report. As a sign of continuing political sensitivity, when in April 2009 it was reported that President Obama's new science adviser John Holdren had said that geoengineering is being vigorously discussed in the White House as an emergency option, he immediately felt the need to issue a 'clarification' claiming that he was expressing only his personal views.[62] Holdren is one of the sharpest minds in the business and would not be entertaining 'Plan B', engineering the planet to head off catastrophic warming, unless he was fairly sure Plan A would fail.

Nevertheless, so anxious are scientists at the escalation of emissions and the tardiness of the response that some now feel emergency measures must be considered. The dam broke with a 2006 editorial by the eminent German atmospheric chemist Paul Crutzen. Crutzen, who won the 1995 Nobel Prize for Chemistry for his work on the hole in the ozone layer, wrote that cutting emissions is 'by far the preferred way' to respond to warming, but in the absence of resolute action it is now time to explore 'the usefulness of artificially enhancing earth's albedo and thereby cooling climate by adding sunlight reflecting aerosol in the stratosphere'.[63] He stressed that plans to alter the chemical composition of the atmosphere should be seen as an escape route if global warming gets out of control. The very best outcome would be for measures to be taken to obviate the need to enhance the Earth's albedo, although this 'looks like a pious wish'. Crutzen is one of the growing number of scientists arguing that we need to consider Plan B. The foremost scientific institutions now agree, with the US National Academy of Sciences organising a conference and the Royal Society issuing a report in September 2009.[64]

As we will see, not all influential advocates of climate engineering adopt a cautious approach; some are gung-ho. When the potentially severe side effects of geoengineering are pointed out the more cavalier climate engineers say they can be managed with other techniques, such as spreading lime in the oceans to counter acidification. (She swallowed a spider ...) They might concede that liming the seas would not be feasible as a generalised response, but it could still be deployed to protect highly valued zones.[65] One idea is to offset acidification by installing a network of undersea pipes that inject alkalis around sites such as the Great Barrier Reef.[66] If, in order to avoid phasing out coal, turning the planet into a museum of natural artifacts while the rest goes to ruin sounds demented then you are clearly neither a scientist channelling Robert Boyle's dream of the 'empire of man' over nature, nor a neoclassical economist confident that we can pick out ecosystems valuable enough to save, nor a coal company executive who has relinquished his soul.

In classical Athens hubris was a crime. In a memorable instance, after Achilles killed Hector he tied the body to a chariot and dragged it around. Humiliation of a corpse, although unique for its brutality, reflected the same hubris that Agamemnon displayed when he desecrated a divine tapestry by walking on it. In modern times, parallels can be seen in the willingness of US soldiers at Iraq's Abu Ghraib prison to take photographs of their captives in humiliating poses.[67] In Ancient Greece Hubris was paired with Nemesis, the god of divine retribution, whose 'blade of vengeance … yields a ripe harvest of repentant wo'[68] on those who imagined themselves to be beyond the reach of the gods or put themselves above the laws of men. Today, we expect hubris to be accompanied by foolishness, a wilful disregard for the consequences of our actions. Messing with Gaia will perhaps provide the material for the legends of the twenty-second century.

We moderns believe implicitly that technology can solve any problem because we understand the world mechanically and because growth based on technological advance has been the easy way to resolve social conflict. Changing technologies always seems easier than changing people or challenging power. In 1959 the philosopher Karl Jaspers wrote in response to the threat to human existence posed by the atom bomb: 'We want to find salvation in a technological conquest of technology—as if the human use of technology might itself be subject to technological direction.'[69]

I have written before of the wealthy Texans who enjoy sitting in front of a log fire.[70] As it is hot in Texas, this can only be done comfortably by turning on the air-conditioner. Geoengineering is akin to those Texans responding to overheating by turning up the air-conditioning while continuing to pile more logs onto the fire. For millions of years the temperature of the Earth and the amount of carbon dioxide in the atmosphere have more or less moved together, creating ice ages and warm epochs. The relationship is governed by primary factors (known as forcings)—notably peaks of solar radiation, volcanic events, methane release and, now, human release of fossil carbon—and secondary feedbacks—especially ice melt changing the Earth's albedo and carbon dioxide release from the land and oceans.[71] Recent research indicates that the interaction is moderated by life forms that benefit from keeping the temperature in a habitable state.[72] Recourse to climate engineering to counter human-induced warming is an unconscious attempt by one species to decouple the great process that links the composition of the atmosphere to the temperature of the Earth and the biotic systems of the land and oceans. Instead of decoupling growth of the economy from growth of carbon emissions, the climate engineers want to decouple global warming from growth of carbon emissions.

The implications are sobering. In August 1883 the painter Edvard Munch witnessed an unusual blood-red sunset over Oslo. He was shaken by it, writing that he 'felt a great, unending scream piercing through nature'. The incident inspired him to create his most famous work, *The Scream*.[73] The sunset he saw that evening followed the eruption of Krakatoa off the coast of Java. The explosion, one of the most violent in recorded history, sent a massive plume of ash into the stratosphere, causing the Earth to cool by more than one degree and disrupting weather patterns for several years. More vivid sunsets would be one of the consequences of using sulphate aerosols to engineer the climate; but a more disturbing effect would be the permanent whitening of daytime skies.[74] A washed-out sky would become the norm. If the nations of the world resorted to climate engineering as an expedient response to global heating, and in doing so relieved pressure to cut carbon emissions, then as the concentration of carbon dioxide in the atmosphere continued to rise so would the latent warming that must be suppressed. It would then become impossible to stop sulphur injections into the stratosphere, even for a year or two, without an immediate jump in temperature. It's estimated that, if we did stop, the backup of greenhouse gases could see warming rebound at a rate 10–20 times faster than in the recent past,[75] a phenomenon referred to, apparently without irony, as the 'termination problem'.[76] Once we start manipulating the atmosphere we could be trapped, forever dependent on a program of sulphur injections into the stratosphere. In that case, human beings may never see a blue sky again.

Geopolitics

The international community has found it difficult to agree on strong collective measures to reduce emissions. Country circumstances are diverse and impacts uncertain. Against this climate engineering is cheap, immediately effective and, most importantly, can be undertaken by a single nation. Among the feasible contenders for unilateral intervention, David Victor names China, the United States, the European Union, Russia, India, Japan and Australia.[77] This is where the politics of geoengineering become disquieting. The situation might be compared to one in which seven people live together in a centrally heated house, each with their own thermostat and each with a different ideal temperature. China will be severely affected by warming, but Russia might prefer the globe to be a couple of degrees warmer. If there is no international agreement an impatient nation suffering the effects of climate disruption may decide to act alone. It is not out of the question that in three decades the climate of the Earth could be determined by a handful of Communist Party officials in Beijing. Or the government of an Australia crippled by permanent drought, collapsing agriculture and ferocious bushfires could risk the wrath of the world by embarking on a climate-control project.

Two of the earliest and most aggressive advocates of planetary engineering were Edward Teller and Lowell Wood. Teller was the co-founder and director of the Lawrence Livermore National Laboratory in San Francisco, said to have a 'near-mythological status as the dark heart of weapons research'.[78] He is often described as the 'father of the hydrogen bomb' and was the inspiration for Dr Strangelove, the wheelchair-bound mad scientist prone to Nazi salutes in Stanley Kubrick's 1964 film of that name.[79] In 1979 Teller blamed Jane Fonda for a heart attack, writing in a full-page advertisement he took out in the *New York Times* that it was brought on by his frenetic efforts to counter anti-nuclear propaganda after the Three Mile Island accident.

Lowell Wood was recruited by Teller to the Lawrence Livermore National Laboratory and became his protégé. For decades Wood was one of the Pentagon's foremost 'weaponeers', leading him to be christened 'Dr Evil' by critics. He led the group tasked with developing the technology for Ronald Reagan's ill-fated Star Wars missile shield, which included plans for an array of orbiting X-ray lasers powered by nuclear reactors. Since 1998 Wood and Teller have been promoting aerosol spraying into the stratosphere as a simple and cheap counter to global warming. A fleet of 747s could do the job. Or, they suggest, the Earth's surface could be linked to the stratosphere by a 15-mile Kevlar tube not much wider than a garden hose and held in place by a high-altitude blimp.[80] Sulphur pollution would be made on the ground and pumped to the top of the pipe.

Teller and Wood epitomise the school of physicists represented by the trio we met in Chapter 4 who established the George C. Marshall Institute to resist the peace and environment movements. Like fellow members of the scientific elite that provided the brainpower for the military–industrial complex in the post-war decades, Teller and Wood believe it is man's duty to exert supremacy over nature. Indeed, Wood is listed as an expert with the Marshall Institute whose first campaign was to promote the Star Wars initiative, for which Teller and Wood were perhaps the most fervent scientific advocates. Wood is better known as a visiting fellow at the right-wing Hoover Institution, a centre of climate scepticism partly funded by ExxonMobil and host to Thomas Gale Moore, the author of *Climate of Fear: Why We Shouldn't Worry About Global Warming*.[81] Edward Teller, who died in 2003, was also affiliated with the Hoover Institution. In addition to sharing personnel, in 2003 the Marshall Institute and Hoover Institution jointly released a book titled *Politicizing Science: The Alchemy of Policymaking* that contained laments on the suppression of 'sound science' from well-known climate sceptics Patrick Michaels and Fred Singer.[82]

Geoengineering is being promoted enthusiastically by a number of right-wing think tanks that are active in climate denialism. In addition to the Marshall Institute and the Hoover Institution, the Competitive Enterprise Institute, the American Enterprise Institute and the Heartland Institute support geoengineering. This is strange. Why would activists who deny warming is occurring and oppose all measures to reduce emissions support the development of a technology aimed at countering global warming? Of course, geoengineering protects their supporters and financiers in the fossil industries because it can be a substitute for abatement and a justification for delay,[83] but I think a deeper explanation lies in their beliefs about the relationship of humans to the natural world. Pursuing abatement is an admission that industrial society has harmed nature while engineering the Earth's climate would be confirmation of our mastery over it, final proof that, whatever minor errors made on the way, human ingenuity and faith in our own abilities will always triumph. Geoengineering promises to turn failure into triumph.

In its 2009 report, the Royal Society argues that there is insufficient evidence to say whether geoengineering would represent a 'moral hazard', that is, undermine efforts to reduce emissions.[84] This goes to the question of whether it is seen or would be seen as a substitute for mitigation or a complement to it. Wood and Teller, and the right-wing think tanks that promote climate manipulation, are unequivocal. Not only should it be pursued instead of reducing emissions, but geoengineering plus rising carbon dioxide concentrations would in fact be a superior outcome compared to a situation in which there was no global warming to worry about.[85] In a reprise of Harrison Brown's belief they argue that food production would be stimulated by 'air fertilization', except that Brown can be forgiven because the enhanced greenhouse effect was not understood in the 1950s. Fossil fuel corporations are currently unwilling to support geoengineering in public for fear of being accused of shirking their responsibilities, but once the approach becomes part of the mainstream debate and gains political traction we can expect to see the commitment to cut greenhouse gas emissions diluted. The promise of geoengineering is the perfect excuse for decades of delay. If, as the Stern report says, climate change is the biggest market failure we have ever faced, geoengineering is the most serious moral hazard we have ever faced.

Lowell Wood believes that climate engineering is inevitable; it's just a matter of time before the 'political elites' wake up to its cheapness and effectiveness. In a statement that could serve as Earth's epitaph, he declared: 'We've engineered every other environment we live in—why not the planet?'[86] Wood wrote a paper with Teller arguing that the costs of sulphur injections to offset warming would amount to only 1 per cent of the cost of reducing emissions. And, if needed, the technique could be reversed to prevent a new ice age.[87] The paper presents global warming as a problem of pure physics, divorced from the biosphere and with no recognition of the complexities of the carbon cycle or feedback effects. The term 'manifest destiny' was originally used to justify the nineteenth-century conquest of the American west; in the twentieth century it came to be interpreted by conservatives as the civilising mission of the United States around the world. Wood wonders why we must stop at Earth. Why not 'terraform' other planets? 'It is the manifest destiny of the human race!' he told a meeting of the Mars Society. 'In this country we are the builders of new worlds. In this country we took a raw wilderness and turned it into the shining city on the hill of our world.'[88]

Wood is contemptuous of the ability of world leaders to reduce emissions—which he dubs 'the bureaucratic suppression of CO_2'[89]—and of their ability to reach a consensus on trialling geoengineering. In Jeff Goodell's words, Wood predicts popular resistance to the idea of 'toying with the integrity of the Earth's climate just so Americans don't have to give up their SUVs'.[90] So Wood speculates about getting private funding from a billionaire for an experiment. 'As far as I can determine, there is no law that prohibits doing something like this.'[91] Wood is right: there is no law against a private individual attempting to tinker with the Earth's climate. That is, unless they are doing so with hostile intent. For a long time military leaders have dreamed of turning the weather into a weapon. The Cold War saw extensive efforts to control the weather for both aggressive and peaceful purposes. It met with little success, although the US military claims it used weather-modification techniques to impede the flow of soldiers and matériel along the Ho Chi Minh Trail during the Vietnam War.

In 1976 the nations of the world outlawed military manipulation of the weather by adopting the Convention on the Prohibition of Military or Any Other Hostile Use of Environmental Modification Techniques (ENMOD), which has been ratified by the major powers, including China. But the convention does not cover unilateral climate engineering for the 'peaceful' purpose of protecting us from climate chaos. The history of international treaties shows that it is far easier to reach agreement when the stakes are lower. It is unlikely the 1959 Antarctic Treaty—which declares 'in the interests of all mankind that Antarctica shall continue forever to be used exclusively for peaceful purposes and shall not become the scene or object of international discord'—would have been possible with today's commercial pressures. The Moon Treaty, an international accord governing human use of the moon, was developed to assign jurisdiction over the moon to the world community, thereby preventing annexation and limiting development. However, it was defeated after vigorous lobbying by US groups determined to keep open the option of private ownership and commercial exploitation. This suggests that the world community should urgently pursue an agreement that would prevent the unilateral deployment of all geoengineering techniques, perhaps by expanding the terms of ENMOD.

For Teller and Wood the answer to the nuclear arms race was not a negotiated scaling down of the threat but the development of superior technology in order to prevail, to find the 'killer app'. They and their climate sceptic colleagues in conservative think tanks want to respond to climate peril with a grand technological intervention, nothing less than seizing control of the climate system of the globe. It is breathtaking in its audacity and astonishing in its arrogance. The attitude of these planetary engineers is so out of sync with contemporary climate science and so at odds with modern attitudes to the natural world that they appear as throwbacks from another era, perhaps the one captured by Arthur Conan Doyle in his fictional character Professor George Edward Challenger—a mad and pugnacious scientist blessed with a supreme faith in his own intellectual capabilities. In a short story first published in 1928 Conan Doyle has Professor Challenger seized by a Lovelockian insight—that 'the world upon which we live is itself a living organism, endowed ... with a circulation, a respiration, and a nervous system of its own'.[92] Deducing that this sentient Earth must be oblivious to the presence of Lilliputian creatures crawling over its outer rind, the professor resolves to 'let the earth know that there is at least one person, George Edward Challenger, who calls for attention—who, indeed, insists upon attention'. So in the Sussex countryside he orders a shaft dug through the crust eight miles deep. When the pit reaches the soft, heaving body of the giant organism he orders a sharp, hundred-foot drill to be suspended just above it. When all is ready, including the assembly up above of a bevy of dignitaries and a throng of curious members of the public, the iron dart is 'shot into the nerve ganglion of old Mother Earth'. The effect? 'It was a howl in which pain, anger, menace, and the outraged majesty of Nature all blended into one hideous shriek.' The Earth trembled and the great pit closed over like a wound being healed. As the tumult settled and the multitude gathered their wits, all eyes turned to Challenger as 'the mighty achievement, the huge sweep of the conception, the genius and wonder of the execution, broke upon their minds'. The triumphant professor bowed to their acclaim. 'Challenger the super scientist, Challenger the arch pioneer, Challenger the first man whom Mother Earth had been compelled to recognize.'

Chapter 7

The four-degree world

So what can we expect, and when are we likely to feel the impacts of a changing climate? Of course, the effects are already manifesting the world over. Droughts in Africa and Australia, shifting seasons in England, heatwaves in France, hurricanes in the Caribbean and sinking Pacific atolls have all been linked to global warming. But for most people in affluent countries climate change remains an abstraction, something that is reported by the media and argued over by politicians but seems remote from daily life. And so it is likely to remain for some time. Yet if the analysis set out in the first chapter is right our lives are going to be radically transformed. Although precise predictions are impossible, some recent books have provided graphic descriptions of what a warming world will look like over this century. In his acclaimed book *Six Degrees*, Mark Lynas provides a comprehensive and compelling synthesis of the best estimates of climate scientists around the world of the impacts of a world under successive degrees of warming. An equally forceful but shorter account is provided by David Spratt and Philip Sutton in the first part of their book *Climate Code Red*. In *Climate Wars*, the esteemed geopolitical analyst Gwynne Dyer constructs a series of future scenarios in which warming-induced droughts, floods, cyclones, epidemics, famine and massive population movements spark political and military conflicts. In one, melting Himalayan glaciers in Indian territory see the rivers dry up in Pakistan, resulting in widespread crop failure. Tensions over access to water escalate into nuclear war. Based on detailed interviews with strategic analysts and military planners around the world, the plausibility of Dyer's book makes it the most frightening I have ever read.

Quite apart from the uncertainties, it is not feasible here to provide a detailed description of what we can expect, but a flavour of the future can be provided another way—an account of what the leading climate scientists are saying to each other. For three days in late September 2009 some 100 or so climate scientists met in Oxford to discuss the end of the world as we know it. Alarmed at the acceleration of global greenhouse gas emissions and the glacial pace of national and international action, the organisers of the meeting—titled '4 degrees and beyond: Implications of a global change of 4+ degrees for people, ecosystems and the earth-system'—put the choice starkly in their conference rationale: 'either instigate an immediate and radical reversal in existing emission trends or accept global temperature rises well beyond 4°C'.[1] So dilatory has been the response to the scientific warnings, they believe, that the only choice we now have is between 'extreme' rates of emissions reduction and 'extreme' impacts of a hot world. It seemed to me that there would be no better way of forming a picture of the world we now face than by hearing the latest thoughts of some of the world's foremost scientists. So I went along.

Opening the conference, Mark New of the University of Oxford told the participants that when the idea for the conference was first mooted some twelve or eighteen months earlier the objective was to explore the 'end of the probability distribution that people don't like thinking about'. But by the time the conference came around, scientific knowledge had developed to the point where the likelihood of the world warming by four or more degrees had moved from the edge to the middle of the probability distribution. Based on all of the evidence, an extreme scenario had become the most likely one. Initially, he said, the organisers were worried that by holding a conference on four-plus degrees they would be accused of being alarmist, and wondered whether the media should be barred. Instead they decided to include a session entitled 'Four degrees of climate change: alarmist or realist?'

When that session came around, Mark Lynas asked those present whether they believed talking of a four-degree world was alarmist or realistic. The answer was unambiguous: in a show of hands everyone indicated they believed four degrees is realistic rather than alarmist. Summing up the view of leading climate scientists, Lynas described the official target of two degrees above the pre-industrial average as optimistic verging on unattainable. Now, expecting three to four degrees is regarded as realistic, five to six degrees pessimistic, and seven to eight degrees alarmist. One of the obstacles we must confront is that most people, including policy-makers, think of three degrees as a bit worse than two degrees and four degrees as a bit worse than three degrees. This thinking reflects a 'false linearity', said Lynas, because the difference is enormous. A planet four degrees warmer would be hotter than at any time since the Miocene era some 25 million years ago.[2] The world was virtually ice-free then. So we are staring into the abyss, said Lynas, the more so when we remember that a global average warming of four degrees means an average of five to six degrees across land surfaces, and even hotter, seven to eight degrees, in the more northerly latitudes. As Kevin Anderson, the highly respected director of the Tyndall Centre for Climate Change Research, later put it: 'The future looks impossible.'

As the conference progressed and became more relaxed, the participants began admitting their deeper feelings about the research being reported. In both formal sessions and the breaks they talked of being on an emotional roller-coaster, of despairing and of having trouble sleeping. The chairs introduced sessions with the hope that one of the speakers would give some good news, but it was hard to find.

How hot and how soon?

In his keynote address, Professor Hans Schellnhuber, the director of the Potsdam Institute for Climate Impact Research and a man regarded with some awe by those present, reminded us that at its meeting in L'Aquila in July 2009, the Group of Eight wealthy nations finally agreed to adopt the two-degree target. Two or three years ago this would have been regarded as a breakthrough, but by mid-2009 it was clear to the climate science community that aiming for two degrees would not meet the aim of the Framework Convention of avoiding 'dangerous climate change'. When the world warms by two degrees, Schellnhuber observed, we will lose all coral reefs. 'But who needs coral reefs?' he added, the first instance of the grim humour that seems to go naturally with reflection on climate science. He showed us a diagram mapping the historical relationship between global temperature and sea levels. A planet 2.5 degrees warmer means most of the ice eventually melts, leaving the oceans 50 metres higher than they are today. Already the Arctic is melting, as are the Himalayan glaciers (sometimes referred to as the 'third pole') that feed the rivers of South Asia. Without the summer run-off a billion people will be without water. The 'really big giant', he noted, is the methane trapped in the permafrost in Siberia and northern Canada, estimated to be equivalent to twice the total amount of carbon dioxide in the atmosphere. 'If this is ever released we will be toast,' Schellnhuber said in his soft German accent.

Kevin Anderson later developed the theme. Until recently it was heresy to question the two-degree target; it is, after all, official European Union policy. But two degrees of warming 'will kill a lot of poor people', he said, although we in the northern hemisphere think we can get away with it. The international community is fixated on setting emissions-reduction targets like 80 per cent by 2050, but the scientific understanding has now shifted. (I confess to a pang of sympathy for the policy-makers, for the political process inevitably moves more slowly than the science in a rapidly evolving area like climate change.) Just getting emissions down at some point is not enough; it is cumulative emissions that matter. Total carbon dioxide added by humans to the atmosphere over the next decades will determine our fate. This is the so-called budget approach that had emerged over the previous year or two. It was adopted by Oxford physicist Myles Allen and colleagues in their analysis showing that total anthropogenic emissions must not exceed a trillion tonnes of carbon if warming is to be limited to two degrees. The first half of that trillion has already been emitted and at current rates of emissions the entire budget will be spent sometime between 2030 and 2050.

The budget approach rewrites the chronology of mitigation

efforts, said Anderson, because it rules out delay; a tonne of carbon dioxide emitted now counts as much as one emitted in 2050, so setting a target for emissions levels in 2050 is folly if it allows governments to postpone emission cuts. A number of speakers referred to the striking paper by Susan Solomon and others (which, along with the paper by Allen et al., I referenced in Chapter 1) showing that, unlike other greenhouse gases, most carbon dioxide stays in the atmosphere for a thousand years and more so that any warming will be with us for many centuries. Overshooting strategies such as that advocated in the Stern review are based on bad science because they are physically impossible, unless methods are found to extract large amounts of carbon from the atmosphere cheaply, permanently and quickly. Yet, such is its allure that overshooting seems to have embedded itself into political negotiations, with consequences that will prove disastrous.

The presentations from Schellnhuber, Anderson and Allen impressed on us that there are two numbers on which the future of humanity rests—the year in which global emissions peak and the rate of reduction of emissions thereafter. The curves that can be drawn to reflect different combinations of these two numbers describe what Schellnhuber called 'vicious integrals', because the areas underneath them are the carbon budgets we have to gamble with. The later the peak occurs, the faster emissions must fall for the world to remain within its emissions budget. So the peak year matters enormously; to have any chance of limiting warming to two degrees global emissions must peak in 2015, with rich countries starting to cut their emissions right now and pushing them to 25–40 per cent below 1990 levels by 2020. It is the imminence of 2015—and the need by then to transform the way we generate and use energy—that inspired a May 2009 meeting of Nobel laureates to urge the world to recognise 'the fierce urgency of now'.[3]

Anderson outlined the task with devastating simplicity. If developing-country emissions peak in 2030 and decline at 3 per cent per year thereafter (where 3 per cent is probably the maximum rate of fall consistent with continued economic growth), and developed-country emissions peak in 2015 and decline by 3 per cent a year thereafter, then the world has a 50:50 chance of limiting warming to four degrees. Read that again: four degrees. In his view, we will limit warming to four degrees 'if we're lucky'. As may have been apparent in Chapter 1, in my view Kevin Anderson is the scariest man on the planet. Yet we must be grateful for his unblinking honesty and compassion.

The pace of climate change thus depends on the trajectory of global emissions over the next couple of decades. The biggest influences will be the rate of growth of the world economy, driven disproportionately by growth rates in China, India and Brazil, and the extent of efforts by governments in the major economies to restrain emissions.

Climate scientists are not political analysts but the more savvy ones know enough about the world to understand that peaking in 2015, with rich countries cutting emissions by 25–40 per cent in 2020, is impossible. A 2020 peak in global emissions seems out of the question too. Without some unforeseeable stroke of luck, a warming of four degrees and more appears very likely. The best estimate is that we will reach that level in the 2070s or 2080s, although if things go badly it could be as soon as the 2060s. In other words, children alive today can expect to be living in a world on average four degrees warmer. Because the oceans warm more slowly, this means five to six degrees hotter on land.

It all comes down to the politics. Schellnhuber told us that he has several times had the opportunity to 'speak the unspeakable' to German Chancellor Angela Merkel—she was a physicist and seems to grasp what is at stake—but he believes it will be another decade before our political leaders collectively understand and are willing to act. So we will definitely go beyond two degrees and perhaps as high as five degrees, he said, confessing his deepest worry that the politicians may then say 'Well, let's just let it [the climate] go and adapt to it'. The only response, he argued, is to 'bombard politicians with scientific information every day'.

Some impacts

Global averages conceal an enormous variability in climate impacts across the regions of the world. As Schellnhuber said: 'If you have your head in the oven and your feet in the freezer, your average temperature may be unchanged but you are still pretty uncomfortable.' The larger part of the conference was given over to reports of what a four-degree world will be like to live in, with most emphasis on sea-level rise, water availability and changes to forests. The Paleoclimate record shows that small temperature changes are associated with large sea-level rises. As we saw, although the impact takes a long time to work its way through, a world 2–2.5 degrees warmer is a world with seas 25 metres higher. Pier Vellinga of Wageningen University in the Netherlands—a nation with more than its fair share of experts on sea-level rise—reminded us that during the last interglacial or warm period 122,000 years ago sea levels were ten metres higher than today. But then it was only 1.5–2 degrees warmer. Alarmingly, the rate of sea-level rise in that period was at times 2.5 centimetres a year, or 2.5 metres a century, so that quantum of sea-level rise is proven possible by the end of the twenty-first century.

The seas are rising due both to thermal expansion of the oceans and the melting of ice. (Interestingly, the world's oceans are three centimetres lower than they would otherwise be because humans have stored a lot of water behind dams over the last 50 years or so.) The record indicates that once the ice begins to melt it cannot be stopped; it becomes 'temperature independent', as Vellinga put it. 'I hesitate to say this,' he admitted, 'but it is a very important implication for today from what has happened in the past.' His assessment is that beyond two degrees the probability of the Greenland icesheet disintegrating is 50 per cent or more, which would mean an additional rise of seven metres in sea levels over the next 300–1000 years. Above two or three degrees the West Antarctic icesheet is also likely to disintegrate, adding another five metres to sea levels on top of this. Due to gravitational effects, sea-level rise is expected to be less than the average in the southern hemisphere and more than the average in the northern hemisphere. Although slowly rising seas are themselves a threat to low-lying areas, they are much more likely to be affected by big storm surges on top of higher seas.

Stefan Rahmstorf, professor of ocean physics at Potsdam University, noted that the best recent estimate is that by the end of the century sea levels will be 75–190 centimetres above 1990 levels (with the minimum level four times higher than the 18–59 centimetres projected in the 2007 Fourth Assessment Report of the IPCC), although under a four-degree scenario it is more likely to be in the range 98–130 centimetres. Of course, that would only be the level through which the seas pass on their way to something much higher because, even if we stabilise the temperature at some level, the seas will continue to rise for hundreds of years. Even cutting emissions to zero would not stop it.

Surprisingly, only 7–10 per cent of the global population lives within ten metres of the coast—that is, ten metres vertically—although the percentage is much higher in South and East Asia. Robert Nicholls of the University of Southampton estimates that this includes 136 port cities with populations of a million or more. (Rahmstorf observed that many nuclear power plants are located on coasts because they use sea water for cooling.) Nicholls gave the only up-beat talk of the conference, an optimistic account of how humans could adapt to rising seas if, by the end of the century, 'the whole world is like the Netherlands'. 'Is it mad,' he asked, 'to think we can put dikes around the world's coasts?' Some might think so. He believes it would be expensive but 'manageable'. Of course, most coastal wetlands would be lost, and countless living species along with them.

The ability of nations to defend against rising seas depends on their resources. Vellinga told us that the annual cost of coastal protection on the Netherlands is around 0.2 per cent of GDP. It's estimated that a one-metre rise in sea levels would double the cost as a percentage of GDP, although I could not help thinking that it is hard to imagine these figures have any relevance for Bangladesh. Naturally enough, thinking about how to respond to sea-level rise is most advanced in Holland, where there is now talk of establishing towns on top of raised dikes and of building floating cities, including floating greenhouses for food cultivation, a comment that stimulated discomforting memories of the post-apocalyptic film *Waterworld*. Another option being mooted, said Vellinga, is to raise the height of the entire country by taking vast quantities of sand from the North Sea, a suggestion greeted with some incredulity. Stefan Rahmstorf reminded participants that dikes will not save low-lying small island states from inundation. It is hard to imagine the citizens of the Pacific Island Tuvalu living on an atoll surrounded by a two- or three-metre high concrete wall.

Ultimately, with enough foresight and resources, we can defend against or retreat from rising seas. The availability of fresh water will be a more intractable determinant of survival in a four-degree world. It's expected that, overall, a warmer world will be more humid, with rainfall increasing by perhaps 25 per cent. But Professor Nigel Arnell from the University of Reading reminded us that changes in precipitation will be highly variable by region. Higher rainfall will be concentrated in northerly latitudes, with large parts of the world nearer the tropics suffering a severe decline. On the maps, areas shaded darker yellow (including Australia, southern Europe, western and central-southern United States) indicate precipitation declines of 10–30 per cent in a four-degree world. The red areas start to look like no-go zones with rainfall declines of 40–50 per cent expected in North Africa, southern Africa and great swathes of territory across the north of Latin America, including the Amazon. Run-off will decline by more than precipitation because of higher rates of evaporation before the water reaches streams and rivers. Arnell estimates that in a four-degree world around 1 billion people (a sixth of the current global population) will be exposed to increased water-resource stress. Cruelly, half of those already prone to flood will face an increased flood hazard.

The models indicate that 15 per cent of land currently suitable for cultivation will become unsuitable, while in cold regions the area suitable for cultivation increases by 20 per cent. This is reassuring perhaps for Siberia and Canada but disastrous for eastern and southern Africa, where land suitable for cultivation declines by around a third. As Schellnhuber drily observed: 'Two hundred million people will not move smoothly between a dry Sahel and a wet Siberia.' The relentless logic of the models proves over and over that the poor and vulnerable will be hardest hit by climate change, even though they are not responsible for causing it and are in the weakest position to defend themselves against it. Phillip Thornton, an agriculture expert from Nairobi, describes the prognosis for food supply in sub-Saharan Africa as 'appalling' because rain-fed agriculture in many areas would cease to be viable by the end of the century. Although the effects are way beyond the capacity for adaptation, we must nevertheless do all we can, including expanding investment in technology and strengthening institutions.

In one of the conference breaks, a scientist from Siberia told me that most people from where she comes from are looking forward to global warming. Arnell produced a chart showing estimated changes in heating and cooling requirements. In a four-degree world heating requirements in cold regions will decline by around 50 per cent; but in warm and hot areas the demand for cooling will double. When we remember that nearly 15,000 people, mainly elderly, died as a result of the August 2003 heatwave in France, cooling no longer seems to be a luxury.

Oxford University professor Yadvinder Malhi is an expert in tropical forests. In a fascinating talk he told us that organisms that have evolved in tropical regions are much less tolerant of temperature changes than those from temperate regions where temperatures show much larger daily and seasonal variation. High latitude species have a much greater thermal tolerance. Yet to accommodate a one-degree increase in temperature, tropical organisms have to travel three times as far horizontally as temperate ones. In the tropics this means moving 380 kilometres further from the equator. Currently, trees in the Andes are migrating at 25–35 metres a decade. Instead of moving horizontally, they can find cooler climates by migrating vertically. Moving a mere 180 metres up a mountain to accommodate a one-degree temperature rise is equivalent to a 380-kilometre trek across land. The problem is that mountains that begin as refugia become traps as warming continues and vertically migrating species discover that mountains have peaks.

Malhi posed the problem of global warming in an arresting way. Referring to the intricate patterns of interdependence of all living things and the systems in which they live, he explained that we are 'reweaving the web of life'. The way organisms respond to climate change will depend on the plasticity of their physiological thresholds (lower for tropical species), their capacity for rapid evolutionary adaptation, changes in behaviour and the opportunities for migration. Organisms have always been forced to adapt to changing climates or die, as they did when ice ages ended in the past. What is uniquely worrying now is that the rate of climatic change is too fast for many species to adapt to the new conditions.

The prospect of more fires in the Amazon is the object of great scientific concern. An average warming of four degrees across the globe would translate into five or six degrees in Amazonia. Deforested areas exposed to the sun become much hotter—an additional five degrees, making those areas a scorching ten degrees hotter. The figures powerfully reinforce the importance of ending deforestation. But it is not only tropical forests that will be affected by warming. Professor David Karoly of the University of Melbourne described the effects of the freakish fires that swept across parts of Victoria in February 2009, the conditions for which were created by a prolonged drought and an extreme heatwave. On 7 February Melbourne recorded its highest-ever maximum of 46.4°C (115.5°F). Brush-tailed possums fell dead from the trees. Flying foxes, unable to cool their bodies, dropped from the sky. Australia's traditional fire danger warning scale, posted on large signs around the country, indicated risks ranging from 'low' to 'extreme'. The 2009 wildfires were off the scale, forcing the development of a new one. Now, above the old 'extreme' are two new categories, the top one being 'catastrophic' or 'code red'. The advice of fire authorities is that the only sensible response to a fire in those conditions is to run for your life. If this sort of devastating fire can occur when the Earth is only 0.8 degrees warmer than it was a century ago, observed Karoly, imagine what is possible when it is four degrees hotter. 'We are unleashing hell on Earth,' he said.

Britain is not expected to become hot and dry like Australia in a four-degree world, although it will undoubtedly be warmer and water shortages are expected in the south and east of England. Although forest fires in Britain are virtually unknown today, forest researcher Andy Moffat believes that planning should begin for their possibility. He suggested that changing conditions might increase interest in planting eucalypts in England, which would be seen by some as 'a crime'. Of course, eucalypts are notorious for their propensity for a hot burn.

Adapting to the unknown

By this stage of the conference, many participants seemed to feel that the emotional roller-coaster had many more downs than ups.

One, a woman in her early thirties, told the conference that she was feeling smug: 'I don't have any children and many of my friends don't want to have children.' I leave the reader to think through the implications of this declaration. One participant, who is a parent, reported that his thirteen-year-old daughter had said we just have to accept the reality of climate change and deal with it, a mature understanding that most adults are a long way from grasping.

One way or another, humans will have to adapt to life in a hotter world. Many plausible scenarios suggest a sharp decline in the number of people that will survive in the long term. Some suggest a billion or a few hundred million will remain in a century or two, but one guess is as good as the next. One thing is certain: the transition to some new stage of stability will be long and brutal, especially for the poorest and most vulnerable whose survival will be threatened by food shortages, extreme weather events and disease. Yet in a world that is now densely interlinked, everyone will be affected profoundly. More autonomous financial systems ought not to be too difficult, but untangling trade networks and returning to a more autarkic world seems from here to be almost inconceivable. Yet shortages and more expensive transport might impose it on us.

For many, only by moving will they survive. It is sometimes said that people will migrate before they die, but in truth people frequently die in large numbers before they have the impetus or means to move. Nevertheless, the volume of migrants heading north into Europe and the United States—not to mention southern Europeans looking to resettle in more hospitable northern climes—could easily overwhelm the capacity of those states to regulate and accommodate it. François Gemenne, a

French expert on migration patterns, told the conference that most migration due to environmental factors has in the past been internal rather than across borders. And it will not be easy to separate climate migrants from those moving for other reasons; or rather, climate impacts are likely to aggravate existing problems, which makes it difficult to estimate numbers. While most migration today is voluntary, climate extremes are likely to make more and more of it forced. Gemenne pointed out that migration flows do not always match the peak of an environmental crisis because relocating permanently requires resources that, in times of drought, for example, need to be devoted to immediate survival. The poorest and most vulnerable often lack the means to migrate, so migrants are more likely to be those who are better off. Gemenne believes that governments will need to encourage and facilitate the migration of the most vulnerable. One severe typhoon now could kill everyone on Tuvalu, yet the residents are understandably reluctant to move. In rich countries, too, people are often reluctant to move after surviving a severe flood, a hurricane or an intense bushfire, even when experts warn that catastrophic events will become more frequent.

Some low-lying islands are expected to disappear under rising seas by the end of the century. The membership of the Commonwealth of Nations (formerly the British Commonwealth) seems likely to shrink from 54 to 50 or 51.[4] Gemenne suggests that this will demand innovation in international law, so that people can remain citizens of nations that no longer exist. Tuvaluans living in New Zealand, Australia and Fiji may hold passports from a 'virtual state' under the Pacific Ocean. (Perhaps we could call them the 'New Atlanteans'.) Can such a ghost nation remain a member of the United Nations and protect the interests of its citizens?

Humans are generally conservative creatures, finding it easier to hope for the best than prepare for the worst. We are at a stage where few accept that climate impacts will become severe. Most believe they can adapt to some known shift in climatic conditions, and that climate risk is just one risk to be balanced against others. But runaway climate change renders such an attitude untenable. As environmental consultant Lisa Horrocks argued at the conference, we will need to abandon the traditional idea of adaptation and shift to a strategy of continuous transformation, one that accounts for the biggest impacts, plans for the long term and takes a system-wide approach. The language now used—'risk management', 'adapting', 'building resilience', 'no regrets', 'win–win'—reflects the belief that to accommodate a warmer world we need only tinker at the edges of the system. This is now a dangerous delusion because adapting to a limited amount of climate change may prove maladaptive for a world at four degrees and beyond. If we change our housing, infrastructure, farming systems and forest management to accommodate a two-degree world we may be in a weaker position to adapt to a four-degree world. Resources spent building dikes to defend against a one metre rise in sea levels will be wasted if seas rise above that level.

It almost goes without saying that the capacity of individuals to adapt is limited, the more so if social order breaks down. Societies must collectively transform themselves if we are to manage and alleviate the impacts of a world at four degrees and beyond. Although the Oxford conference was dominated by biophysical scientists, there were mentions of 'social tipping points'. To date the term has been mainly applied by marketers and popular social commentators to the questions of how social trends begin and how public opinion is changed. As societies struggle to cope with a world under four degrees of warming we can expect much deeper social stresses, something I take up in the next chapter.

At the conference, French sociologist Bertrand Guillaume gave some hints at possible futures. He noted that high awareness of the dangers of global warming does not necessarily translate into action to stop it, that catastrophe can be 'both inevitable and impossible'. This reminded me of the third evolutionary 'f' in response to danger—fight, flight or freeze. Nevertheless, said Guillaume, avoiding catastrophe demands radical measures including drastic wartime-style rationing of emissions-intensive commodities like meat, milk and petrol. The question is whether such measures would be met with voluntary compliance, as often occurs in wartime as societies unite to resist a common threat. If not, and a large proportion of citizens refuse to comply, then slashing emissions may require a 'benevolent tyranny'.

Guillaume posed the question that has begun to haunt others: Can we continue to gamble with democracy? Yet, I have often thought, those who suggest that in the face of an existential crisis the democratic system is too cumbersome to respond do not explain the process by which a society could make the transition from democracy to some form of emergency government. Who would seize the reins of power? An enlightened intelligentsia? A vanguard of concerned citizens? The intelligence services, perhaps in alliance with progressive business interests? What would be the source of their power? How would the military forces, charged with protecting the elected government, respond? How would the new administration gain legitimacy or exercise authority? And, of course, the problem with tyrannies is that, whatever their initial purpose, they are rarely benevolent. The answer is not to abandon democracy but to radicalise it.

Reflecting on the three days, conference organiser Diana Liverman, director of Oxford University's Environmental Change Institute, told of some acquaintances who, on hearing of the conference, said that it sounded like more of the same old thing. 'They couldn't see that we are saying something new,' she said despairingly. If being blasé is a device used by members of the public to ignore the truth, scientists too crave ways of escaping. Professor Liverman said that she sometimes just wants to 'immerse myself in academic work' in order to distance herself from its implications. But she knows that climate scientists have an obligation to tell the world about their research, to make sure the politicians have no excuse to pretend things will turn out differently. She urged those present to make their voices heard in the lead-up to the Copenhagen conference and at the meeting itself. Alas, three months later in the Danish capital those in command of the facts were drowned out by industry lobbyists and ignored by timorous politicians.

Chapter 8

Reconstructing a future

Despair

A few decades hence perhaps historians will characterise the last three centuries as the era of struggle between political philosophies, each of which promised a utopian vision of the future. Certainly in the century and a half to 1989 world history was in large measure the story of the contest between the opposing forces of capitalism and socialism, with fascism interceding for two decades in the twentieth century. In the twenty-first century, climate disruption will increasingly push all utopian visions and ideological disputes into the background. Abandoning the pursuit of utopias, including the last great utopian vision of endless growth, our task will be to avoid a dystopia. The triumph of liberal capitalism, which was hailed prematurely as the 'end of history', coincided precisely with the dawning realisation that industrial progress has been transforming the physical environment in a way that threatens the demise of the world that liberal capitalism promised to create. Distracted by the triumphalism of the 'end of history' there crept up on us the end of progress, so that now we are staring at a century and more of regress, an unwinding of the revolution that began three centuries ago with the liberation of the forces of science, technology and economic expansion. We can now see that, like a teenage boy who suddenly acquires the strength of a man, humans proved insufficiently mature to be entrusted with the powers they unleashed.

Awakening to the prospect of climate disruption compels us to abandon most of the comfortable beliefs that have sustained our sense of the world as a stable and civilising place. We are now led to question our faith in human advancement—the constant we have used to connect the past with the future—and the psychological stability it has provided. We will have to accommodate the fact that, due to our own actions, Nature has turned against us and can no longer be relied upon to provide the conditions for the flourishing of life. The foundational beliefs of modernity—the unlimited scope of human achievement, our capacity to control the world around us, our belief in the power of knowledge to solve whatever discomforts us—will collapse. Science and technology—which we moderns take to be the grandest testimony of human superiority, our claim to some form of divinity—will be turned from a celebration of our improving powers into our only means of saving ourselves and staving off the ravages unleashed by our hubris. If the great forces of Nature on our home planet turn against us, who will not feel abandoned and alone in the cosmos?

Relinquishing our rosy view of how the future will unfold is a task more difficult than it may appear because the vision of a stable and sympathetic future undergirds our sense of self and our place in the world. On a small scale we see this in daily life. We have all constructed in our minds future worlds based on an expectation of securing a new job, building a new business or making the perfect marriage. Over weeks and months we assemble a picture of a new future in our minds and the new life becomes incorporated into our conception of self. When the expected event does not occur we can feel crushed. Even though our lives are unchanged, our dreams have been shattered. The loss is no less real psychologically than if it had actually occurred, so that the process of bringing our newly constructed self back into conformity with an unchanged reality can be traumatic. Subtly, our hopes for our lives and those of our children and grandchildren all depend on an expectation that the world will unfold in a certain way, as an enhanced version of the world we have now. If the evidence is that the future will in fact be a diminished version of what we have now—that life will be harsher and more unpredictable as the patterns of weather that govern the rhythms of daily life can no longer be relied upon—then our conception of the future and the hopes that are built on it are illusory. When we recognise that our dreams of the future are built on sand the natural human response is to despair.

In the face of the evidence of climate disruption, clinging to hopefulness becomes a means of forestalling the truth. Sooner or later we must respond and that means allowing ourselves to enter a phase of desolation and hopelessness, in short, to grieve.[1] Climate disruption will require that we change not only how we live but how we conceive of our selves; to recognise and confront a gap between our inner lives—including our habits and suppositions about how the world will evolve—and the sharply divergent reality that climate science now presents to us. The process of bringing our inner experience into conformity with the new external reality will for many be a long and painful emotional journey. What are the likely elements of this mourning for a lost future?

Rather than passing through well-defined stages, grief is characterised by strong episodic feelings and a persistent sense of background disturbance.[2] When a loved one is diagnosed with a terminal illness, many people embark on a process of anticipatory mourning; for those who confront the facts and emotional meaning of climate change, the 'death' that is mourned is the loss of the future. The first phase of grief is often marked by shock and disbelief, followed by a mixture of emotions: anger, anxiety, longing, depression and emptiness.[3] To regulate the flood of unpleasant emotions, humans deploy a number of strategies to suppress or buffer them. Among them John Archer includes numbness, pretence that the loss has not occurred, aggression directed at those seen as responsible for the loss, and self-blame, which are similar to the methods we use to deny or filter climate science. This suggests that the widespread prevalence of forms of denial and avoidance among the population may indeed be defences against the feelings of despair that the climate science rationally entails. The study of grief suggests that accepting a loss is more difficult when there is room for doubt about the death or when someone can be blamed for it,[4] both of which apply to the loss of the future under climate change.

While attention is usually focused on the emotional expressions of grief, the process is as much a cognitive one as we first learn to cope with the severe disruption to our conception of the world, and then begin to build a new conception of the world that we can live by. It is sometimes feared that those who grieve too early will experience premature detachment—or 'decathexis', as the professionals call it. In a famous example from the 1940s, an English bride whose husband went off to war was convinced he would be killed. She grieved so deeply that when he returned alive she divorced him.[5] Those who say we should not despair but always remain hopeful in the face of climate science are perhaps afraid we will detach ourselves from the future completely, and then sink into apathy or go on a binge. It seems to be a recipe for a kind of nihilism, like that glamourised in the Sex Pistol's song lamenting 'no future'.

It is true that, in the words of one expert, healthy grieving requires a gradual 'withdrawal of emotional investment in the hopes, dreams, and expectations of the future' on which our life has been constructed.[6] Yet after facing up to the truth and detaching from the future few of us will just call a halt and remain trapped in a slough of despond or refuse to think beyond today. Humans are not built that way. After detaching from the old future we will construct and attach to a new future, just as we eventually do when a loved one dies. Yet we cannot build a new conception of the future until we allow the old one to die, and Joanna Macy reminds us that we need to have the courage to allow ourselves to descend into hopelessness, resisting the temptation to rush too soon into a new future.[7] She quotes T.S. Eliot:

> I said to my soul, be still, and wait without hope,
> For hope would be hope of the wrong thing.

Waiting, I will suggest, does not mean we should be passive. The nature of the mourning process will vary with the individual, depending in part on the strength of their attachment, conscious or unconscious, to the future. Some people live largely for today and give little thought to tomorrow. Others have a deep sense of attachment to the healthy evolution of their societies, the natural world or civilisation. Those with an interdependent or metapersonal self-construal are more likely to feel distressed by the threat posed by climate disruption to the future welfare of other people or the natural world. In some cultures, people feel a much stronger attachment to their ancestors and descendants. How we mourn will be influenced by how our society and those around us are responding to the loss. At present, the early mourners feel lonely and isolated, sometimes keeping their thoughts to themselves for fear of alienating those around them with their anxieties and pessimism. It is as if the doctors had declared there is no hope of recovery for a sick child, yet all around friends and family are saying, 'Don't worry, she will be fine'.

Against this, I expect to see a new genre of humour, not as a way of ridiculing but of accommodating the facts. Here is the first one I have come across:[8]

> I, for one, welcome the coming apocalypse. We can have a world where all a man needs to make his way is some stubble, a mullet and a sawn off shotgun, and women are beautiful, deadly and clad in leather. One can live by your wits and your nerve, fending off hordes of mutants, cannibals and assorted beasts.
>
> Much like Basingstoke on a Saturday night, in fact.

In addition to a rash of gallows humour and post-apocalyptic novels, at some point we can expect to see a period of nostalgia for the future lost, including a 'life review' that may take the form of an outpouring of books and public discussion reflecting on the era that is passing, an era that will glow more golden in retrospect.

Acceptance

The trauma arising from recognising the gap between our self-concept and the disrupted future we now face can be thought of as an instance of 'positive disintegration', the term used by psychiatrist Kazimierz Dabrowski to capture the idea of our world 'falling apart' when the situation makes untenable the assumptions we have used to construct an integral sense of self.[9] The inner struggle to adapt ourselves to changed circumstances requires that we go through a painful process of disintegration involving strong emotions, including excitability, anger, anxiety, guilt, depression, hopelessness and despair. But the ability to navigate them and reconstruct our selves is a sign of mental health. Accelerated psychic development requires a difficult transition in which the individual becomes an active agent in his or her own disintegration, a process in which we assess and reintegrate the broken pieces of ourselves into a new and more robust whole.[10] It is an adaptive coping strategy.

Climate disruption has the smell of death about it. It threatens to bring to the surface that which we work so hard to suppress. Fear of death, wrote Ernest Becker, 'is the mainspring of human activity—activity designed largely to avoid the fatality of death, to overcome it by denying in some way that it is the final destination for man'.[11] The desire for immortality is perhaps the best answer to the riddle of why the affluent are driven to accumulate more. There is evidence for this. Studies using 'terror management theory' have shown that when given fleeting reminders of their own mortality, people are more likely to seek out means of enhancing their self-esteem, especially by attaching greater importance to money, image and status.[12] They are also more likely to punish those who do not agree with their worldview.[13] Sheldon and Kasser suggest that humans may be 'hard-wired' to pursue extrinsic goals of wealth, attractiveness and position because they improve the chances of survival in times of uncertainty and threat.[14] There is, therefore, a risk that the threat posed by climate change will see a greater emphasis on the sorts of consumer values that have aggravated global warming. We seem to be trapped: materialism exacerbates climate change, and talking about climate change makes us retreat further to materialism. Does this mean we should not talk about the climate crisis? Fortunately, the answer is 'no'.

While fleeting reminders of death are shown to promote self-interested and materialistic behaviour, folklore, philosophy and religion have long taught that reflection on death 'concentrates the mind' in a way that makes possessions and social standing appear trivial and causes us to reflect on those deeper aspects of life that give our existence meaning. Those who have had near-death experiences or life-threatening illnesses are often transformed so that they see their previous lives as empty and self-centred. 'Post-traumatic growth theory' suggests that confrontation with one's mortality typically brings about a change in priorities, away from greed and vanity and towards a greater emphasis on intimate relationships, a greater sense of personal strength, more openness to change and a deeper appreciation of life.[15] Tests of the theory indicate that more sustained and considered reflection on death does indeed stimulate more intrinsic goals centred on building close relationships, personal growth and community betterment. So while fleeting reminders of death tend to induce a retreat to self-gratification, more conscious and careful processing of death brings about the opposite reaction. When the reality of death cannot be avoided, prolonged reflection causes us to transcend our defensive reactions and accept both life and death more maturely.

The expected effects of a changing climate over this century naturally stimulate thoughts of mortality—our own and that of our descendents, the vulnerable in poor countries and other species. We reflect too on the prospects for more abstract things like civilisation and progress. While it is tempting to suppress such thoughts, the evidence suggests that an open public engagement with notions of impermanence and death could have a salutary effect and contribute to a shift in value orientation that is both more mature and more protective of the environment. Reluctance to draw attention to the threats to survival implied by climate science fails to counter the tendency for people to resort to self-focused and materialistic goals. Contrary to the prevailing 'don't scare the horses' approach of governments and environmental organisations, more conscious reflection on the meaning of climate disruption is likely to encourage more pro-social and less materialistic goals.

There are many uncertainties in how climate change will play out over this century and beyond, except that each decade will be marked by greater disruption to everyday lives. For most people in poor countries there will be no redeeming features of climate disruption, just hard lives being made harder, and the daily struggle punctuated by catastrophic weather events and political eruptions that may burden them even more. For many citizens of affluent nations it is possible that accepting the future will be marked by greater hardships and tests of our capacity to adapt could be the stimulus to a new orientation to life with more attention to higher goals. Isn't that the lesson of history? Certainly, we know that levels of mental illness declined in London during the Blitz in World War II, perhaps due to the effect of group bonding at a time of peril for everyone.[16] For all of its material benefits, which few would repudiate, affluence has not been notable for its promotion of psychological health. It is now well established, by Tim Kasser and others, that those who pursue intrinsic life goals of self-acceptance, personal development and community orientation lead more fulfilling lives than those who pursue extrinsic goals of material acquisition, physical attractiveness and celebrity.[17] Just as the new values of the Protestant ethic helped usher in the era of capitalism, there is a chance that fresh values will emerge in the era of the hot Earth—values of moderation, humility and respect, even reverence, for the natural world. And in place of self-pity and instant gratification, we could see a resurgence of resourcefulness and selflessness. 'Resilient people', writes Shelley Taylor, 'tend to find some meaning and interest in whatever they are involved in; they are actively engaged and infrequently bored, apathetic or alienated. … They rarely feel like passive victims'.[18]

It is true that the shift could be in the opposite direction, a retreat to self-preservation in which the ruthless and the wealthy use their power to control dwindling resources and exclude others from sharing in them. It is to prevent this from happening that, in the last section of this chapter, I urge the mobilisation of a mass movement to build a countervailing power to the elites and corporations that have captured government. In short, a revived democracy is the only means of fighting the effects of climate change in a humane way.

Meaning

Morris Berman has observed that during periods of rapid transformation in human history, such as the Renaissance, 'the meaning of individual lives begins to surface as a disturbing problem'.[19] As the climate crisis unfolds, and poses the question of the future of humankind, the meaning of our lives will come increasingly to the fore. After a long period of psychological disruption stability will return only with the emergence of a new understanding of the Earth, a story to replace the one in which the globe is seen as a repository of resources to fuel endless growth. The new narrative will reflect a world no longer subject to human will but governed by forces largely beyond our control. In that sense, the new story will be closer to those of pre-modern cultures where daily lives and destiny were in the hands of all-powerful invisible forces. In the West little changed from Ancient Greece to Shakespearean England. Caught in a storm at sea, Pericles declaimed:

> Wind, rain and thunder, remember earthly man
> Is but a substance that must yield to you.

As much as anything else, Shakespeare's plays are about the weather—its fickle capacity to disrupt the plans of mortals, its moods as symbolic of ours, and its utility as the chief weapon of the gods.

I have suggested that we now face a profound threat not because of our beliefs or even our attitudes, but because of the very way we see and understand the world, our way of being in the world. The scientific revolution taught us to understand ourselves in a new way, to feel radically separated from the world around us, to experience ourselves as isolated egos inside our bodies which must understand and act on the 'world out there'. The alternative is simply a different way of experiencing ourselves out of which a distinctive understanding and set of values arises. It involves reconceptualising the Earth in a way that supersedes the idea that it exists to meet our needs, to accept that it is not a storehouse to be raided at will but our only home.

Of all humans, we moderns alone have lived in a radically desacralised cosmos.[20] We saw that, on the eve of the scientific revolution, Isaac Newton himself was an avid participant in an animate universe. Newton, and almost all of those who came before him, differed from us not so much because of what they believed but because of their mode of being in the world.[21] For them, in addition to its practical consequences, the disruption of the climate by human activity would have had religious meaning. Climate change would have meant sky trouble. For pre-modern men and women the sky was powerfully symbolic. It represented the infinite, the transcendent; it is where the gods dwell and where we aim to ascend after we have cast off our mortal form. As Mircea Eliade writes: '… a religious sense of the divine transcendence is aroused by the very existence of the sky'.[22] With climate change mortal humans have violated the domain of the gods, disturbed the home of the transcendent. Why wouldn't the deities retaliate, the more so as we have aroused the heavens by digging into and releasing the energy of the underworld?

I am not sure this is such a primitive understanding of the meaning of climate change, for the signs that the sky retains its divine symbolism are everywhere: it is where the prayerful look; where the eyes of the goal-scorer turn; its moods impose themselves on ours; and it still feels eerie to fly in it. And nothing can better evoke a sense of cosmic mystery than the night sky. It is one thing, therefore, to foul our own realm on the surface of the Earth but quite another to violate the celestial vault, the realm of the gods.

Eliade has noticed that in early cultures, after the act of creation the Supreme Being withdraws. As men and women become increasingly occupied with their own discoveries, the divine becomes more remote and other religious forces come into play—fertility, sexuality, money and personal creativity. These are more practical mythologies. Today in the West, meaning is found above all in the commitment to progress, technology and consumption. We have not lost our religious sensibility, for secularisation can be understood as 'the disembedding of faith from an encompassing religious culture'.[23] But the god of gods can always stage a return. Eliade wrote:[24]

> In cases of extreme distress and especially in cases of disaster proceeding from the sky—drought, storm, epidemic—men turn to the supreme being again and entreat him ... [I]n an extremely critical situation, in which the very existence of the community is at stake, the divinities who in normal times ensure and exalt life are abandoned in favor of the supreme god.

The lesser divinities could reproduce and augment life but they could not save life in moments of crisis. Perhaps these archaic patterns remain implanted within us, structuring our deeper consciousness so that, as the climate disruption unfolds and the sky seems to turn against us, we will abandon the lesser gods of money, growth and hedonism and turn to the celestial god, the creator god who alone has the power to save us. Is not the tentative turn to Gaia just such an appeal? If our scientific understanding and technological control over the world allowed us to discard the gods, will the reassertion of Nature's power see us turn again to the sacred for protection? Will the late surge of militant atheism come to be seen as a Homeric burst of pride before the fall?

Act

Climate disruption's assault on all we believed—endless progress, a stable future, our capacity to control the natural world with science and technology—will corrode the pillars that hold up the psyche of modern humanity. It will be psychologically destabilising in a way exceeded in human history perhaps only by the shift to agriculture and the rise of industrial society. Already we find psychiatrists and psychologists issuing guidelines on how to respond to the emotional and psychological distress associated with awareness of climate change, although the leading therapeutic recommendation of 'be optimistic about the future' suggests that the mental health professionals have yet to grasp the seriousness of the threat posed by global warming.[25] We can expect that, for a time, the loss of faith in the future and in our ability to control our lives will see a proliferation of mental disturbance characterised by depression, withdrawal and fearfulness. It is well known, however, that one of the most effective responses to depression is to act. Helplessness is immiserising, and we should not capitulate to it even when things appear irredeemable. As Pablo Casals is reputed to have said: 'The situation is hopeless; we must now take the next step.' Finding meaning in adverse circumstances is one of the most remarkable human qualities.[26]

If it is too late to prevent climate disruption there is still much we can influence. Any success in reducing emissions is better than doing nothing, because warming and its effects can at least be slowed down. Resisting those who want to capitulate is a fight worth having. And we can begin preparing for the impacts of climate disruption not by self-protection but by vigorous political engagement aimed at collectively building democracies that can ensure the best defences against a more hostile climate, ones that do not abandon the poor and vulnerable to their fate while those who are able to buy their way out of the crisis do so for as long as they can. For we should remember that once the dramatic implications of the climate crisis are recognised by the powerful as a threat to themselves and their children they will, unless resisted, impose their own solutions on the rest of us, ones that will protect their interests and exacerbate unequal access to the means of survival, leaving the weak to fend for themselves. This is how it has always been. We must democratise survivability.

Climate change represents a failure of modern politics. Elected government should execute the people's will yet, in this greatest threat to our future, governments around the world have not represented the interests of the people but have allowed themselves to be held in the thrall of a powerful group of energy companies and the ideology of growth fetishism they embody. It is apparent to even the most dim-witted observer that these corporations are 'more interested in commerce than humanity', as Thoreau wrote, and are run by executives who are, to put it most charitably, misguided and self-interested. This is truer today after the remoulding of democratic political systems to give greater influence to lobbyists and insiders. The climate crisis is upon us because democracy has been corrupted; influence has replaced representation, and spin now substitutes for honest communication. The 'professionalisation' of the major political parties has turned them into finely tuned vote-getting machines. Instead of being the expressions of competing social forces and ideologies they are driven by polls, focus groups and minute demographic analysis. Political campaigns now occur largely in the mass media, a channel between the people and their leaders that is filled by an army of specialists whose task is to craft messages and cultivate editors. This is possible because the power of social movements has waned, and visionary politics has been swamped by the lure of affluence. For the most part, environment organisations too have been sucked into the political game of influence-peddling and media management, with their leaders resigned to incrementalism, a strategy now mocked by Nature's powers.

The passivity of the public has allowed our political representatives to become more and more dominated by a professional class of power-seeking individuals who stand for little other than self-advancement. Political parties have been hollowed out, with memberships shrinking and those remaining deprived of all influence. In Britain, for example, with the expectation that after years of New Labour the Conservatives will form the next government, lobbying companies are relinquishing staff close to the Labour Party and hiring Conservatives with a view to having instant access. The *Sunday Times* reports that 'more than 50 prospective candidates chosen by the main parties are already working as lobbyists and public relations executives and are deeply enmeshed in the world of spin and politics'.[27] PR veterans describe the two career paths, lobbying and politics, as 'a natural fit'. The influence of corporate lobbyists is checked only when it becomes too transparent or when the pressure to ease up on regulation jeopardises the system as a whole, such as occurred with the deregulation of finance on the United States before the crisis of 2008. Reclaiming democracy for the citizenry is the only way to temper the effects of climate disruption and ensure that the wealthy and powerful cannot protect their own interests at the expense of the rest. To do so requires a new radicalism, a radicalism that refuses to be drawn into short-term electoral trade-offs and aims to shift the ground of politics itself.

We all value and benefit from a law-abiding society. Yet at times like these we have a higher duty and are no longer bound to submit to the laws that protect those who continue to pollute the atmosphere in a way that threatens to destroy the habitability of the Earth. When just laws are used to protect unjust behaviour our obligation to uphold the laws is diminished. In the usual course of affairs, it is right to allow the normal democratic process, however slowly its wheels may turn, to change the laws to reflect the new reality. In 2008 the truth of this was acknowledged in the case of six Greenpeace protestors arrested for causing criminal damage to the Kingsnorth coal-fired power plant in Kent, to wit, scaling its smokestack and painting a slogan on it. Persuaded by the defence's argument that the protesters had a lawful excuse—for in causing damage they were trying to prevent the greater harm being done by the power plant to the climate—the jury of ordinary citizens acquitted the six.

Global warming presents us with a uniquely challenging historical predicament. In the great struggles for universal suffrage and civil liberties, and against slavery and unjust wars, victory meant the end of the problem, or at least the beginning of the end of the problem. In the case of climate change victory can come too late. A sudden awakening in a decade by governments and the people to the dangers of climate change will be too late; the global climate system will have shifted course and the future will have been taken out of our hands. In such times we have moral obligations other than obedience to the law. We feel we owe obedience to a higher law even though we have to accept the consequences of disobeying the ones in the statute books. It is for this reason that those who engage in civil disobedience are usually the most law-abiding citizens—those who have most regard for the social interest and the keenest understanding of the democratic process.

With runaway climate change now jeopardising the stable, prosperous and civilised community that our laws are designed to protect, the time has come for us to ask whether our obligations to our fellow humans and the wider natural world entitle us to break laws that protect those who continue to pollute the atmosphere in a way that threatens our survival.

Despair, Accept, Act. These are the three stages we must pass through. Despair is a natural human response to the new reality we face and to resist it is to deny the truth. Although the duration and intensity of despair will vary among us, it is unhealthy and unhelpful to stop there. Emerging from despair means accepting the situation and resuming our equanimity; but if we go no further we risk becoming mired in passivity and fatalism. Only by acting, and acting ethically, can we redeem our humanity.

Appendix: Greenhouse gases

It's worth clarifying a technical detail that leads to much confusion. Each greenhouse gas has a different potential to cause climate warming, first because of its molecular structure, which determines just how effective it is in absorbing and emitting heat at different wavelengths, and secondly because each gas has a different atmospheric residence time before being chemically changed or absorbed by the oceans or biosphere.

To measure their relative warming effects, climate scientists convert greenhouse gases other than carbon dioxide (CO_2) into a 'carbon dioxide equivalent' (CO_2-e). So, for example, in terms of its heat-trapping potential a molecule of methane (CH_4) is (over 20 years) 23 times more potent than a molecule of CO_2. Together they are measured by the number of parts per million (ppm) of carbon dioxide equivalent (CO_2-e) in the atmosphere. In the scientific literature and the policy discussion it is common for people to switch without notice between talking about CO_2 concentrations and concentrations of all greenhouse gases, measured in CO_2-e. The confusion has even found its way into official documents, yet it is vitally important.

For easy reference, the following table sets out the

Level	CO_2 concentration in the atmosphere (ppm)	Corresponding CO_2-e concentration (ppm)	Eventual warming most likely associated with this concentration (°C)
Pre-industrial	280	—	0°C
Hansen target	350	445[a]	2.0°C
Current (2009)	387	455[b]	2.2°C
EU target	380	450	2.0°C
Stern target	450	550	3.0°C
Anderson and Bows' 'optimistic' scenario	530	650	4.0°C

Source: IPCC, 'Summary for Policymakers' in *Climate Change 2007: Mitigation. Contribution of Working Group III to the Fourth Assessment Report of the Intergovernmental Panel on Climate Change*, Cambridge University Press, Cambridge, 2007, Table SPM5 and various others.

a. If annual CO_2 emissions were reduced to below zero to get to 350 ppm (i.e. net withdrawals from the atmosphere using some form of carbon sequestration) then non-CO_2 gases would in all likelihood be lower than indicated.

b. The Stern report notes it is currently (2006) at 430 ppm CO_2-e. If account is taken of aerosols and other offsetting factors the net effect of all anthropogenic forcing is estimated to be 375 ppm CO_2-e (Stern, *The Economics of Climate Change*, p. 193).

equivalence levels for CO_2 and CO_2-e along with the expected levels of warming associated with the levels most commonly discussed. (The temperatures are mean estimates and should be regarded as having considerable uncertainty.) The corresponding levels of CO_2-e can only be approximations as they depend on the emissions of non-CO_2 gases over the period taken for CO_2

to reach the indicated concentrations. If, for example, methane emissions were reduced by more than anticipated then a lower level of CO_2-e would be associated with each level of CO_2.

Notes

Preface

1 Quoted by George Marshall from Levi's *Beyond Judgement*.

2 For example, Ross Gelbspan in *Boiling Point* (Basic Books, New York, 2004) and Guy Pearse in *High & Dry* (Penguin, Camberwell, 2007).

Chapter 1 No escaping the science

1 For example, Tim Lenton et al., 'Tipping elements in the Earth's climate system', *Proceedings of the National Academy of the Sciences*, vol. 105, no. 6, 12 February 2008.

2 Jørgen Peder Steffensen et al., 'High-Resolution Greenland Ice Core Data Show Abrupt Climate Change Happens in Few Years', *Science*, vol. 321, no. 5889, 1 August 2008. Graeme Pearman notes that these abrupt changes may have been due to rapid deglaciation coming out of the last ice age, 'a process that would not be applicable to Earth which is already substantially more deglaciated' (pers. comm.).

3 James Hansen, 'Scientific reticence and sea level rise', *Environmental Research Letters*, April–June 2007.

4 Hansen, 'Scientific reticence and sea level rise', p. 5. Slightly modified.

5 Others, such as the UK Met Office's Vicki Pope, believe the recent sharp decline could be due to natural variation but that over the longer term human-induced warming will lead to the disappearance of Arctic sea-ice in the summer. Vicki Pope, 'Scientists must rein in misleading climate change claims', *Guardian*, 11 February 2009.

6 Quoted in Deborah Zabarenko, 'Arctic ice second-lowest ever; polar bears affected', *Reuters*, 27 August 2008.

7 Quoted in the *New York Sun*, 22 December 2007.

8 Andrew Weaver of the University of Victoria in British Columbia quoted by Richard Monastersky, 'A Burden Beyond Bearing', *Nature*, vol. 458, 30 April 2009, p. 1094.

9 Ross Garnaut, *The Garnaut Climate Change Review*, Cambridge University Press, Melbourne, 2008, Table 3.1, p. 56.

10 Garnaut, *The Garnaut Climate Change Review*, p. 66.

11 Garnaut, *The Garnaut Climate Change Review*, Table 3.2, p. 65. In which year, the United States is expected to account for 11 per cent (down from 18) and India 8 per cent (up from 4.6 per cent). Everything is going the wrong way in China: it has the biggest population, the fastest rate of economic growth and its energy is overwhelmingly based on fossil fuels.

12 Garnaut, *The Garnaut Climate Change Review*, p. 58.

13 National Oceanic and Atmospheric Administration, 'Trends in Atmospheric Carbon Dioxide—Mauna Loa', http://www.esrl.noaa.gov/gmd/ccgg/trends/.

14 Susan Solomon, Gian-Kasper Plattner, Reto Knutti and Pierre Friedlingstein, 'Irreversible climate change due to carbon dioxide emissions', *Proceedings of the National Academy of Sciences*, vol. 106, no. 6, 10 February 2009.

15 Richard Monastersky, 'A Burden Beyond Bearing', *Nature*, vol. 458, 30 April 2009, p. 1094.

16 Garnaut, *The Garnaut Climate Change Review*, p. 64.

17 Steve Connor and Chris Green, 'Climate scientists: it's time for plan B', *Independent*, 2 January 2009, http://www.independent.co.uk/environment/climate-change/climate-scientists-its-time-for-plan-b-1221092.html.

18 The extent to which higher concentrations of greenhouse gases in the atmosphere lead to warming is known as climate sensitivity. The best estimate is that a doubling of CO_2 concentrations from 280 to 560 will bring about warming of 3°C, with a likely range of 1.5°C to 4.5°C, although this has been challenged as much too conservative. See David Spratt and Philip Sutton, *Climate Code Red* (Scribe, Melbourne, 2008), pp. 45–8.

19 Bjorn Lomborg, *The Skeptical Environmentalist*, Cambridge University Press, Cambridge, 2001, pp. 284, 286.

20 Lomborg, *The Skeptical Environmentalist*, p. 286.

21 See also Katherine Richardson et al., *Synthesis Report*, from the Climate Change: Global Risks, Challenges & Decisions conference, University of Copenhagen, Copenhagen, 2009, Box 2.

22 Recent observed climate trends are compared to the model projections contained in the 2001 IPCC report in S. Rahmstorf, A. Cazenave, J.A. Church, J.E. Hansen, R.F. Keeling, D.E. Parker and R.J.C. Somerville, 'Recent climate observations compared to projections', *Science*, vol. 316, no. 5825, 2007.

23 IPCC, 'Summary for Policymakers', *Climate Change 2007: Mitigation. Contribution of Working Group III to the Fourth Assessment Report of the Intergovernmental Panel on Climate Change*, Cambridge University Press, Cambridge, Table SPM1, p. 8. See also V. Ramanathan and Y. Feng, 'On avoiding dangerous anthropogenic interference with the climate system: Formidable challenges ahead', *Proceedings of the National Academy of Sciences*, vol. 105, no. 38, 23 September 2008.

24 Although it in turn has a range of 2.4–6.4°C above 1990 levels, or 3.0–7.0°C above pre-industrial levels.

25 David Archer, *The Long Thaw*, Princeton University Press, Princeton, 2009, p. 1; Solomon et al., 'Irreversible climate change due to carbon dioxide emissions'.

26 Archer, *The Long Thaw*, p. 6. Anthropogenic forcing is currently at around 1.6 Watt/m^2 relative to 1750 (accounting for all gases), to

which should be added the short-term masking effect of aerosols, 1.2 Watt/m^2, and the effects of Arctic and other albedo loss, and open-water infrared radiative gain, totalling 3 Watt/m^2 or more. The natural orbital forcing associated with the end of glacial periods was around 6 Watt/m^2. So to date we have had about half the impact that led to the end of the last ice age (Andrew Glikson, pers. comm., based on James Hansen et al., 'Target Atmospheric CO_2: Where Should Humanity Aim?', *The Open Atmospheric Science Journal*, vol. 2, pp. 217–31, 2008).

27 David Adam, 'Amazon could shrink by 85% due to climate change, scientists say', *Guardian*, 11 March 2009.

28 Global Carbon Project, 'Carbon budget and trends 2007', 26 September 2008, www.globalcarbonproject.org.

29 IPCC, *Climate Change 2007: Synthesis Report, Contribution of Working Groups I, II and III to the Fourth Assessment Report of the Intergovernmental Panel on Climate Change*, Core writing team, R.K. Pachauri and A. Reisinger (eds), IPCC, Geneva, 2007, p. 67.

30 See, for example, Ramanathan and Feng, 'On avoiding dangerous anthropogenic interference with the climate system'. Graeme Pearman points out that setting a target like this is not a rigorous process because it involves estimating risks associated with a wide range of impacts across the globe. Some of the risks embodied in it are very large for some impacts in some parts of the world (pers. comm.).

31 The IPCC report shows that there is almost a 50 per cent chance of exceeding 2°C warming if the concentration stabilises at 450 ppm.

32 Richardson et al., *Synthesis Report*, p. 18.

33 Richardson et al., *Synthesis Report*, p. 18.

34 Lenton et al., 'Tipping elements in the Earth's climate system', Table 1.

35 James Hansen, 'Global Warming Twenty Years Later: Tipping Points Near', Speech to the National Press Club, Washington, 23 June 2008.

36 Richardson et al., *Synthesis Report*, p. 18.

37 J.C. Zachos, G.R. Dickens and R.E. Zeebe, 'An early Cenozoic perspective on greenhouse warming and carbon-cycle dynamics', *Nature*, vol. 451, 2008, pp. 279–83.

38 Hansen et al., 'Target Atmospheric CO_2'.

39 See, for example, Bill Hare, Michiel Schaeffer and Malte Meinshausen, 'Emission reductions by the USA in 2020 and the risk of exceeding 2°C warming', *Climate Analytics*, March 2009.

40 Hansen et al., 'Target Atmospheric CO_2'.

41 Richardson et al., *Synthesis Report*, p. 18.

42 Kevin Anderson and Alice Bows, 'Reframing the climate change challenge in light of post-2000 emission trends', *Philosophical Transactions of the Royal Society*, Royal Society, 2008.

43 All figures below are taken from the analysis by Anderson and Bows.

44 Anderson and Bows, 'Reframing the climate change challenge', p. 5.

45 Also called a gigatonne. It is organic carbon rather than CO_2 that is locked up in forests, but the analysis here expresses it in terms of the CO_2 that results from oxidising the carbon through burning or decay.

46 Anderson and Bows, 'Reframing the climate change challenge', p. 7. After rising for many years, in 1999 global methane emissions plateaued. They began to rise again in 2007, possibly due to the melting of the Siberian permafrost. See M. Rigby et al., 'Renewed growth of atmospheric methane', *Geophysical Research Letters*, vol. 35, L22805, 2008.

47 Anderson and Bows, 'Reframing the climate change challenge', pp. 8–9.

48 In 2007 the world's population was 6.6 billion and the UN's middle estimate for 2050 is 9.2 billion (United Nations, *World Population Prospects: The 2006 Revision*, UN Department of Economic and Social Affairs, New York, 2007).

49 It is, for example, the most optimistic outcome modelled by Hare et al., 'Emission reductions by the USA in 2020 and the risk of exceeding 2°C warming'.

50 United Nations, *World Population Prospects.*

51 Robert Socolow and Steve Pacala, 'Stabilisation Wedges: Solving the Climate Problem for the Next Fifty Years with Current Technology', *Science*, vol. 305, 13 August 2004.

52 Nicholas Stern, *The Economics of Climate Change: The Stern Review*, Cambridge University Press, Cambridge, 2007, Box 8.3, p. 231. Anderson and Bows also draw from it.

53 See the World Bank figures reported by the BBC (http://news.bbc.co.uk/2/shared/spl/hi/guides/457000/457038/html/default.stm).

54 Stern, *The Economics of Climate Change*, p. 232.

55 Anderson and Bows, 'Reframing the climate change challenge', Table 7, p. 14.

56 One study concluded that, to keep warming from exceeding 2°C, total anthropogenic emissions must be limited to 3.67 trillion tonnes of CO_2 (ignoring non-CO_2 forcing agents). Half of this amount has already been emitted since the start of the Industrial Revolution in the eighteenth century, leaving a budget of 1.85 trillion tonnes for the twenty-first century, or 1.46 trillion tonnes if non-CO_2 forcings are taken into account (Myles Allen et al., 'Warming caused by cumulative carbon emissions towards the trillionth tonne', *Nature*, vol. 458, 30 April 2009). Anderson and Bows' analysis shows that, if global emissions peak in 2020 and fall by 3 per cent per annum thereafter, an additional 3 trillion tonnes of CO_2-e will be added to the atmosphere—60 per cent more than allowed by the 2°C target.

57 Anderson and Bows, 'Reframing the climate change challenge', p. 13.

58 See especially, Joel B. Smith et al., 'Assessing dangerous climate change through an update of the Intergovernmental Panel on Climate Change (IPCC) "reasons for concern"', *Proceedings of the National Academy of Sciences*, Early edition, 26 February 2009.

59 Alice Bows, Kevin Anderson and Sarah Mander, 'Aviation in turbulent times', *Technology Analysis & Strategic Management*, vol. 21, no. 1, 2009, pp. 17–37.

60 J.G. Canadell et al., 'Contributions to accelerating atmospheric CO_2 growth from economic activity, carbon intensity, and efficiency of natural sinks', *Proceedings of the National Academy of Sciences*, vol. 104, 2007, pp. 18866–70; M.R. Raupach, J.G. Canadell and C. Le Quéré, 'Anthropogenic and biophysical contributions to increasing atmospheric CO_2 growth rate and airborne fraction', *Biogeosciences*, vol. 5, 2008, pp. 1601–13.

61 Stern, *The Economics of Climate Change*, p. 194.

62 I am grateful to Andrew Glikson and Graeme Pearman for discussions on these themes.

63 Other factors driving abrupt climate changes include vulcanism, asteroid and comet impacts, methane releases from sediments and the effects of radiation from supernovae. G. Keller, 'Impacts, Volcanism and Mass Extinction: Random coincidence or cause and effect?', *Australian Journal of Earth Sciences*, vol. 52, issues 4 & 5, 2005, pp. 725–57; Andrew Glikson, 'Asteroid/comet impact clusters, flood basalts and mass extinctions: Significance of isotopic age overlaps', *Earth and Planetary Science Letters*, vol. 236, 2005, pp. 933–7; Archer, *The Long Thaw*; Steffensen et al., 'High-Resolution Greenland Ice Core Data Show Abrupt Climate Change Happens in Few Years'; Hansen et al., 'Target Atmospheric CO_2'.

64 Lenton et al., 'Tipping elements in the Earth's climate system'; Ramanathan and Feng, 'On avoiding dangerous anthropogenic interference with the climate system'.

65 Solomon et al., 'Irreversible climate change due to carbon dioxide emissions', pp. 1704–9.

66 Solomon et al., 'Irreversible climate change due to carbon dioxide emissions', pp. 1708–9.

67 IPCC, *Climate Change 2007: Mitigation of climate change, Working Group III Contribution to the Fourth Assessment Report of the IPCC*,

Cambridge University Press, Cambridge, 2007, p. 173.

68 Lenton et al., 'Tipping elements in the Earth's climate system', p. 1792.

69 David King, Speech to the Decarbonising the UK conference, Church House, Westminster, 21 September 2005. King, of course, is one of the more enlightened policy advisers. He accepts that aiming even for 450 ppm is a big risk. In 2007 he was urging the world to aim at somewhere between 450 and 550 ppm (*Science*, vol. 317, no. 5842, 31 August 2007, pp. 1184–7).

70 Stern, *The Economics of Climate Change*, p. 194.

71 Todd Stern, 'Keynote Remarks at U.S. Climate Action Symposium', Senate Hart Office Building, Washington, DC, 3 March 2009.

72 J.A. Lowe, C. Huntingford, S.C.B. Raper, C.D. Jones, S.K. Liddicoat and L.K. Gohar, 'How difficult is it to recover from dangerous levels of global warming?', *Environmental Research Letters*, vol. 4, 2009. In the simulation where emissions are set to zero in 2050 as concentrations reach 550 ppm CO_2, the temperature rises by an additional 0.2°C through to 2150.

73 Ramanathan and Feng, 'On avoiding dangerous anthropogenic interference with the climate system'.

74 Hans Joachim Schellnhuber, 'Global warming: Stop worrying, start panicking?', *Proceedings of the National Academy of the Sciences*, vol. 105, no. 38, 23 September 2008, pp. 14239–40.

75 See, for example, A. Dupont and G.I. Pearman, *Heating up the Planet: Climate Change and Security*, Lowy Institute Paper 12, Lowy Institute, Sydney, 2007; and R. Schubert et al., *Climate Change as a Security Risk*, Earthscan, London, 2008.

76 See, for example, J. Overpeck, D.C. Whitlock and B. Huntley, 'Terrestrial biosphere dynamics in the climate system: Past and future', in K.D. Bradley and R.S. and T.F. Pedersen (eds), *Paleo-climate, Global Change and the Future*, Springer-Verlag, Berlin, 2003.

Chapter 2 Growth fetishism

1 Global Footprint Network, http://www.footprintnetwork.org/gfn_sub.php?content=overshoot.

2 http://dccc.org/blog/archives/the_american_way_of_life/.

3 Gary Kroll, 'Rachel Carson—Silent Spring: A Brief History of Ecology as a Subversive Subject', Online Ethics Center for Engineering, National Academy of Engineering, 6 July 2006, www.onlineethics.org.

4 *Newsweek*, editorial, 13 March 1972.

5 Quoted by Rex Weyler at http://rexweyler.com/2008/11/28/attacking-margaret-atwood-are-limits-to-growth-real/.

6 Donella Meadows, Dennis Meadows, Jørgen Randers and William Behrens, *The Limits to Growth*, Earth Island Ltd, London, 1972, p. 23.

7 Although it's worth noting that the authors' 'prediction' that CO_2 concentrations in the atmosphere would reach 380 ppm by 2000 (Meadows et al., *The Limits to Growth*, p. 73) was almost exactly right.

8 Meadows et al., *The Limits to Growth*, p. 157.

9 Meadows et al., *The Limits to Growth*, pp. 157, 184.

10 Meadows et al., *The Limits to Growth*, p. 167.

11 Bjorn Lomborg, *The Skeptical Environmentalist*, Cambridge University Press, Cambridge, 2001.

12 George W. Bush, 'President Bush Discusses Global Climate Change', White House, June 2001, http://www.whitehouse.gov/news/releases/2001/06/20010611–2.html.

13 World Commission on Environment and Development, *Our Common Future*, Oxford University Press, Oxford, 1987.

14 Quoted in David Stern, 'The Rise and Fall of the Environmental Kuznets Curve', *Rensselaer Working Papers in Economics No. 0302*, Rensselaer Polytechnic Institute, October 2003.

15 Quoted by Stern, 'The Rise and Fall of the Environmental Kuznets Curve'.

16 Lomborg, *The Skeptical Environmentalist*, p. 33. Lomborg shows a graph plotting for dozens of countries the relationship between GDP per capita and an index of environmental sustainability (Figure 9, p. 33). There is a definite upward trend, but among the 18 richest countries, all with incomes clustered around $30,000, the index ranges from 45 to 80. In other words, above that threshold there is no relationship between higher incomes and environmental quality.

17 Paul A. Murtaugh and Michael G. Schlax, 'Reproduction and the carbon legacies of individuals', *Global Environmental Change*, vol. 19, 2009, pp. 14–20.

18 Of course, since the population of China is so enormous (four times bigger than that of the United States), any policy that limits fertility will have a large global impact. Although not part of the plan, China's much-maligned one-child policy means global greenhouse gas emissions will be substantially lower in the twenty-first century, a fact for which we should be grateful.

19 Thomas Robert Malthus, *Essay on the Principle of Population*, Volume 1, 2nd Edition, Cosmo Classics, n.d., p. 55.

20 United Nations, *World Population Prospects: The 2006 Revision*, UN Department of Economic and Social Affairs, New York, 2007. Depending on fertility rates, the estimates range from a low of 7.8 billion to a high of 10.8 billion.

21 Clive Hamilton and Hal Turton, 'Determinants of emissions growth in OECD countries', *Energy Policy*, vol. 30, 2002, pp. 63–71.

22 Tim Jackson, *Prosperity without Growth: Economics for a Finite Planet*, Earthscan, London, 2009, pp80–81

23 Income, and the technology factor (T), are measured in constant year-2000 US dollars at market prices.

24 Jackson, *Prosperity Without Growth?*, p. 54. The analysis excludes non-CO_2 emissions. We saw in Chapter 1 that Anderson and Bows set the non-CO_2 floor of their analysis at 7.5 billion tonnes by 2050.

25 United Nations, *World Population Prospects.*

26 These figures are based on Nicholas Stern, *The Economics of Climate Change: The Stern Review*, Cambridge University Press, Cambridge, 2007, p. 209. Stressing China's expected influence, the Garnaut report is much more bullish, suggesting per capita GDP growth of around 2.75 per cent (Ross Garnaut, *The Garnaut Climate Change Review Final Report*, Cambridge University Press, Melbourne, 2008, Figure 3.6, p. 60).

27 Interviewed by Jeff Goodell, 'Geoengineering: The Prospect of Manipulating the Planet', *Yale Environment 360* magazine, Yale School of Forestry and Environmental Studies, January 2009.

28 See Lisa Sellin Davis, 'Malls, the Future of Housing?', *HousingWire.com*, 29 December 2008.

29 IPCC, *Climate Change 2007: Mitigation. Contribution of Working Group III to the Fourth Assessment Report of the Intergovernmental Panel on Climate Change*, edited by B. Metz, O.R. Davidson, P.R. Bosch, R. Dave and L.A. Meyer, Cambridge University Press, Cambridge, 2007. See also T. Barker et al., 'Technical Summary', in *Climate Change 2007: Mitigation.*

30 IPCC, *Climate Change 2007: Mitigation*, Table SPM 6, p. 18. To be precise, the target in question is 445 ppm and the 5.5 per cent is the upper end of the 10th and 90th percentile range of the analysed data.

31 In annual terms it means the growth rate of global GDP would be 0.12 per cent (a little over one tenth of 1 per cent) lower than otherwise.

32 Stern, *The Economics of Climate Change*, p. 208.

33 Stern, *The Economics of Climate Change*, p. 209.

34 The 2050 figure is only a crude estimate. In practice, changes in exchange rates will invalidate a simple scaling up, but attempting

more accuracy would not change the essential point being made (Stern, *The Economics of Climate Change*, Box 7.2). For the 2007 figure see World Bank, http://siteresources.worldbank.org/DATASTATISTICS/Resources/GDP.pdf.

35 United Nations, *World Population Prospects.*

36 While many have criticised the models for overstating the economic costs of abatement, occasionally they are accused of understating them. Among the latter Dieter Helm suggests that the true cost of cutting emissions may be 'several percentage points higher' than the 1 per cent argued by the Stern report ('Climate-change policy: why has so little been achieved?', *Oxford Review of Economic Policy*, vol. 24, no. 2, 2008, p. 227). That might take the costs up to 5 per cent of increased GDP, still an insignificant number in the scheme of things, as I have argued above. To suggest, as Helm does, that the reality of 'significantly higher' abatement costs is responsible for nations failing to take emissions reductions seriously overlooks the fact that, if it is true, it has been unknown to governments.

37 This is the estimated cost to GDP of stabilising at around 500–550 ppm (Stern, *The Economics of Climate Change*, p. 267).

38 'Our actions over the coming decades could create risks of major disruption to economic and social activity, on a scale similar to those associated with the great wars and the economic depression of the first half of the twentieth century' (Stern, *The Economics of Climate Change*, p. xv).

39 Stern, *The Economics of Climate Change*, p. 27.

40 Nicholas Stern, Address to the Royal Economic Society, November 2007, http://www.guardian.co.uk/environment/2007/nov/29/climatechange.carbonemissions.

41 Stern, *The Economics of Climate Change*, p. 267. After the release of the IPCC's *Fourth Assessment Report*, Stern doubled his estimate to 2 per cent.

42 Stern, *The Economics of Climate Change*, p. 276.

43 Stern, *The Economics of Climate Change*, pp. 276, 338.

44 Quoted in an interview with The Climate Group, 29 June 2004, http://www.theclimategroup.org/news_and_events/professor_sir_david_king/.
45 Garnaut, *The Garnaut Climate Change Review.*
46 Garnaut, *The Garnaut Climate Change Review*, p. 271.
47 Garnaut, *The Garnaut Climate Change Review*, p. 272.
48 Stern, *The Economics of Climate Change*, Figure 13.4, p. 330.
49 William Nordhaus, 'The *Stern Review* on the Economics of Climate Change' (unpublished paper, 3 May 2007) reprinted as Chapter 9 in William Nordhaus, *A Question of Balance: Weighing the Options on Global Warming Policies* (Yale University Press, New Haven, 2008) from which all quotes are taken.
50 Nordhaus, *A Question of Balance*, pp. 167, 174.
51 This point is made in the context of the scientific revolution by Morris Berman, *Coming to Our Senses: Body and Spirit in the Hidden History of the West*, Bantam Books, New York, 1990, pp. 112–13.
52 Julie A. Nelson, 'Economists, value judgments, and climate change: A view from feminist economics', *Ecological Economics*, vol. 65, no. 3, April 2008.
53 Nelson, 'Economists, value judgments, and climate change', p. 445.
54 Quoted by Robert Kuttner, 'The Poverty of Economics', *Atlantic Monthly*, February 1985, pp. 74–84.
55 Nordhaus, *A Question of Balance*, p. 15.
56 Right wing and insufferable: responding to the Stern report Tol said: 'If a student of mine were to hand in this report as a Masters thesis, perhaps if I were in a good mood I would give him a "D" for diligence; but more likely I would give him an "f" for fail.' Quoted by Simon Cox and Richard Vadon, 'Running the rule over Stern's numbers', BBC Radio 4, *The Investigation*, 26 January 2007.
57 Nordhaus, *A Question of Balance.*
58 All estimates are taken from Nordhaus, *A Question of Balance*,

Table 5–1, and are rounded. In fact, there is a very small cost of abatement associated with this option, for reasons that are not explained.

59 In fact, the present value of climate damage under the do-nothing policy is $22.55 trillion, while the present value of abatement costs under 'do nothing' is an unexplained $0.04 trillion.

60 See the commentary by Jeffrey Sachs in *Yale Symposium on the Stern Review*, Yale Center for the Study of Globalization, February 2007, p. 113, http://www.ycsg.yale.edu/climate/forms/FullText.pdf.

61 The costs of the Stern proposal amount to 0.8 per cent of future income, and this Nordhaus describes as 'extremely expensive' (*A Question of Balance*, p. 87).

62 Nordhaus refers to them as 'worse-than-nothing cases' (*A Question of Balance*, p. 88).

63 Nordhaus would claim that his model incorporates the possibility of catastrophic events but John Quiggin shows that, even within the economic framework, Nordhaus's treatment of catastrophic events is deficient. It uses conservative estimates of the probabilities of catastrophes, incorporates a low measure of risk aversion, excludes events with very low probability but very high losses and mis-specifies the damage function. He also observes that Nordhaus uses 'trivially low' estimates of the cost of species extinction. John Quiggin, 'Stern and his critics on discounting and climate change', *Climatic Change*, vol. 89, nos 3–4, 2008, pp. 195–205; John Quiggin, 'Counting the cost of climate change at an agricultural level', *CAB Reviews: Perspectives in Agriculture, Veterinary Science, Nutrition and Natural Resources*, vol. 2, no. 092, 2008, pp. 1–9.

64 Quoted by Ed Pilkington in 'The carbon catcher', *Guardian*, 24 May 2008.

65 W.S. Broecker, 'Unpleasant surprises in the greenhouse?', *Nature*, vol. 328, 1987, pp. 123–6.

66 Clive Hamilton, *Growth Fetish*, Allen & Unwin, Sydney, 2003 and Pluto Press, London, 2004; Richard Layard, *Happiness*, Allen Lane, London, 2005.

Chapter 3 The consumer self

1 This is spelled out in more detail in Clive Hamilton, 'Consumerism, self-creation and prospects for a new ecological consciousness', *Journal of Cleaner Production* (forthcoming, 2010).

2 See Martin Lindstrom, *Brand Sense*, Free Press, New York, 2005; Naomi Klein, *No Logo*, HarperCollins, London, 2001; Clive Hamilton, *Growth Fetish*, Allen & Unwin, Sydney, 2003 and Pluto Press, London, 2004.

3 Robert Frank, *Luxury Fever: Money and happiness in an era of excess*, Princeton University Press, New Jersey, 1999.

4 Ulrich Beck, *Democracy without Enemies*, Polity Press, Cambridge, 1998; Ulrich Beck and E. Beck-Gernsheim, *Individualization: Institutionalized Individualism and its Social and Political Consequences*, Sage, London, 2002.

5 Zygmund Bauman, *Consuming Life*, Polity Press, Cambridge, 2007; Russell Belk, 'Are We What We Own?', in April Lane Benson (ed.), *I Shop, Therefore I Am: Compulsive buying and the search for self*, Rowman & Littlefield, Maryland, 2004.

6 Helga Dittmar, 'The costs of the consumer culture and the "cage within"', *Psychological Inquiry*, vol. 18, no. 1, 2007.

7 Anon., 'Global house price boom: The greatest bubble in history', *Economist*, 19 June 2005.

8 Robert Samuelson, 'Homes As Hummers', *Washington Post*, 13 July 2005.

9 For Britain see Clive Hamilton, *Overconsumption in Britain: A culture of middle-class complaint?*, Discussion Paper No. 57, The Australia Institute, Canberra, 2003. For Australia see Clive Hamilton, *Overconsumption in Australia: The rise of the middle-class battler*, Discussion Paper No. 49, The Australia Institute, Canberra, 2002.

10 http://www.selfstorages.net/storage/guide/self-storage-industry.html.

11 http://www.allbusiness.com/construction/building-renovation/5268603–1.html.

12 For Australia see Hamilton, *Overconsumption in Australia*, and for Britain see Hamilton, *Overconsumption in Britain*.

13 Josh Fear, *Stuff happens: Unused things cluttering up our homes*, Research Paper No. 52, The Australia Institute, Canberra, 2008.

14 Marcus Walker, 'Behind Slow Growth in Europe: Citizens' Tight Grip on Wallets, A Thicket of Laws to Protect People Damps Spending', *Wall Street Journal*, 10 December 2004, p. A1.

15 Catherine Rampell, 'Shift From Spending To Saving May Be Slump's Lasting Impact', *New York Times*, 10 May 2009.

16 Although this does not include compulsory savings due to superannuation.

17 Rampell, 'Shift From Spending To Saving'.

18 http://www.ftc.gov/bcp/workshops/debtcollection/presentations/hampel.pdf; http://src.senate.gov/public/_files/graphics/Household DebtDisposF03E0D.pdf.

19 Bill Hampel (Chief Economist, Credit Union National Association), 'Overview of Household Debt Exposure', FTC Debt Collection Workshop, 10 October 2007 http://www.ftc.gov/bcp/workshops/debtcollection/presentations/hampel.pdf. Among the wealthiest 10 per cent of the population the share of income was 43 per cent while the share of debt was 32 per cent.

20 Anon., 'Will you still love your new iPhone next month?', *Business Wire*, 9 September 2008.

21 This section is based on Clive Hamilton, Richard Denniss and David Baker, *Wasteful Consumption in Australia*, Discussion Paper No. 77, The Australia Institute, Canberra, 2007. Figures are in Australian dollars. In 2009 an Australian dollar was worth approximately 80 US cents and 50 British pence.

22 James Garvey, 'Environmental morality in the present', *New Statesman* online, 10 January 2008.

23 http://www.ucsusa.org/global_warming/what_you_can_do/ten-personal-solutions-to.html.

24 Paul Kellstedt, Sammy Zahran and Arnold Vedlitz, 'Personal Efficacy, the Information Environment, and Attitudes Towards

Global Warming and Climate Change in the United States', *Risk Analysis*, vol. 28, no. 1, 2008. On the other hand, the study is vitiated by the fact that the extent to which respondents were knowledgeable about global warming was based on 'self-reported informedness' when other studies have shown that there is virtually no correlation between how informed people believe themselves to be and how informed they actually are. The 'best informed' may be the most ignorant, which is certainly the case with climate sceptics.

25 Michael Maniates, 'Individualization: Plant a Tree, Buy a Bike, Save the World?', in T. Princen, M. Maniates and K. Conca (eds), *Confronting Consumption*, MIT Press, Cambridge, 2002, p. 57.

26 http://www.alacrastore.com/storecontent/datamonitor-premium-profiles/BFEN0374.

27 Quoted by Per Gyberg and Jenny Palm, 'Influencing households' energy behaviour—how is this done and on what premises?', *Energy Policy*, vol. 37, 2009, p. 2810. The statement is on E.ON's Swedish website.

28 Maniates, 'Individualization: Plant a Tree'.

29 Mark Sagoff, *Price, Principle, and the Environment*, Cambridge University Press, Cambridge, 2004, Chapter 4.

30 Gyberg and Palm, 'Influencing households' energy behaviour'.

31 http://www.fineliving.com/fine/our_specials/episode/0,,FINE_5916_50485,00.html.

32 http://www.corpwatch.org/section.php?id=102.

33 http://www.asa.org.uk/asa/adjudications/Public/TF_ADJ_44828.htm.

34 http://www.energycurrent.com/index.php?id=3&storyid=17187.

35 See also Fred Pearce, 'Greenwash: E.ON's "integrated" technology claim is shameless spin', *Guardian*, 9 April 2009.

36 See, for example, American Coal Council, 'Coal—Environmentally Sound', www.clean-coal.info/drupal/environ.

37 David Roberts, 'The Essential "Clean Coal" Scam: Politico lets shill get away with the basic dodge at the center of the "clean coal" campaign', *Grist*, 23 December 2008.

38 David Roberts, 'The Essential "Clean Coal" Scam'.

39 Sheldon Rampton, 'The Clean Coal Bait and Switch', *PR Watch*, 27 December 2008.

40 Jad Mouawad, 'Lessons on How to Guzzle Less, from Europe and Japan', *New York Times*, 5 April 2009.

41 Anon., 'GM exec stands by calling global warming a "crock"', *Reuters*, 22 February 2008.

42 Robert Siegel, 'At Auto Show, GM Seeks To Shift Perceptions', *All Things Considered*, National Public Radio, 12 January 2009.

43 Veronica Dagher, 'Extreme Measures: So, you think you've cut your spending? Here are some ideas you probably haven't thought of', *Wall Street Journal*, 7 April 2009, p. R3.

44 Survey commissioned by the Center for a New American Dream, http://www.newdream.org/about/pdfs/PollResults.pdf.

45 John Maynard Keynes, 'Economic Possibilities for Our Grandchildren', in *Essays in Persuasion*, W.W. Norton, New York, 1963, p. 362.

46 Adriana Barbaro and Jeremy Earp (writers and directors), *Consuming Kids: The Commercialization of Childhood*, DVD produced by the Media Education Foundation, http://www.mediaed.org/assets/products/134/presskit_134.pdf.

47 Barbaro and Earp, *Consuming Kids.*

48 See C. Hamilton and R. Denniss, *Affluenza*, Allen & Unwin, Sydney, 2005, p. 53.

49 Quoted in Hamilton and Denniss, *Affluenza*, p. 53. Juliet Schor writes that in preparing her book, *Born to Buy* (Scribner, 2004), she found marketers feeling 'immense guilt and ambivalence about using their skills to target kids with inappropriate messages, questionable products, and insidious techniques'.

50 Richard Monastersky, 'A Burden Beyond Bearing', *Nature*, vol. 458, 30 April 2009, p. 1094.

51 Dabo Guan, Klaus Hubacek, Christopher Weber, Glen Peters and David Reiner, 'The drivers of Chinese CO_2 emissions from 1980 to 2030', *Global Environmental Change*, vol. 18, 2008, pp. 626–34.

52 Ross Garnaut, *The Garnaut Climate Change Review*, Cambridge University Press, Melbourne, 2008, p. 66.

53 Guan et al., 'The drivers of Chinese CO_2 emissions from 1980 to 2030'.

54 Garnaut, *The Garnaut Climate Change Review*, Table 3.2, p. 65.

55 Christopher Weber, Glen Peters, Dabo Guan and Klaus Hubacek, 'The contribution of Chinese exports to climate change', *Energy Policy*, vol. 36, 2008, pp. 3572–7.

56 Guan et al., 'The drivers of Chinese CO_2 emissions from 1980 to 2030'.

57 Guan et al., 'The drivers of Chinese CO_2 emissions from 1980 to 2030'.

58 Xin Zhao and Russell Belk, 'Politicizing Consumer Culture: Advertising's Appropriation of Political Ideology in China's Social Transition', *Journal of Consumer Research*, vol. 35, August 2008.

59 Tu Weiming, 'The Continuity of Being: Chinese Visions of Nature', in Mary Evelyn Tucker and John Berthrong (eds), *Confucianism and Ecology*, Harvard University Press, Cambridge, 1998. Weiming writes (p. 113): '… the notion of humanity as forming one body with the universe has been so widely accepted by the Chinese, in popular as well as elite culture, that it can very well be characterized as a general Chinese worldview … [H]uman life is part of the continuous flow of the blood and breath that constitutes the cosmic process. Human beings are thus organically connected with rocks, trees, and animals.'

60 The next few paragraphs draw heavily on the excellent study by Elisabeth Croll, 'Conjuring goods, identities and cultures', in Kevin Latham, Stuart Thompson and Jakob Klein (eds), *Consuming*

China: Approaches to cultural change in contemporary China, Routledge, London, 2006.

61 John Quelch, a marketing professor at Harvard Business School, quoted by Sean Silverthorne, 'China, Consumerism, and the Red Pepsi Can', *BNet*, Harvard Business School, 12 August 2008.

62 Croll, 'Conjuring goods, identities and cultures', p. 24.

63 Paul Solman, 'China's Vast Consumer Class', *Public Broadcasting Service* (US), 5 October 2005.

64 Croll, 'Conjuring goods, identities and cultures', p. 26 (slightly modified).

65 Quoted by Ariana Eunjung Cha, 'Chinese Consumers Eager to Excel at the American Pastime', *Washington Post*, 15 November 2008.

66 Solman, 'China's Vast Consumer Class'.

67 Edmund L. Andrews, 'Snow Urges Consumerism on China Trip', *New York Times*, 14 October 2005.

Chapter 4 Many forms of denial

1 Leon Festinger, *A Theory of Cognitive Dissonance*, Stanford University Press, Stanford, 1957.

2 C.S. Lewis, *God in the Dock*, William B. Eerdmans Publishing Co., Grand Rapids, 1970.

3 See Peter Jacques, Riley E. Dunlap and Mark Freeman, 'The organisation of denial: Conservative think tanks and environmental scepticism', *Environmental Politics*, vol. 17, no. 3, June 2008.

4 See Timothy W. Luke, 'A Rough Road out of Rio: The right-wing reaction in the United States against global environmentalism', Department of Political Science, Virginia Polytechnic Institute and State University, Blacksburg, nd (1998?). Luke writes: 'the split over international ecology agreements, like those propounded at the Rio Summit, express some of the most fundamental divisions now splitting the American body politic during the post-Cold War era.'

5 Quoted by Luke, 'A Rough Road out of Rio'. This opinion has been echoed more recently by Czech President and climate sceptic Vaclav Klaus: 'The largest threat to freedom, democracy, the market economy and prosperity is no longer socialism. It is, instead, the ambitious, arrogant, unscrupulous ideology of environmentalism.' Quoted by Charles Krauthammer, 'Carbon chastity', *New York Times*, 30 May 2008. Krauthammer adds his own take: 'Just as the ash heap of history beckoned, the intellectual left was handed the ultimate salvation: environmentalism. Now the experts will regulate your life not in the name of the proletariat or Fabian socialism but—even better—in the name of Earth itself.'

6 Richard Darman, President Bush's chief of the Office of Management and Budget, quoted by Luke, 'A Rough Road out of Rio'.

7 Interviewed on *Frontline*, Public Broadcasting Service (US), 3 April 2006.

8 Quoted by Jacques et al., 'The organisation of denial', pp. 362–3.

9 Myanna Lahsen, 'Experience of modernity in the greenhouse: A cultural analysis of a physicist "trio" supporting the backlash against global warming', *Global Environmental Change*, vol. 18, 2008, pp. 204–19.

10 Lahsen, 'Experience of modernity in the greenhouse', p. 211.

11 Lahsen, 'Experience of modernity in the greenhouse', p. 214.

12 Interviewed on *Frontline*, Public Broadcasting Service (US), 3 April 2006. The first part of Seitz's statement is true. A survey of members of the American Association for the Advancement of Science found that 55 per cent of scientists identified as Democrats and only six per cent as Republicans, with the balance Independents (Pew Research Center for the People & the Press, 'Public Praises Science; Scientists Fault Public, Media: Scientific Achievements Less Prominent Than a Decade Ago', 9 July 2009).

13 Lahsen, 'Experience of modernity in the greenhouse', p. 212.

14 Nicholas Dawidoff, 'The Civil Heretic', *New York Times Magazine*, 29 March 2009.

15 Simon Baron-Cohen et al., 'Autism occurs more often in families of physicists, engineers, and mathematicians', *Autism*, vol. 2, 1998, pp. 296–301.

16 Seitz wrote of 'the scientific base on which our current civilization rests' (Lahsen, 'Experience of modernity in the greenhouse', p. 214). Civilisation is built not on political rights, or a commitment to social welfare, let alone the arts, but on scientific progress of which he and his colleagues are the custodians.

17 Lahsen, 'Experience of modernity in the greenhouse', p. 216.

18 Lahsen, 'Experience of modernity in the greenhouse', p. 210.

19 Mark Hertsgaard, 'While Washington Slept', *Vanity Fair*, May 2006. When asked about funding for the Marshall Institute by oil companies, including Exxon, Seitz said: 'There's nothing wrong with oil money', having previously argued that all funding is without strings: 'When money changes hands it's the new owner that decides how it's used, not the old' (*Frontline*, Public Broadcasting Service (US), 3 April 2006). Other prominent deniers, such as Fred Singer and Sallie Balliunas, also gravitated to the Marshall Institute.

20 http://www.marshall.org/category.php?id=6.

21 Aaron McCright and Riley Dunlap, 'Defeating Kyoto: The conservative movement's impact on U.S. climate change policy', *Social Problems*, vol. 50, no. 3, 2003.

22 Chris Mooney, *The Republican War on Science*, Basic Books, New York, 2005.

23 McCright and Dunlap, 'Defeating Kyoto'.

24 George Monbiot, *Heat: How to stop the planet burning*, Allen Lane, London, 2006, pp. 31 ff. See also Clive Hamilton, *Scorcher: The dirty politics of climate change*, Black Inc., Melbourne, 2007.

25 Monbiot, *Heat*, p. 32.

26 Monbiot, *Heat*, p. 32.

27 Monbiot, *Heat*, p. 129.

28 Mark Hertsgaard, 'While Washington Slept'. When asked about the ethics of his position Seitz said: 'I'm not quite clear about this moralistic issue ... I'll leave that to the philosophers and priests.'

29 McCright and Dunlap, 'Defeating Kyoto'.

30 http://www.onenewsnow.com/Politics/Default.aspx?id=210502.

31 Kate Galbraith, 'Michele Bachmann Seeks "Armed and Dangerous" Opposition to Cap-and-Trade', *New York Times*, 26 March 2009.

32 In a survey across 30 countries, three quarters of respondents said there should be a legally binding international agreement. Of the 92 per cent of Americans who had heard of global warming, 88 per cent supported the Kyoto Protocol. Anthony Leiserowitz, *Public Perception, Opinion and Understanding of Climate Change—Current Patterns, Trends and Limitations*, Occasional Paper for the Human Development Report Office, United Nations Development Program, 2007.

33 Jacques et al., 'The organisation of denial', p. 352.

34 Jon A. Krosnick, Allyson L. Holbrook and Penny S. Visser, 'The impact of the fall 1997 debate about global warming on American public opinion', *Public Understanding of Science*, vol. 9, 2000, pp. 239–60.

35 Riley Dunlap and Aaron McCright, 'A Widening Gap: Republican and Democrat views on climate change', *Environment Magazine*, vol. 50, no. 5, September/October 2008.

36 Edward Maibach, Connie Roser-Renouf and Anthony Leiserowitz, *Global Warming's 'Six Americas' 2009: An audience segmentation*, Yale Project on Climate Change and George Mason University Center for Climate Change Communication, 2009.

37 Maibach et al., *Global Warming's 'Six Americas' 2009*, p. 24.

38 Data are from Maibach et al., *Global Warming's 'Six Americas' 2009*, Table 20, p. 113. Note that I have reversed the order of the Cautious and Disengaged samples given by Maibach et al. Among both groups only 49 per cent agree that most scientists think global warming is happening (Table 1). The Cautious are a little more

likely than the Disengaged to believe that warming is happening (Table 1), but less likely to support policies and personal actions to reduce warming (Table 2).

39 Maibach et al., *Global Warming's 'Six Americas' 2009*, Table 21, pp. 114–15.

40 Maibach et al., *Global Warming's 'Six Americas' 2009*, Figure 32, p. 37.

41 Maibach et al., *Global Warming's 'Six Americas' 2009*, Table 28, p. 128.

42 Hamilton, *Scorcher*, Chapter 10.

43 Anon., 'Telegraph YouGov poll: Labour leads Conservatives, *Telegraph*, 12 April 2008. Twenty three per cent disagree.

44 Jonathan Fowlie, 'Majority opposes B.C. carbon tax', *Vancouver Sun*, 17 June 2008.

45 Leiserowitz, *Public Perception, Opinion and Understanding of Climate Change.*

46 Maibach et al., *Global Warming's 'Six Americas' 2009*, Table 21, p. 116.

47 Leiserowitz, *Public Perception, Opinion and Understanding of Climate Change.*

48 Levels of concern in the United States rose to almost 50 per cent in 2006, but they rose too in other countries.

49 Leiserowitz, *Public Perception, Opinion and Understanding of Climate Change*, p. 9.

50 Leiserowitz, *Public Perception, Opinion and Understanding of Climate Change.*

51 David Lester, 'National differences in neuroticism and extraversion', *Journal of Personality and Individual Differences*, vol. 28, issue 1, January 2000.

52 Brendan O'Neill, 'Stupid, feckless, greedy: that's you, that is', *Spiked*, 16 March 2009. In another article, editor Brendan O'Neill describes environmentalism as 'a largely elitist project, beloved of politicians, priests and prudes keen to control people's behaviour

and curb our excessive lifestyles' (*Spiked*, 4 March 2009). The RCP diverges from most Trotskyist groups which accept the science and campaign on global warming.

53 Frank Furedi, 'Climate change and the return of original sin', *Spiked*, 25 February 2009.

54 Writing on *Spiked*, some of Furedi's colleagues have characterised climate science as the 'New Scientism', science that is perverted for political purposes, made incontrovertible, put on a pedestal and then used to close down debate (James Woudhuysen and Joe Kaplinsky, 'A man-made morality tale', *Spiked*, 5 February 2007).

55 Anon., 'Global warming labeled a "scam"', *Washington Times*, 6 March 2007. Its director, Martin Durkin, characterised global warming as 'a multibillion-dollar worldwide industry, created by fanatically anti-industrial environmentalists, supported by scientists peddling scare stories to chase funding, and propped up by compliant politicians and the media'.

56 Brendan O'Neill, 'Apocalypse my arse', *Spiked*, 9 March 2007.

57 The links between Furedi, Durkin, *Against Nature* and the RCP were first made by George Monbiot in 'The Revolution Has Been Televised', *Guardian*, 18 December 1997.

58 The far-right conspiracist organisation established by Lyndon LaRouche actively promoted *Swindle* on university campuses.

59 O'Neill, 'Stupid, feckless, greedy' (emphasis added).

60 To avoid the grievous charge of 'self-plagiarism' I declare that this paragraph is similar to one in my book *Scorcher*.

61 A raging climate denialist, Phillips also stands for moral absolutes against 'the prevailing amorality and nihilism which is now promoted by the Gramscian left', reminding her readers that 'I have been banging on for the past two decades about our de-moralised society, the way morality has been turned into a dirty word through non-judgmentalism and moral relativism which have inverted right and wrong, good and bad, truth and lies, and the terrible damage to individuals and society which has resulted from the collapse of

moral responsibility' ('A moral revival?', *Spectator* website, 8 July 2008).

62 This point is made by Bruno Latour, 'Why has critique run out of steam? From matters of fact to matters of concern', *Critical Inquiry*, vol. 30, no. 2, Winter 2004.

63 Ian Plimer, *Heaven and Earth: Global Warming: The Missing Science*, Connor Court Publishing, 2009; Barry Brook, 'Ian Plimer—*Heaven and Earth*', 23 April 2009, www.bravenewclimate.com.

64 See, for example, Ross Gelbspan, *Boiling Point*, Basic Books, New York, 2004. The most detailed and revealing study of the power of the fossil fuel lobby has been told for Australia by Guy Pearse in *High & Dry*, Penguin, Camberwell, 2007.

65 Tim Kasser, Steve Cohn, Allen Kanner and Richard Ryan, 'Some Costs of American Corporate Capitalism: A Psychological Exploration of Value and Goal Conflicts', *Psychological Inquiry*, vol. 18, no. 1, 2007, pp. 2–3.

66 Ian Langford, 'An Existential Approach to Risk Perception', *Risk Analysis*, vol. 22, no. 1, 2002. The other main defence is a belief in some form of ultimate rescuer.

67 The seminal article in this area is George Lowenstein, Christopher Hsee, Elke Weber and Ned Welch, 'Risk as Feelings', *Psychological Bulletin*, vol. 127, no. 2, 2001.

68 Lowenstein et al., 'Risk as Feelings', p. 279.

69 Anthony Leiserowitz, 'Climate Change Risk Perception and Policy Preferences: The Role of Affect, Imagery, and Values', *Climate Change*, vol. 77, 2006, pp. 45–72.

70 Maibach et al., *Global Warming's 'Six Americas' 2009.*

71 Pew Research Center, 'Jobs Trump All Other Policy Priorities in 2009', 22 January 2009.

72 See especially Andreas Homburg, Andreas Stolberg and Ulrich Wagner, 'Coping With Global Environmental Problems: Development and First Validation of Scales', *Environment and*

Behavior, vol. 39, no. 6, November 2007; Kari Marie Norgaard, '"People Want to Protect Themselves a Little Bit": Emotions, Denial, and Social Movement Nonparticipation', *Sociological Inquiry*, vol. 76, no. 3, August 2006. In August 2009 the American Psychological Association released a draft report containing a compendious review of relevant research (Janet Swim et al., *Psychology and Global Climate Change: Addressing a Multi-faceted Phenomenon and Set of Challenges*, A Report by the American Psychological Association's Task Force on the Interface between Psychology and Global Climate Change (Draft), 2009, www.apa.org/science/).

73 Clive Hamilton and Tim Kasser, 'Psychological Adaptation to the Threats and Stresses of a Four Degree World', A paper for 'The World at Four Plus Degrees' conference, Oxford University, 28–30 September 2009.

74 Tom Crompton and Tim Kasser, *Meeting Environmental Challenges: The Role of Human Identity*, WWF-UK, Godalming, 2009.

75 Anna Freud, *The Ego and the Mechanisms of Defence*, International Universities Press, New York, 1967.

76 Discussed especially by Norgaard, 'People Want to Protect Themselves a Little Bit'.

77 Homburg et al., 'Coping With Global Environmental Problems'.

78 Anthony Leiserowitz, 'Climate Change Risk Perception and Policy Preferences'.

79 Tal Eyal, Michael Sagristano, Yaacov Trope, Nira Liberman and Shelly Chaiken, 'When Values Matter: Expressing values in behavioural intentions for the near vs. distant future', *Journal of Experimental Social Psychology*, vol. 45, 2009, pp. 35–43.

80 Quoted by Ciar Byrne, 'Scourge of the greens: Clarkson branded "a bigoted petrolhead"', *Independent*, 31 May 2006.

81 Donald MacLeod, 'Denise Morrey: Engineer steps up a gear', *Guardian*, 20 December 2005.

82 See, for example, M. Finucane, P. Slovic, C.K. Mertz, J. Flynn and T. Satterfield, 'Gender, race, and perceived risk: The "white male" effect', *Health, Risk & Society*, vol. 2, no. 2, 2000; Paul Kellstedt, Sammy Zahran and Arnold Vedlitz, 'Personal Efficacy, the Information Environment, and Attitudes Towards Global Warming and Climate Change in the United States', *Risk Analysis*, vol. 28, no. 1, 2008.
83 A website called '500 Places to See Before They Disappear' was created to enable 'passionate travelers and the eco-conscious to learn about and plan a visit to see rare cultural, historic, and natural places before they are irrevocably altered or even gone forever' (http://www.itineraryguide.com/tag/500-places-to-see-before-they-disappear/).
84 Homburg et al., 'Coping With Global Environmental Problems'.
85 Norgaard, 'People Want to Protect Themselves a Little Bit', p. 379.
86 Kraig R. Naasz, 'Climate Change and the Energy Industry—the Role for Coal', Address to the USEA, 16 January 2008.
87 Crompton and Kasser, *Meeting Environmental Challenges*, pp. 20–1.
88 http://www.raptureready.com/faq/faq90.html.
89 http://www.raptureready.com/faq/faq403.html.
90 James Lovelock, *The Ages of Gaia: A biography of our living Earth*, Oxford University Press, Oxford, 1989.
91 In fact the original story was of 'Pandora's jar', but 'jar' was mistranslated as 'box' in the sixteenth century.
92 In some versions of the myth Pandora, whose name means 'all-giving', is a goddess similar to Gaia who rises out of the ground and is the source of all fertility.
93 Renée Lertzman, 'The myth of apathy', *The Ecologist*, 19 June 2008.
94 Joanna Macy, 'Despair Work', in *World As Lover, World As Self*, Parallax Press, Berkeley, 1991, p. 15.

95 Norgaard, 'People Want to Protect Themselves a Little Bit'.
96 See Christopher Peterson, 'The Future of Optimism', *American Psychologist*, vol. 55, no. 1, January 2000, pp. 44–55, who considers the 'uniquely American brand of optimism'.
97 Peterson, 'The Future of Optimism'.
98 Shelley Taylor, *Positive Illusions: Creative self-deception and the healthy mind*, Basic Books, New York, 1989.
99 Taylor, *Positive Illusions*, p. xi.
100 Homburg et al., 'Coping With Global Environmental Problems', p. 774.
101 Sheena Sethi and Martin Seligman, 'Optimism and fundamentalism', *Psychological Science*, vol. 4, no. 4, July 1993.
102 Taylor, *Positive Illusions*, p. 33.
103 Taylor, *Positive Illusions*, p. 32.
104 Taylor, *Positive Illusions*, p. 64.
105 N.S. Jacobson, C.R. Martell and S. Dimidjian, 'Behavioral activation treatment for depression: Returning to contextual roots', *Clinical Psychology: Science & Practice*, vol. 8, 2001, pp. 255–70.
106 Taylor, *Positive Illusions*, p. 36.
107 Martin Seligman, *Learned Optimism*, Knopf, New York, 1991, p. 292.
108 http://www.hopenhagen.org.

Chapter 5 Disconnection from Nature

1 P. Wesley Schultz, Chris Shriver, Jennifer Tabanico and Azar Khazian, 'Implicit Connections With Nature', *Journal of Environmental Psychology*, vol. 24, 2004, pp. 31–42.
2 Schultz et al., 'Implicit Connections With Nature', p. 41. See also P. Wesley Schultz, 'Environmental Attitudes and Behaviors Across Cultures', in W.J. Lonner, D.L. Dinnel, S.A. Hayes and D.N. Sattler (eds), *Online Readings in Psychology and Culture*, Center for Cross-Cultural Research, Western Washington University, Bellingham, 2002.

3 Schultz et al., 'Implicit Connections With Nature'; Kathryn Williams and David Harvey, 'Transcendent Experience in Forest Environments', *Journal of Environmental Psychology*, vol. 21, 2001, pp. 249–60.
4 Robert Bixler and Myron Floyd, 'Nature is Scary, Disgusting and Uncomfortable', *Environment and Behavior*, vol. 29, no. 4, July 1997.
5 See Clive Hamilton, 'The Rebirth of Nature and the Climate Crisis', A Sydney Ideas Lecture, University of Sydney, 7 July 2009.
6 See Richard Westfall, *Never At Rest: A Biography of Isaac Newton*, Cambridge University Press, Cambridge, 1980, p. 184.
7 Plato, *Timaeus*.
8 Mircea Eliade, *The Sacred and the Profane: The nature of religion*, Harper & Row, New York, 1961, p. 151. Eliade goes on: 'For others, nature still exhibits a charm, a mystery, a majesty in which it is possible to decipher traces of ancient religious values. No modern man, however irreligious, is entirely insensible to the charms of nature.'
9 William Wordsworth, *The Tables Turned* [1798].
10 Johann Goethe, *Faust*, Part One, Penguin, London, 1949 [1808], p. 95.
11 Catherine Pickstock, *After Writing: On the Liturgical Consummation of Philosophy*, Blackwell, Oxford, 1998; Catherine Pickstock, 'Duns Scotus: His historical and contemporary significance', *Modern Theology*, vol. 21, no. 4, October 2005.
12 Pickstock, *After Writing*, pp. 62, 63.
13 Pickstock notes that experimental philosophers like Boyle did recognise force in matter but identified it as a direct presence of a divine causality, as if a remote god had decided to inject his own influences into a universe also controlled by mechanical forces (Pickstock, *After Writing*, p. 80).
14 G.W.F. Hegel, *Encyclopedia of the Philosophical Sciences*, quoted by Kate Rigby in *Topographies of the Sacred: The Poetics of Place in*

European Romanticism, University of Virginia Press, Charlottesville, 2004, p. 31.

15 Quoted by Arthur Zajonc, 'The Wearer of Shapes: Goethe's Study of Clouds and Weather', *Orion Nature Quarterly*, vol. 3, no. 1, Winter 1984.

16 From his journal, quoted by David Skrbina, *Panpsychism in the West*, MIT Press, Cambridge, 2007, p. 224.

17 Pickstock, *After Writing*, pp. 74 ff. Also Steven Shapin and Simon Schaffer, *Leviathan and the Air-Pump: Hobbes, Boyle, and the Experimental Life*, Princeton University Press, Princeton, 1985.

18 Robert Boyle, *A Free Enquiry into the Vulgarly Received Notion of Nature*, edited by Edward B. Davis and Michael Hunter, Cambridge University Press, Cambridge, 1996 [1686].

19 Boyle, *A Free Enquiry*, p. 13. In 1605 Kepler had written that his aim was 'to show that the celestial machine is to be likened not to a divine organism but to a clockwork' (quoted by Carolyn Merchant, *The Death of Nature: Women, Ecology, and the Scientific Revolution,* Harper & Row, San Francisco, 1980).

20 William C. Placher, *The Domestication of Transcendence*, Westminster John Knox Press, Louisville, 1996.

21 Thanks to Scott Cowdell for discussions on this point.

22 Boyle, *A Free Enquiry*, p. 15.

23 Quoted by Merchant, *The Death of Nature*, p. 249.

24 There is now an extensive literature on Newton's alchemy. See especially Betty Jo Teeter Dobbs, *The Foundations of Newton's Alchemy, or 'The Hunting of the Greene Lyon'*, Cambridge University Press, Cambridge, 1975; P.M. Rattansi, 'Newton's Alchemical Studies', in Allen G. Debus (ed.), *Science, Medicine and Society in the Renaissance*, Heinemann, London, 1972; Richard Westfall, *Never At Rest: A Biography of Isaac Newton*, Cambridge University Press, Cambridge, 1980; Richard S. Westfall, 'Newton and the Hermetic Tradition', in Allen G. Debus (ed.), *Science, Medicine and Society in the Renaissance*, Heinemann, London, 1972; and

David Kubrin, 'Newton's Inside Out! Magic, Class Struggle, and the Rise of Mechanism in the West', in Harry Woolf (ed.), *The Analytic Spirit: Essays in the history of science*, Cornell University Press, Ithaca, 1981.

25 Quoted by Westfall, *Never At Rest*, p. 285.

26 Newton, *The Correspondence of Isaac Newton*, Cambridge University Press, for the Royal Society, London, 1959, vol. I, p. 366.

27 A point made by Rattansi, 'Newton's Alchemical Studies', p. 176. Newton distinguished carefully between 'vegetable' actions and 'purely mechanical' ones, with the reactions of ordinary chemistry falling into the latter category. Vegetation was a process by which the seeds of things, interacting with the aether or spirit, mature. The alchemists seemed to combine the two in the notion of the 'vegetation of metals', a process of change involving purification which ultimately could reveal the universal spirit.

28 Westfall, *Never At Rest*, pp. 185–6, 194.

29 The following relies heavily on Kubrin, 'Newton's Inside Out!', pp. 96–121.

30 Kubrin, 'Newton's Inside Out!', pp. 115–16. See also Margaret Candee Jacob, 'John Toland and the Newtonian Ideology', *Journal of the Warburg and Courtauld Institutes*, vol. 32, 1969, pp. 307–31.

31 Kubrin, 'Newton's Inside Out!', p. 116.

32 Merchant, *The Death of Nature*, p. 29 ff.

33 Merchant, *The Death of Nature*, p. 3.

34 Kubrin, 'Newton's Inside Out!', p. 100.

35 Kubrin, 'Newton's Inside Out!', p. 100.

36 Max Weber, *The Protestant Ethic and the Spirit of Capitalism*, Unwin University Books, London, 1930, pp. 26–7. He argued that economic self-interest is not unique to modern capitalism and can be found in all ages. After all, it was Jesus who cast the money-lenders from the temple steps.

37 The words are those of R.H. Tawney in his foreword to Weber's *The Protestant Ethic and the Spirit of Capitalism*, p. 2.

38 David Landes, *The Unbound Prometheus*, Cambridge University Press, Cambridge, 1969.

39 Jan Smuts, *Holism and Evolution*, Macmillan, London, 1926, pp. 108–9. In 1970 the Master of Christ's College, where Smuts was an undergraduate in the early 1890s, said that in the College's 500-year history only three students had been 'truly outstanding': John Milton, Charles Darwin and Jan Smuts.

40 James Lovelock, *The Ages of Gaia: A biography of our living Earth*, Oxford University Press, Oxford, 1989; James Lovelock, *The Revenge of Gaia*, Penguin, London, 2007; James Lovelock, *The Vanishing Face of Gaia*, Allen Lane, Camberwell, 2009.

41 Lovelock, *The Ages of Gaia*, p. 12.

42 Lovelock, *The Ages of Gaia*, p. 33.

43 See, for example, the discussion of 'Life' in the *Stanford Encyclopedia of Philosophy*.

44 Lovelock, *The Ages of Gaia*, p. 27. It might be thought that the capacity to reproduce must be included in the definition of 'life'. Lovelock suggests that life on a planetary scale regulates itself so effectively it is 'near immortal' and so does not need to reproduce (p. 63).

45 Lovelock, *The Ages of Gaia*, pp. 214–15.

46 Lovelock, *The Ages of Gaia*, pp. 35–8.

47 Lovelock, *The Ages of Gaia*, p. 31.

48 Lovelock, *The Ages of Gaia*, p. 79.

49 Lovelock, *The Revenge of Gaia*, pp. 21–2.

50 Lovelock, *The Vanishing Face of Gaia*, p. 162.

51 Lovelock, *The Vanishing Face of Gaia*, p. 21.

52 Judith Wright, *Australia 1970*.

53 Below I rely especially on Steven Arnocky, Mirella Stroink and Teresa DeCicco, 'Self-construal predicts environmental concern, cooperation and conservation', *Journal of Environmental Psychology*, vol. 27, 2007, pp. 255–64.

54 Arnocky et al., 'Self-construal predicts environmental concern'. See also Teresa DeCicco and Mirella Stroink, 'A Third Model of Self-Construal: The metapersonal self', *International Journal of Transpersonal Studies*, vol. 26, 2007, pp. 82–104.
55 My thanks to Tim Kasser for provoking this distinction.
56 Robert Putnam, *Bowling Alone: The Collapse and Revival of American Community*, Simon & Schuster, New York, 2000.
57 DeCicco and Stroink, 'A Third Model of Self-Construal'; Mirella Stroink and Teresa DeCicco, 'A Third Self-Construal: Cultural differences and underlying value dimensions', unpublished, November 2008; Arnocky et al., 'Self-construal predicts environmental concern'.
58 Arnocky et al., 'Self-construal predicts environmental concern', p. 256.
59 P. Wesley Schultz, 'The Structure of Environmental Concern: Concern for self, other people, and the biosphere', *Journal of Environmental Psychology*, vol. 21, 2001, pp. 327–39.
60 Arnocky et al., 'Self-construal predicts environmental concern', p. 258; Schultz, 'The Structure of Environmental Concern', p. 336.
61 Sonja Utz, 'Self-Construal and Cooperation: Is the interdependent self more cooperative than the independent self?', *Self and Identity*, vol. 3, 2004, pp. 177–90.
62 Wendi Gardner, Shira Gabriel and Angela Lee, '"I" Value Freedom, But "We" Value relationship: Self-construal priming mirrors cultural difference in judgment', *Psychological Science*, vol. 10, no. 4, July 1999.
63 Jacob Hirsch and Dan Dolderman, 'Personality Predictors of Consumerism and Environmentalism: A preliminary study', *Personality and Individual Differences*, vol. 43, 2007, pp. 1583–93.
64 Hirsch and Dolderman, 'Personality Predictors of Consumerism and Environmentalism'.
65 Arnocky et al., 'Self-construal predicts environmental concern'.

66 Tom Crompton and Tim Kasser, *Meeting Environmental Challenges: The Role of Human Identity*, WWF-UK, Godalming, 2009, p. 19. Note that this result is associated with *brief* reminders of mortality; when people are asked to reflect at more length on their mortality, they tend to adopt less self-focused values, a subject I return to in Chapter 8.

67 Daniel McGuire, 'More People: Less Earth, the Shadow of Mankind', in Daniel McGuire and Larry Rasmussen, *Ethics for a Small Planet*, State University of New York Press, Albany, 1998, p. 48.

Chapter 6 Is there a way out?

1 The World Energy Council estimates economically recoverable reserves of coal, excluding non-conventional sources, at 850 billion tonnes. At current usage rates that would last 150 years. Adding in known potentially exploitable reserves at least doubles this estimate. The United States has the greatest reserves, followed by Russia, China and Australia (Judy Trinnaman and Alan Clarke (eds), *Survey of Energy Resources 2007: Coal*, World Energy Council, London, 2007).

2 http://www.onedigitallife.com/2009/02/26/the-awesome-power-of-the-word-clean.

3 Anon., 'Trouble in store', *Economist*, 5 March 2009.

4 http://www.youtube.com/watch?v=GehK7Q_QxPc.

5 Roland Nelles, 'Germany Plans Boom in Coal-Fired Power Plants Despite High Emissions', *Der Spiegel Online*, 21 March 2007.

6 Matthew Franklin, 'Obama supports Rudd on clean coal', *Australian*, 26 March 2009.

7 Nicholas Stern, *The Economics of Climate Change*, Cambridge University Press, Cambridge, 2007, p. 251.

8 Jeffrey Sachs, 'Living with Coal: Addressing Climate Change', Speech to the Asia Society, New York, 1 June 2009. Mike

Stephenson, head of science at the British Geological Survey, says: 'It does not matter what we say in the west about what they should do, they will always want to exploit their coal ... The only way round the problem is to make the use of coal safe and environmentally friendly' (Robin McKie, 'Coal at the centre of fierce new climate battle', *Observer*, 15 February 2009).

9 Ross Garnaut, *The Garnaut Climate Change Review*, Cambridge University Press, Melbourne, 2008, p. 392.

10 Anon., 'Trouble in store'; http://www.themoneytimes.com/20090518/carbon-capture-storage-projects-funded-id–1068423.html.

11 Christian Kerr, 'Carbon capture to save industry', *Australian*, 13 May 2009.

12 Anon., 'Trouble in store'.

13 For coal see Guy Pearse, *Quarry Vision: Coal, climate change and the end of the resources boom*, Quarterly Essay, no. 23, Black Inc., Melbourne, 2009, p. 84. For wool see Australian Wool Innovation, *Annual Report 2008*, AWI, 2008, p. 4.

14 World Business Council for Sustainable Development, 'Facts and Trends: Carbon capture and storage', WBCSD, 2006.

15 Treasury, *Australia's Low Pollution Future: The Economics of Climate Change Mitigation*, Commonwealth of Australia, Canberra, 2008, p. 179.

16 Anon., 'Trouble in store'.

17 International Energy Agency, *Energy Technology Perspectives 2008*, International Energy Agency, Paris, 2008, http://www.iea.org/Textbase/subjectqueries/ccs/what_is_ccs.asp.

18 Cooperative Research Centre for Greenhouse Gas Technologies (Australia), 'Sleipner Project Overview', http://www.co2crc.com.au/demo/sleipner.html.

19 Jeff Goodell, 'Coal's New Technology: Panacea or risky gamble?', *Yale Environment 360*, 14 July 2008.

20 Quoted by Goodell, 'Coal's New Technology'.

21 CSIRO, *Submission to the House of Representatives Inquiry into Geosequestration Technology*, CSIRO, Australia, August 2006.

22 IPCC, *Summary for Policymakers, Special Report: Carbon Dioxide Capture and Storage*, IPCC, 2005, p. 4 and Figure SPM.2; Anon., 'Trouble in store'.

23 Greenpeace, *False Hope: Why carbon capture and storage won't save the climate*, Greenpeace International, Amsterdam, 2008, p. 35; Anon., 'Trouble in store'.

24 http://www.geology.sdsu.edu/how_volcanoes_work/Nyos.html.

25 Greenpeace, *False Hope*, p. 31.

26 Stern, *The Economics of Climate Change*, p. 251.

27 Greenpeace, *False Hope.*

28 Anon., 'Trouble in store'; Anon., 'The illusion of clean coal', *Economist*, 5 March 2009.

29 Mark Milner, '"Without commercial carbon capture, it's 'game over'", E.ON boss tells government', *Guardian*, 17 March 2009.

30 Anon., 'UK—no new coal without CCS', *Carbon Capture Journal*, May–June 2009, http://www.carboncapturejournal.com/issues/CCJ9web.pdf.

31 See especially European Renewable Energy Council and Greenpeace International, *Energy [R]evolution: A sustainable global energy outlook*, 2008.

32 Quoted in Melanie Warner, 'Is America ready to Quit Coal?', *New York Times*, 15 February 2009.

33 For the next several paragraphs I'd like to thank George Wilkenfeld and Hugh Saddler for allowing me to draw on George Wilkenfeld, Clive Hamilton and Hugh Saddler, *'Clean coal' and other greenhouse myths*, Research Paper No. 49, The Australia Institute, Canberra, August 2007.

34 'Technical reliability of single generating units is not the issue: modern wind turbines are ~98–99% available, far better than any thermal plant. The issue is rather the aggregate effect of some renewables' variability' (Amory Lovins and Imran Sheikh, 'The

Nuclear Illusion', Rocky Mountains Institute, 27 May 2008, p. 22).

35 Lovins and Sheikh, 'The Nuclear Illusion', p. 22, n. 88.

36 Anon., 'Offshore wind farms could meet a quarter of the UK's electricity needs', *Guardian*, 25 June 2009.

37 'Research is increasingly showing that if we properly diversify renewable energy supplies in type and location, forecast the weather (as hydropower and windpower operators now do), and integrate renewables with existing demand- and supply-side resources on the grid, then renewables' electrical supplies will be more reliable than current arrangements' (Lovins and Sheikh, 'The Nuclear Illusion', p. 24).

38 See, for example, James Kanter, 'European Solar Power From African Deserts?', *New York Times*, 18 June 2009.

39 http://www.energy.ca.gov/siting/solar/index.html.

40 European Renewable Energy Council and Greenpeace International, *Energy [R]evolution: A sustainable global energy outlook*, p. 144.

41 See, for example, Greenpeace International, 'Changing lifestyles and consumption patterns', *The Greenpeace Climate Vision*, Background Note No. 8, May 2009.

42 Amory Lovins and Imran Sheikh, 'The Nuclear Illusion', p. 8, n. 39.

43 Greenpeace International, 'Nuclear Power: An expensive waste of time', Greenpeace, Amsterdam, 2009.

44 Lovins and Sheikh, 'The Nuclear Illusion', p. 20.

45 Generation IV nuclear energy includes several designs for power plants that are safer and produce much less radioactive waste than conventional plants. The technologies are not expected to be commercial until 2030, although one is planned for completion in 2021.

46 Royal Society, *Geoengineering the Climate: Science, governance and uncertainty*, Royal Society, London, 2009, p. 1.

47 Royal Society, *Geoengineering the Climate*, p. 1.

48 James Lovelock, *The Vanishing Face of Gaia*, Penguin, Camberwell, 2009, p. 98.
49 Robert Kunzig and Wallace Broecker, *Fixing Climate*, Green Profile, London, 2008, pp. 234–45.
50 Royal Society, *Geoengineering the Climate*, p. 32.
51 Royal Society, *Geoengineering the Climate*, p. 25; David Adam, 'Paint it white', *Guardian*, 16 January 2009.
52 Royal Society, *Geoengineering the Climate*, pp. 2, 24.
53 Paul Crutzen, 'Albedo enhancement by stratospheric sulfur injections: A contribution to resolve a policy dilemma?', *Climatic Change*, vol. 77, nos 3–4, pp. 211–20.
54 Scott Barrett, 'The Incredible Economics of Geoengineering', *Environmental and Resource Economics*, vol. 39, 2008, pp. 45–54.
55 Although soot particles can also amplify warming.
56 Crutzen, 'Albedo enhancement by stratospheric sulfur injections'.
57 David J. Travis, Andrew M. Carleton and Ryan G. Lauritsen, 'Contrails reduce daily temperature range', *Nature*, vol. 418, 8 August 2002, p. 601.
58 H.D. Matthews, L. Cao and K. Caldeira, 'Sensitivity of ocean acidification to geoengineered climate stabilization', *Geophysical Research Letters*, vol. 36, 2009.
59 Kunzig and Broecker, *Fixing Climate*, p. 262.
60 Alan Robock, Luke Oman and Georgiy Stenchikov, 'Regional climate responses to geoengineering with tropical and Arctic SO_2 injections', *Journal of Geophysical Research*, vol. 13, 2008.
61 Barrett, 'The Incredible Economics of Geoengineering'.
62 'Obama's science chief eyes drastic climate steps', Associated Press, 8 April 2009, http://www.thebreakthrough.org/blog/2009/04/john_holdrens_minor_geoenginee.shtml.
63 Crutzen, 'Albedo enhancement by stratospheric sulfur injections'.
64 Royal Society, *Geoengineering the Climate*. As we saw in Chapter 5, in the late seventeenth century the Royal Society was instrumental in unleashing the powers of Prometheus, so there is an irony in the

fact that in the twenty-first century it is leading the campaign to counter the consequences.

65 David Victor, 'On the regulation of geoengineering', *Oxford Review of Economic Policy*, vol. 24, no. 2, 2008, p. 327.

66 Kurt House, Christopher House, Daniel Schrag and Michael Aziz, 'Electrochemical acceleration of chemical weathering as an energetically feasible approach to mitigating anthropogenic climate change', *Environmental Science and Technology*, vol. 41, no. 24, 2007, p. 8467.

67 Philip Gourevitch and Errol Morris, *Standard Operating Procedure*, Penguin, Harmondsworth, 2008.

68 Aeschylus, *The Persians.*

69 Karl Jaspers, *The Future of Mankind*, University of Chicago Press, Chicago, 1961, p. viii.

70 Clive Hamilton, 'Building on Kyoto', *New Left Review*, no. 45, May–June 2007.

71 In the glacial/interglacial period of the last 34 million years changes in global carbon dioxide levels have in the main been due to solar radiation triggering ice melt/water interactions, causing warming oceans and carbon dioxide release. Climate deniers have mischievously claimed that the paleoclimate record showing carbon dioxide increases trailing warming 'proves' that recent warming is the cause of rising carbon dioxide levels rather than the other way round.

72 Timothy Lenton and Werner von Bloh, 'Biotic feedback extends the life span of the biosphere', *Geophysical Research Letters*, vol. 28, 2001; James Lovelock, *The Revenge of Gaia*, Penguin, London, 2007, p. 40.

73 Donald Olson, Russell Doescher and Marilynn Olson, 'When the Sky Ran Red: The Story Behind "The Scream"', *Sky & Telescope*, February 2004, pp. 29–35.

74 Crutzen, 'Albedo enhancement by stratospheric sulfur injections'.

75 H. Damon Matthews and Ken Caldeira, 'Transient climate-carbon simulations of planetary geoengineering', *Proceedings of the National Academy of Science*, vol. 104, no. 24, 12 June 2007.

76 Royal Society, *Geoengineering the Climate*, p. 24.

77 Victor, 'On the regulation of geoengineering', p. 331, n. 14.

78 Jeff Goodell, 'Can Dr. Evil Save The World?', *Rolling Stone*, 3 November 2006.

79 Although Teller was Jewish and left Europe in 1935. Teller had a prosthetic foot while Dr Strangelove had a prosthetic hand. See the Wikipedia entries on Teller and Dr Strangelove.

80 E. Teller, L. Wood and R. Hyde, 'Global Warming and Ice Ages: I. Prospects for Physics-Based Modulation of Global Change', Paper to the 22nd International Seminar on Planetary Emergencies, Italy, August 20–23 1997; Goodell, 'Can Dr. Evil Save The World?'.

81 Alex Steffen, 'Geoengineering and the New Climate Denialism', *Worldchanging*, 29 April 2009, http://www.worldchanging.com/archives/009784.html.

82 http://media.hoover.org/documents/0817939326_283.pdf.

83 Steffen, 'Geoengineering and the New Climate Denialism'.

84 Royal Society, *Geoengineering the Climate*, p. 45.

85 Edward Teller, Roderick Hyde and Lowell Wood, 'Active Climate Stabilization: Practical Physics-Based Approaches to Prevention of Climate Change', paper submitted to the National Academy of Engineering Symposium, Lawrence Livermore National Laboratory, April 2002.

86 Goodell, 'Can Dr. Evil Save The World?'.

87 Teller et al., 'Global Warming and Ice Ages'.

88 Quoted by David Grinspoon, 'Is Mars Ours? The logistics and ethics of colonizing the red planet', *Slate*, 7 January 2004, http://www.slate.com/id/2093579/.

89 Quoted in James R. Fleming, 'The Climate Engineers: Playing god to save the planet', *Wilson Quarterly*, vol. 31, no. 2, 2007, p. 48.

90 Goodell, 'Can Dr. Evil Save The World?'. The quote is slightly modified.

91 Goodell, 'Can Dr. Evil Save The World?'.

92 Arthur Conan Doyle, 'When the World Screamed', in *The Lost World & Other Stories*, Wordsworth Editions Ltd, Hertfordshire, 1995.

Chapter 7 The four-degree world

1 See http://www.eci.ox.ac.uk/4degrees. Abstracts, PowerPoint presentations, audio and, in some cases, full papers from the conference can all be found on the site.

2 Although the global deep-ocean temperature was 4°C warmer than today 15 million years ago. See James Hansen et al., 'Target Atmospheric CO_2: Where Should Humanity Aim?', *The Open Atmospheric Science Journal*, vol. 2, 2008, pp. 217–31, Figure 3b.

3 In the St James's Palace Memorandum of May 2009.

4 Clive Hamilton, 'The Commonwealth and Sea-Level Rise', *The Roundtable*, September 2003.

Chapter 8 Reconstructing a future

1 Joanna Macy, 'Working Through Environmental Despair', in Theodore Roszak, Mary Gomes and Allen Kanner (eds), *Ecopsychology*, Sierra Club, San Francisco, 1995.

2 John Archer, *The Nature of Grief: The evolution and psychology of reactions to loss*, Routledge, London, 1999, p. 67. See also George Bonnano and Stacey Kaltman, 'Toward an Integrative Perspective on Bereavement', *Psychological Bulletin*, vol. 125, no. 6, 1999, pp. 760–76.

3 Archer, *The Nature of Grief*, p. 66 *passim*.

4 Archer, *The Nature of Grief*, p. 115. A third blockage can arise when the circumstances of the death are traumatic.

5 Eric Lindemann, 'Symptomatology and Management of Acute Grief', *American Journal of Psychiatry*, vol. 101, 1944, pp. 142–8.

6 The quote, slightly modified, is from Therese Rando, *How to Go On Living When Someone You Love Dies*, Bantam Books, New York, 1991, p. 97.

7 Macy, 'Working Through Environmental Despair', p. 26.

8 From blogger 'savagedave', 'Is there any point in fighting to stave off industrial apocalypse?', *Guardian* website, 17 August 2009, http://www.guardian.co.uk/commentisfree/cif-green/2009/aug/17/environment-climate-change (slightly modified).

9 Kazimierz Dabrowski, *Positive Disintegration*, Little Brown & Co, Boston, 1964.

10 Kazimierz Dabrowski, *Psychoneurosis is not an illness*, Gryf Publications, London, 1972, p. 220.

11 Ernest Becker, *The Denial of Death*, The Free Press, New York, 1973, p. ix.

12 Kennon Sheldon and Tim Kasser, 'Psychological threat and extrinsic goal striving', *Motivation and Emotion*, vol. 32, 2008, pp. 37–45; S. Solomon, J. Greenberg and T. Pyszczynski, 'A terror-management theory of social behaviour: The psychological functions of self-esteem and cultural worldviews', in M.P. Zanna (ed.), *Advances in Experimental Social Psychology*, Academic Press, San Diego, 1991.

13 P. Cozzolino, A.D. Staples, L.S. Meyers and J. Samboceti, 'Greed, death, and values: From terror management to transcendence management theory', *Personality and Social Psychology Bulletin*, vol. 30, no. 3, 2004.

14 Sheldon and Kasser, 'Psychological threat and extrinsic goal striving', p. 38.

15 E. Lykins, S. Segerstrom, A. Averill, D. Evans and M. Kemeny, 'Goals shift following reminders of mortality: reconciling post-traumatic growth and terror management theory', *Personality and Social Psychology Bulletin*, vol. 33, no. 8, 2007; Cozzolino et al., 'Greed, death, and values'.

16 Judd Marmor, *Psychiatry in Transition*, 2nd edition, Brunner/Mazel, New York, 1974, p. 21.
17 Tim Kasser, *The High Price of Materialism*, MIT Press, Cambridge, 2002.
18 Shelley Taylor, *Positive Illusions: Creative Self-Deception and the Healthy Mind*, Basic Books, New York, 1989, p. 83, quoting Salvador Maddi.
19 Morris Berman, *The Reenchantment of the World*, Cornel University Press, Ithaca, 1981, p. 9.
20 Mircea Eliade, *The Sacred and the Profane: The nature of religion*, Harper & Row, New York, 1961, p. 17.
21 Eliade, *The Sacred and the Profane*, p. 14.
22 Eliade, *The Sacred and the Profane*, p. 119.
23 Scott Cowdell, *Abiding Faith: Christianity Beyond Certainty, Anxiety, and Violence*, Cascade Books, Eugene, Oregon, 2009, p. 9.
24 Eliade, *The Sacred and the Profane*, pp. 126–7.
25 For example, Australian Psychological Society, 'Tip Sheet: Climate change—what you can do', Melbourne, 2007. 'Reminding ourselves that there is a lot that we can personally do, and starting to take action to manage the environment better, can help us move from despair and hopelessness to a sense of empowerment.'
26 Taylor, *Positive Illusions*, p. 193. 'One of the ways in which people achieve control in threatening circumstances is by becoming actively involved in the decisions that are made concerning the circumstances' (p. 188).
27 Marie Woolf, 'Spin doctors swoop on "safe" Tory seats', *Sunday Times*, 9 August 2009.

Index